Simplicity's®

SIMPLY THE BEST SEWING BOOK

Simplicity's

SIMPLY THE BEST

SEWING BOOK

Fashion Illustrations by Martha Vaughan

Simplicity Pattern Co., Inc.

ACKNOWLEDGMENTS

A book of this scope depends on a special pool of talents. From conceptual stage to finished books, SIMPLICITY'S® SIMPLY THE BEST SEWING BOOK involved many individuals working together, contributing their creative best.

Judy Raymond, Simplicity's Senior Vice President, first saw the merit of a new, simplified approach to sewing and provided the editorial objectives for the book.

Anne Marie Soto, Senior Copywriter and Associate Editor, wrote the main text and worked closely with the technical artists to illustrate it. She also originated the editorial concept for the color pages.

M. Grace McMahon-Johnson and *Janice S. Saunders*, Contributing Writers and Overlock/Serger Experts, developed most of the serger techniques in the book and generously shared their sewing expertise in both conventional and overlock sewing.

Nancy Nix, of The Tacony Corporation, provided valuable, expert advice on overlock/serger techniques.

Ann Marie Timinelli, freelance writer and editor with Simplicity's Primer Department, assisted in developing the basic "patternless wardrobe" concept and text for Part Three as well as the sewing techniques represented in color (examples of which she prepared for photography).

Betty Ann Pillsworth, Director of Simplicity's Consumer Services and Publishing, contributed many editorial ideas throughout the book and generously helped with the countless routine procedures involved. She supervised the progress and development of Part Three, and contributed to the concept and development of the color pages, overseeing dressmaking, styling and photography.

Fashion illustrations throughout the text were done by *Martha Vaughan*, whose talent and creativity rose above and beyond expectations.

Photographs in the color sections were taken by *Louise Boekenheide, Ralph Bogertman, Alan Price, Peter Sakas* and *Theo.*

Terry Baldessari produced the technical art for Chapters Four and Five; *Ada Cruz* did the technical art for all the projects in Part Three. Both artists are on staff in Simplicity's Primer Department. *Helen Pettee–Keeley*, Assistant Art Director of the Simplicity Catalog, did the technical art for Chapter Six.

Harriet Ripinsky, of Ripinsky & Company, produced the book for Harper & Row; *Beri Greenwald, Dorothy Gordineer* and *Christine Swirnoff* at Libra Graphics, Inc., designed it.

Special credit goes to *Marlene Connor* of the Connor Literary Agency, who acted as agent for this book and brought many of the above-mentioned contributors together to develop it.

Julie Houston, Editorial Director
and Project Coordinator

SIMPLICITY'S SIMPLY THE BEST SEWING BOOK.

Copyright © 1988
Simplicity Pattern Co., Inc., 200 Madison Avenue, New York, N.Y. 10016
In Canada, Dominion Simplicity Ltd., 7 Curity Avenue, Toronto, Ontario M4B 318
Simplicity ® is a registered trademark of Simplicity Pattern Co., Inc.

FIRST EDITION

Designed by Christine Swirnoff/Libra Graphics, Inc.

Library of Congress Cataloging-in-Publication Data

Simplicity's simply the best sewing book / by the Simplicity Pattern Co. Inc.
Includes index.

1. Dressmaking. 2. Sewing. I. Simplicity Pattern Co.
TT515.S595 1988
646.4'304—dc19   87-24940

88 89 90 91 92 10 9 8 7 6 5 4 3 2

CONTENTS

PART TWO

SIMPLY THE BEST SEWING RESOURCE

PART THREE

SIMPLY THE BEST PATTERNLESS SEWING PROJECTS

INTRODUCTION:
HOW THIS BOOK EVOLVED

DEAR READER:

As a pattern company devoted to being an integral part of the fashion apparel business, we have evolved just as the apparel business has. For us, finding the right fashion looks is just part of the job; then we take pride in making those items as easy for you to sew as possible. The good news is that sewing is getting much easier, much faster, and much more fun than ever before. The sewing industry has undergone an industrial revolution all by itself and the result is some of the most streamlined, state-of-the-art equipment you could ever hope to own—including computerized sewing machines that operate with a touch of the finger and a memory feature that programs sewing techniques; overlock or serger machines that not only stitch and finish a seam all at once but also, for the first time ever, put knits and slippery sheers within the realm of beginner and expert alike—with perfect, ready-to-wear results guaranteed.

Just as food processors and microwave ovens have revolutionized cooking, so the dazzling new sewing equipment introduces speed, convenience and instant, professional results to the world of sewing at home. Along with the new basic equipment, there are other exciting advances as well—new accessories like the rotary wheel which cuts through many layers of fabrics at once; markers that eliminate basting and disappear in the wash; fusibles to use in construction that improve the appearance of a garment in completion; specialized patterns that focus on individual needs and present a whole array of shortcut techniques—to use with both new and conventional sewing equipment.

We at Simplicity® feel that now is the time to show you exactly how to put what's available to good use to simplify your sewing.

The one central source of sewing information you'll ever need, this book not only introduces all the exciting new sewing technology, but it also presents a whole new approach to sewing at home—*regardless* of what kind of sewing equipment you own. Hard-and-fast sewing rules have been replaced wherever possible with the myriad of sewing options now available. At last, there's no "right" or "wrong" way to sew at home—just many different ways to achieve fabulous, speedy results. We've exploited every shortcut, infused the text with hints, tips and suggestions for individual sewing needs and, hopefully, opened up a whole new world of individual creativity based on sewing confidence. And if you are not yet ready to invest your money in new sewing equipment, at least you can get a first-hand glimpse of how easily it can be integrated into sewing today, finding it in the pages of this book alongside the basic, best-ever conventional techniques.

To our delight, untapped sources of valuable information for the book turned up right in the Simplicity® offices. Through our Consumer Relations Department, for example, where questions and calls for help are answered by our experts, we were able to pinpoint the areas of sewing where today's consumer needed guidance. We found that both the rank beginner and those with years of previous sewing skill would benefit greatly from refocusing their sewing objectives, assessing why they sew and where it makes a valid wardrobe contribution. These essentials are covered in *Chapter 1*.

We found that many sewing enthusiasts

plunge into sewing oblivious to the easy but all-important preliminaries that assure ultimate success in any sewing project. In *Chapter 2, Pattern Savvy*, you'll find easy guidelines for selecting a pattern with know-how and confidence, while *Chapter 3* covers everything you need to know about choosing fabric, including how it "behaves," pitfalls to avoid, care considerations and the wonderful effects of color on individual appearance.

Chapter 4, The Easy Way to a Perfect Fit, provides the first simplified approach to fit, with a simple "fit formula" that really works.

Part Two is, without doubt, the ultimate sewing resource. First, in *Chapter 5* come the "universal basics" for all sewing projects—preshrinking the fabric and understanding fabric terms, laying out patterns and cutting methods, stitching, seam and thread choices, pressing as you sew—*everything* you need to know, including new innovations as well as basic information for conventional sewing.

Chapter 6—the heart and soul of the book—is a veritable encyclopedia of sewing techniques for today, chock-full of new information for beginner and expert alike. Each technique is presented as a self-contained unit, complete with all the best and newest ways to accomplish the desired results, along with suggestions about which methods work best for specific needs. Wherever there's a choice between an easy or an easier approach to a technique presented, you'll find it—along with timesaving tips and sewing hints (sometimes so obvious you'll be amazed you didn't think of them yourself).

Part Three is a get-started section of projects created at Simplicity® exclusively for this book—with no complicated grids to enlarge, send-away coupons for patterns or other obstacles to putting all your new sewing skills to practical use. The brilliantly inspired *patternless wardrobe* and its accessories are sized to Simplicity® pattern standards for adults and children, and provide the most rewarding, wearable results you could ever hope for in launching into sewing for today. And there are other projects as well—adorable baby clothes and a super-simple table setting—rounding out the exciting range of today's individual home-sewing objectives.

That's it—SIMPLICITY'S® SIMPLY THE BEST SEWING BOOK— the only guide you'll ever need to get going and *keep* going with fabulous, soul-satisfying sewing at home. There's never been a better time to sew! Whether you're new to sewing, a seasoned expert or coming back to it once again, you've got everything at your fingertips—including this book—to make the most of your sewing time. We wish you the best as you sew along with all of us at Simplicity.

The Simplicity Pattern Company

PART ONE

YOUR OWN SPECIAL SEWING STYLE

How wise you are to sew at home! You'll find it's never been more rewarding or more fun than now, with options readily available to suit every sewing philosophy. Good sewing sense begins with a fresh new analysis of your own priorities and sewing goals; after that, everything falls naturally into place.

The next four chapters provide a new orientation to sewing, aimed at helping you discover—and make the most of—your own special sewing style. All the fundamentals—from analyzing your wardrobe and assessing fashions that suit your figure, to finding and fitting patterns that really work for you, in fabrics that bring out your best—are presented in clear, simple steps that will apply to every sewing project you undertake.

CHAPTER 1

SEWING FOR TODAY

Not long ago, if you asked a group of people why they sewed, you would probably get one of two answers. The first would be "to save money." The second would be "because there's nothing suitable in the stores."

Ask that same question today, and you'll get a rainbow of answers.

"Sewing is a way to express myself."

In this age of advanced technology and mass production, sewing provides the means for expressing individuality. It doesn't matter if you shop in a department store, an expensive boutique or a discount chain . . . or if you shop at the high or the low end of the line. When you buy ready-made clothes, you can always see someone else coming and going in "your" outfit. If you sew, however, you can say to yourself, "No, I'm not a dress designer; I could NEVER design my own garment. But through fabric

and pattern I can have a lot of fun and get a lot of satisfaction expressing myself as an individual."

"Sewing gives me time to unwind."

Sewing is the perfect antidote for stress—it offers the opportunity to escape, even if it's only for half an hour, from the cares and pressures of the day. An activity that occupies both your hands and your brain, sewing absorbs your complete attention. When sewing time is over, you can go back to the "real" world with a cleared head.

"The garments I sew are better made . . . in better fabric than the ones I could afford to buy."

Buttons fall off, seams aren't finished, hems come undone . . .

even on the most expensive ready-to-wear garments. If you invest that same amount of money in quality fabric and a flattering pattern, you'll end up with a garment that will look better and last longer than the one you would have bought. With today's easy sewing techniques, helpful notions and new sewing machine technology, anyone can turn out a professional-looking garment.

In fact, the more you sew, the more discriminating a buyer you will become. You'll be able to recognize quality construction when you see it . . . which means you'll ultimately get more for your ready-to-wear dollars, too.

"I have small children . . . and buying clothes for them is SO expensive."

Sewing children's clothes is a great way to save money—and a great way to create a pint-sized wardrobe with irresistible appeal. Since children's clothes take relatively little fabric, you can frequently use the leftovers from the clothes you sew for yourself. Remnant tables, with yardages that are frequently insufficient for adult garments, provide countless bargains for children's sewing. Sewing children's garments is also a great way to experiment with new techniques—stitch details, appliqués, trims. A small child won't notice, or even care, if the plaids don't match perfectly or the buttonholes aren't exactly straight.

"Sewing is fun . . . and now it's so easy!"

If you learned to sew back in the days when finishing the seams on a garment was a real task, when making a jacket meant hours of laborious padstitching or when reading pattern instructions was like learning a foreign language, you're in for a pleasant surprise. "State-of-the-art" sewing has never been easier.

■ *Computerized sewing machines* require no more than a light touch of the finger to change stitch length, width or configuration, allowing you to go from straight stitch to zigzag stitch to stretch stitch in a matter of seconds. As with all good computers, these sewing machines have a memory, making it possible to program the size, then duplicate the same buttonhole as many times as you wish; or to program a variety of decorative stitches in almost infinite combinations.

■ *Overlock or "serger" sewing machines*, once the exclusive property of the garment industry, are now widely available for home use. These magic machines

are the perfect complement to the conventional sewing machine. They stitch, trim and overcast a seam—all in one operation. They can do narrow rolled hems on anything from linen napkins and tablecloths to lightweight silks and chiffons. They can clean-finish the edge of a garment, eliminating the need for facings, with a stitch that is both functional and decorative. And they perform all these feats at a speed that's twice as fast as the fastest conventional machine. Chapters 5 and 6 are full of examples of how the overlock can enhance your conventional sewing.

■ *Sewing patterns* are easier to use than ever before, and now there are even *special pattern groups,* each identified by its own unique logo, that focus on the needs of the beginner, on overlock sewing, on quick, easy sewing—among others. In addition, many patterns available today include specialized fitting information; Chapter 2 gives further details.

■ *Fusible interfacings* that really stay fused through repeated washings or dry cleanings take the work out of shaping a garment. This holds true whether you are merely adding interfacing to the collar and cuffs of a blouse or constructing a tailored jacket.

■ *Sewing aids and notions* have simplified sewing in ways that your grandmother wouldn't have dreamed possible. Imagine basting thread that dissolves in the wash, disappearing marking pens that make it possible to mark directly on the right side of the fabric, a lightweight, sheer seam binding that automatically curls around the edge of the fabric as you apply it, or a liquid that invisibly seals the raw edges of seams, trim, buttonholes, etc. The tips and techniques in Chapters 5

and 6 include these, and many more, timesaving notions.

CHOOSING YOUR SEWING PHILOSOPHY

Who, in this busy world of ours, has time to sew everything she needs? With so many beautiful fabrics and patterns to choose from, it makes good sense to adopt a sewing philosophy to help you decide where your sewing priorities lie.

BUY HARD, SEW EASY

Sew simple, easy-fitting garments that don't have a lot of complicated details, in fabrics that don't require special handling. For example, you might make the top and the skirt—but buy the co-ordinating tailored jacket to complete the outfit. If you're short on time or experience, this may be the sewing philosophy for you.

BUY EASY, SEW HARD

Put your time and money into the luxury fabrics and special details that greatly increase the cost of a ready-to-wear garment. With this approach, you would buy the top and the pants and use your sewing time to create the jacket.

SEW THE CLASSICS

Choose traditional styles that won't go out of fashion for several seasons. If you're sewing mostly for pleasure, it may not matter how soon the project is finished. Concentrate on seasonless fabrics (See Chapter 3) so the garment can go straight into your wardrobe regardless of when it's finished.

SEW THE "FAD" STYLES

If you want to be the first with the newest fashions, keep up to date on all the latest shortcut techniques. Because you sew a style for today, with the understanding that tomorrow it may be passé, saving time is essential to making this sewing objective a success.

SEW FOR SPECIAL OCCASIONS

If you love "dressing to the nines," you may want to devote your sewing time exclusively to the very satisfying sewing category of evening wear. Not only are the fabrics for formal clothes wonderful and inspiring to work with, but you can also save money by sewing the glamorous parts of your wardrobe.

SEW SIMPLY BECAUSE YOU LOVE TO

If you enjoy the opportunity to experiment with different types of fabrics and patterns, sewing anything that catches your eye, then you're someone who enjoys sewing for the pure pleasure of it. If you're not in this category now, with a little sewing experience you'll soon graduate to it!

FINDING WHAT FLATTERS

Regardless of why you sew or what sewing philosophy you adopt, how do you combine fabric, pattern and fit to achieve the most flattering wardrobe ever?

This is the question that challenges everyone who sews her own clothes. The answer, believe it or not, can be found in the clothes you already own. Open your closets and pull out the items you wear most often. If you're like most people, you wear only 10 percent of your clothes

90 percent of the time. While not immediately apparent, there are some very good reasons why this is so!

ANALYZING YOUR FAVORITE GARMENTS

Examine each garment carefully and try it on—you're going to analyze what it is that makes each one a favorite. Make lots of notes as you go.

■ *Fabric*—Perhaps you like the look and feel of natural fibers . . . or the easy care of a synthetic. Do you wear this garment because it keeps you very warm or very cool? Does the fabric have some "give" (for example, is it a knit or is it cut on the bias) that enhances the fit and adds to the comfort?

■ *Color*—If it's an outfit that brings you lots of compliments, it may just be the color. Even the simplest of garments, in a flattering color, will win rave reviews. Color analysis, a method for determining the colors that compliment you best, is one way some of the smartest dressers make sure that their wardrobes are full of flattering and coordinating colors. In Chapter 3, there's more about the benefits of developing a personal color strategy.

■ *Style*—Do you like the garment because it makes you look taller, shorter or thinner? Because it camouflages wide hips, a thick waist, narrow shoulders, a large bust or a flat chest?

■ *Fit*—You won't feel comfortable in a garment unless it fits well. Notice what features provide you with a good fit. Are the sleeves cut full in the upper arm? Is the dress a no-waistline or elasticized-waist style? Do the trousers have front pleats? Pay particular attention to the proportions. Do many of your favorite jackets and tops end at the waistline or

high hipbone . . . or do you prefer styles that cover up the fullest part of your hips and derrière? What skirt length(s) enhance your proportions and provide the most comfort?

■ *Compatibility*—Do some garments get a lot of wear because they coordinate well with other things in your wardrobe?

As you go through this list, award the garment points for each category: two points if it's a success, one point if it's just okay, no points if it's a flop. Some of the garments in your 10 percent group will score high marks in all five categories. Others will have only one or two features that make it a favorite, such as great fit, comfortable fabric, but a color that does nothing special for you. Pay closest attention to the garments that get the highest scores.

WHAT YOUR WARDROBE CAN TELL YOU

Now go back to your closet and take a look at the things that you seldom wear. As you compare the two sets of clothes, certain themes will begin to emerge. Notice how, when you shopped, you were attracted to a variety of styles, fabrics and colors. However, once you got those garments home, you only wore certain ones; the others were relegated to the far corners of your closet—a waste of time and money.

Analyzing the good and bad points of your current wardrobe gives you clues about where to concentrate your sewing efforts. If you focus on the clothes you love, pinpointing fabric type, color, fashion style and fit, you will have established valuable guidelines to use in choosing patterns, fabrics and sewing techniques.

Remember, the purpose of a

wardrobe analysis is not to look for clothes to duplicate (although that's a fine idea, if that's what you want to do) but rather to give you information about your best personal style. It will help you to make wise choices about what you sew and to avoid repeating the mistakes you found in the clothes you've purchased. Write down the good points and bad points you've discovered about the clothes from your closet. Keep the points handy as you read and act on the information in Chapters 2 and 3 on selecting patterns and fabric.

Don't make the mistake of thinking your best personal style is fixed on one fashion category either. Loose-fitting, tailored, very

FIGURE-WISE STRATEGIES

Because each of us has lived with our body all our life, we instinctively know whether we're short and slender, short and heavy, tall and slender, tall and heavy, top heavy or bottom heavy. However, we may not know how to camouflage—or enhance—these proportions to achieve a balanced look. The following "strategies" or style formulas work well for most women; for more on fit and fabric, turn to Chapters 3 and 4 respectively.

"Sewing provides you with the opportunity to combine good fit, complimentary color, suitable fabric and flattering style, all in one garment. When you sew, every garment in your closet can rate a '10.'"

IF YOU'RE SHORT AND SLENDER . . .

Fashions with vertical lines will seem to add inches to your height. To add softness and curves, choose styles with uncluttered fullness.

Styles that flatter:

■ shirtdresses, narrow tents or tunics with vertical details
■ single-breasted jackets with shawl collars or narrow lapels
■ narrow, slim or slightly flared pants and skirts
■ neat, small details at the top— stand-up collars, shoulder yoke seaming or tiny pockets

Fabrics that flatter:

■ plain, soft, drapable textures
■ light to medium weights
■ small to medium-sized prints, plaids and stripes

Color schemes that flatter:

■ light or pale tones with darker, bolder colors for accents
■ matching or similar colors, when used for coordinates, add height

casual or elegant—there's a wide range of styles, fabrics, color and fit combinations to be discovered—if you're open to them.

As you look over your favorite clothes, don't be dissuaded by thoughts like, "Oh, but I could never sew something like that!" Look more closely. Turn the garment inside out—see how it's constructed and think about what techniques were used. Browse through Chapter 6 to find similar construction techniques. Chances are most garments are well within your sewing abilities, and that includes the ones you love best. If not, begin with something simpler. As your confidence builds, you'll be able to sew all the styles you love.

IF YOU'RE
SHORT AND HEAVY . . .

To appear taller, choose fashions that accent the vertical. Styles that just skim the body will seem to whittle away the inches. Avoid very full styles as they will overwhelm your figure.

Styles that flatter:

■ dresses with contrasting necklines, no waistline seams or narrow, matching belts
■ cardigan jackets or jackets that can be worn open to create the illusion of a narrow waist
■ pants and skirts that are straight but not slim

Fabrics that flatter:

■ smooth, plain, crisp textures
■ light to medium weights
■ small-scale prints, plaids and stripes in muted colors

Color schemes that flatter:

■ solids in dark or dulled tones
■ color-matched schemes for tops and bottoms

IF YOU'RE
TALL AND SLENDER . . .

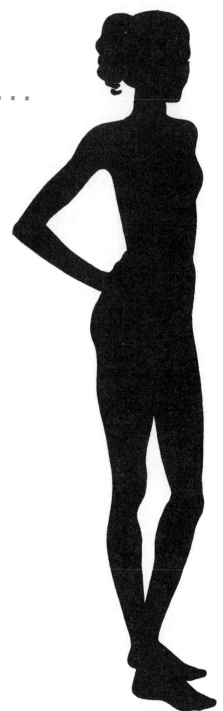

Choose fashions that round out your figure and balance your height.

Styles that flatter:

- pants with hip details and cuffs
- double-breasted, unstructured jackets with wide lapels
- blouses with fullness or tucks at the shoulder seams
- loose, flowing dresses, nipped in at the waist
- skirts with pleats or tucks
- horizontal details, such as flap pockets or yoked seams

Fabrics that flatter:

- highly textured surfaces
- medium to heavy weights, in either soft or crisp fabrics
- bold prints, checks, plaids or stripes

Color schemes that flatter:

- bright, light colors
- contrasting colors for separates

IF YOU'RE
TALL AND HEAVY . . .

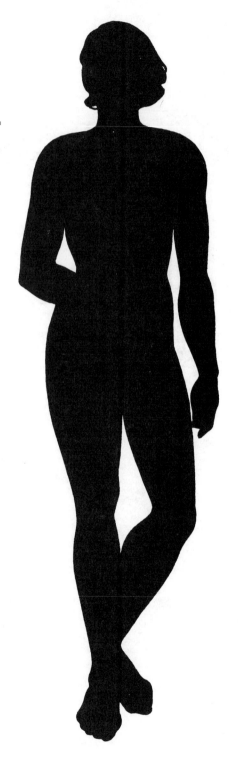

Select fashions that softly skim your body, streamlining your figure and minimizing your weight.

Styles that flatter:

- uncluttered silhouettes with emphasis on vertical lines
- dresses with softly belted waistlines, wrapped closings
- softly tailored separates, such as a flared skirt, bow-tied blouse and midlength, single-breasted jacket
- straight-leg pants
- tunic-length tops

Fabrics that flatter:

- plain, smooth textures
- medium weights
- soft or crisp styles
- medium-scale plaids, prints or stripes in muted shades

Color schemes that flatter:

- cool colors in medium to dark tones
- one-color family for separates

IF YOU'RE
TOP HEAVY . . .

Balance your proportions with contrasting fashions that play up your hips and de-emphasize your bust.

Styles that flatter:

■ easy-fitting shirtdresses

■ pants and skirts with pockets, pleats, tucks and gathers

■ uncluttered, tailored blouses with small collars, softly gathered shoulders and center closings

■ loose-fitting jackets

Fabrics to wear on top have:

■ plain textures, light weights

■ dark, muted colors

■ solids or small prints

Fabrics to wear on the bottom have:

■ medium to heavy textures and weights

■ drapability

■ light, bright colors

■ bold designs

IF YOU'RE
BOTTOM HEAVY . . .

Balance your proportions with lots of detailing and horizontal lines on top, simple and vertical lines on the bottom.

Styles that flatter:

- dresses that skim your hips and have bodice detailing
- simple skirts and pants
- full-blown blouses with unusual design interest
- long, loose-fitting jackets

Fabrics to wear on top have:

- medium to heavy textures and weights
- drapability
- light, bright colors
- eye-catching prints and designs

Fabrics to wear on the bottom have:

- plain textures, light weights
- dark, muted colors
- solid coloring or subtle designs
- small-scale prints

CHAPTER 2

PATTERN SAVVY

Leafing through the pages of a pattern catalog is like being turned loose in a candy store. There are so many goodies to choose from!

FASHION INSPIRATION

The pattern catalog itself is one of your most valuable sources of inspiration. It's full of ideas for co-ordinating separates, combining colors and prints, and picking fabrics. By studying the photographs and sketches carefully, you'll also pick up some good ideas about how to accessorize your finished garment.

In addition to the pattern catalog that is carried in the fabric store, most pattern companies produce their own pattern magazine which is published regularly and is available either on the newsstand or on a subscription basis. With your pattern magazine in hand and in the comfort of your own living room, you can choose your sewing projects from a selection of the newest patterns.

A CLIPPING FILE

Of course when it comes to fashion inspiration, you're not limited to the pattern catalog and pattern magazines. One of the advantages of sewing is that the ultimate choice of pattern and fabric combinations can be all your own. Magazines and newspapers are full of ideas to get your creative juices flowing. Why not start a fashion file? Clip and save anything that catches your eye. Here's one place where price is no object. You can be as equally inspired by an inexpensive outfit as by one that costs several thousand dollars. Look for pleasing design lines, attractive color combinations, unusual fabric mixes, and interesting trims and details. It's fun once you tune in on the possibilities.

SELECTING A PATTERN

For some people, sifting through the pattern catalog, with its wide range of choices, is pure delight. For others, particularly beginners at sewing, the process of choosing a pattern seems a bit over-whelming. It's really very easy if you just keep three simple criteria in mind:
1. Choose a style that you like.
2. Choose design lines that are flattering to your figure.
3. Look for design details that are compatible with your sewing skills.

A STYLE THAT YOU LIKE

Don't select a pattern just because the style is "in" or just because it's easy. How many people do you know who were turned off sewing because they were required to make something way back in junior high school that they would NEVER wear? Make sure you really like what you select. After all, half the fun of sewing is being able to show off what you have made.

A STYLE THAT FLATTERS

Be sure the style you love is also a style that flatters. Use the knowledge you gained from analyzing your current wardrobe, along with the figure-wise strategies you learned in Chapter 1. If the style you're considering is a radical departure from anything you've ever worn, it might be wise to spend some time trying on a few similar ready-to-wear garments before you buy your fabric and pattern.

A STYLE THAT MATCHES YOUR SEWING SKILLS

If you were learning to cook, you wouldn't begin by making a soufflé! Instead, you'd start with something basic and gradually work your way up to the more complicated recipes. Learning to sew is much the same.

As you thumb through the catalog, notice how the patterns are grouped together in various ways. You'll find tabs that indicate *garment* or *other categories*, such as "Dresses," "Coordinates," "Bridal," "Blouses & Tops" or "Home Dec & Crafts," as well as tabs that indicate *special size and age ranges*, such as "Larger Sizes," "Toddlers," "Children" and "Men & Boys."

In addition, there are two other pattern categories, one based on fitting techniques and the other on sewing techniques. They may have their own tab or they may be found under the tabs for particular garment, size or age range categories.

FIT. Patterns with logos such as ADJUST-TO-FIT, PERSONAL FIT™, FUSS-FREE FIT® Mor ADJUSTABLE FOR MISS PETITE are designed to help solve certain fitting dilemmas. (See Chapter 4 for more information.)

SEWING LEVEL. If you're just learning to sew, if you're experimenting with a difficult-to-handle fabric, or if you need to sew something fast, look at patterns with logos such as JIFFY®, BE-

GINNER'S CHOICE® or E-A-S-Y TO SEW. Patterns marked OVERLOCK/SERGER include instructions for sewing on the overlock machine as well as on the conventional machine. Although these are certainly not the only patterns you can use with an overlock, they're a great help when you're just learning to use this fabulous new machine.

Although the above examples are all from the Simplicity® Pattern Catalog, every major pattern company has its own set of terms or logos to indicate their specialized patterns. As the sewing and fashion picture changes, new categories may be developed. If you're not sure what the terms mean, turn to the back of the pattern catalog. You'll usually find a page that includes an explanation of each category. If the category doesn't have its own tab, you'll often find an index that includes a listing of the specialized patterns and their appropriate page numbers.

CREATIVE PATTERN SELECTION

Suppose you've fallen in love with a particular garment from your clipping file and you can't find a pattern that looks like it. Here are a few ideas:

■ If it's a dress, see if you can find a skirt and blouse combination that will give you the same look. The bonus in having a two-piece dress is that you'll have two items that look smashing together or that can go their own separate ways in your wardrobe.

■ If it's a jumpsuit, consider pants and a top of the same fabric. These will be easier to fit, as well as more versatile, than a one-piece garment.

■ If you can find a blouse pattern that has the right lines, consider

lengthening it to make a dress. Be sure to buy enough extra fabric to accommodate the longer length.

THE CATALOG PAGE

The catalog page is a treasure trove of information. If you know how to "read" it properly, you'll be able to pick the pattern that's just right for your needs.

Here's the information you will find, keyed here by number to its location on the sample page at right:

1–A fashion photo of one of the views shows how the pattern will look when it's all sewn up. The garment may have been altered slightly to fit the model's individual proportions, but no more so than for anyone else, and you can consider the photograph an accurate guide as to how the pattern should fit. It also provides you with visual clues about what fabric weights and textures are suitable for the design.

2–Fashion drawings show what other views or versions are included in the pattern. They're illustrated in different colors, prints or fabric types than the photo to inspire you with more fashion and fabric ideas that are compatible with the design.

3–Identification information includes the pattern number, a

> **TIP** *Although your pattern view may not use every piece, the total number of pattern pieces is one way to evaluate the amount of time or sewing skill a pattern will require. Use it as a guide when you're trying to decide which of two similar designs is the easiest.*

E-A-S-Y TO SEW

0000 Simplicity® MISSES' SLIM–FITTING PULL-ON PANTS AND SKIRT AND LOOSE–FITTING UNLINED JACKET
. . . SIZED FOR STRETCH KNITS ONLY: 10 PIECES **$5.00**

Fabrics–Cotton interlock, lightweight double knits, cotton and wool jerseys, ribbed knits, sweatshirt knits. (SEE PICK–A–KNIT® RULE for pants and skirt.) Extra fabric needed to match plaids, stripes or one-way design fabrics. For pile, shaded or one-way design fabrics, use with nap yardages/layouts. Not suitable for obvious diagonals.

BONUS
How to cover shoulder pads.

OVERLOCK/SERGER

TimeSaver® instructions included for sewing on an Overlock/Serger or conventional machine.

BODY MEASUREMENTS							
Bust	30½	31½	32½	34	36	38	Ins.
Waist	23	24	25	26½	28	30	"
Hip	32½	33½	34½	36	38	40	"
Sizes	6	8	10	12	14	16	
Pants							
52″ / 54″**	1½	1¾	1⅞	2⅛	2⅛	2⅛	Yds.
58″ / 60″**	1¼	1¼	1¼	1½	1¾	2	"

Sizes	6	8	10	12	14	16	
Skirt							
52″ / 54″ or 58″ / 60″**	⅞	⅞	⅞	⅞	⅞	⅞	Yd.
Jacket							
52″ / 54″**		2⅛	2⅛	2⅛	2⅛	2⅛	2⅛	Yds.
58″ / 60″**		1⅞	1⅞	1⅞	1⅞	2	2⅛	"
Pants leg width		11½	12	12½	13	13½	14	"
Skirt width		35½	36½	37½	39	41	43	"

*without nap   **with nap   ***with or without nap

MULTI-SIZE PATTERN
HH(6 + 8 + 10 + 12) NN(10 + 12 + 14 + 16)

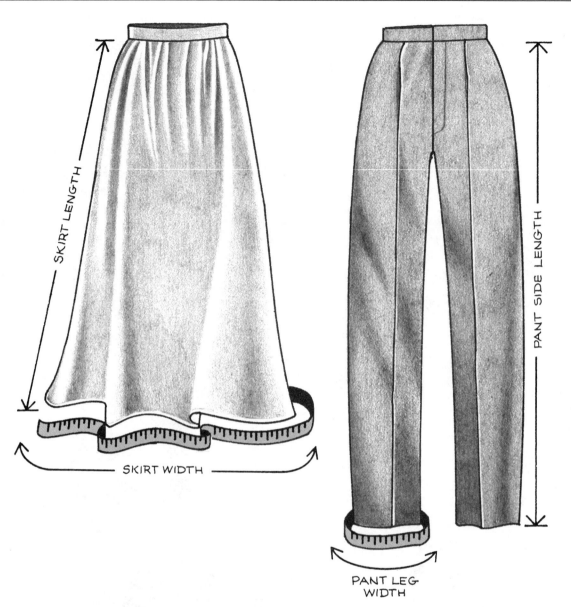

SKIRT LENGTH

SKIRT WIDTH

PANT SIDE LENGTH

PANT LEG
WIDTH

very brief description, pattern category (such as JIFFY or OVERLOCK/SERGER), the total number of pattern pieces, and the price.

4—*A chart* tells you which sizes the pattern comes in and how much fabric is needed for each size, fabric width and view. Yardages for fabrics "with nap" are also included. This chart is especially handy if you've come to the fabric store for fabric and you've forgotten to bring your pattern . . . or if you're looking for a pattern to go with a piece of fabric you already own.

In addition to the yardage requirements, this chart may also include some actual garment measurements that will help you judge the length or fullness of the design. For example, "Skirt Width" and "Skirt Length" may be included on a dress or skirt pattern; "Pants Leg Width" or "Pants Side Length" may be included on trousers, shorts or culotte patterns. It will be helpful if you take these measurements on several garments you already own, as shown above. Write them down and take them with you when

you pick out your pattern. That way, you'll have a meaningful reference point for comparison.

5—*Fabric types* that will work best with the style are suggested. You might also find a note about which ones to avoid, such as "Not suitable for obvious diagonal fabrics." Don't ignore these notes, no matter how much you love a particular fabric, or you're sure to be disappointed with the results.

6—*Special alerts*, such as "Sized for stretch knits only," "Two sizes on same pattern tissue," or "BONUS—Pattern includes special chart on how to work with plaids," as well as other helpful fabric selection information, are included on the catalog page.

7—Back views show you fashion details, such as zipper, pocket or button locations, seams and darts that are not visible from the front.

THE PATTERN ENVELOPE

The pattern envelope contains much the same information as the catalog page but in greater detail.

THE ENVELOPE FRONT

The front of the envelope includes the same sketches and photographs that were featured on the catalog page, as well as the pattern number, the price, the size and any identifying logos for special pattern categories.

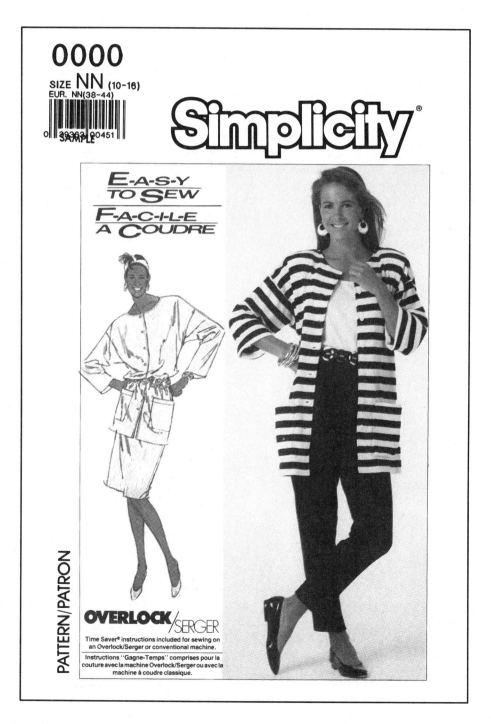

0000

SIZE **NN** (10-16)
EUR. NN(38-44)

0 39363 00451
SAMPLE

Simplicity®

E·A·S·Y TO SEW
F·A·C·I·L·E A COUDRE

OVERLOCK/SERGER

Time Saver® instructions included for sewing on an Overlock/Serger or conventional machine.

Instructions "Gagne-Temps" comprises pour la couture avec la machine Overlock/Serger ou avec la machine à coudre classique.

PATTERN/PATRON

> **TIP** *Patterns are not returnable so make sure you've got the pattern you want, in the size and figure type you need, before you pay for it.*

THE ENVELOPE BACK

The back of the envelope serves as a convenient shopping list for the fabric and notions you'll need to make the pattern. It repeats some of the information that was on the catalog page, such as the pattern identification number, the number of pattern pieces and the back views. Other information is not only repeated, but also expanded upon. (Numbers on sample below correspond to numbers in text.)

1—*Garment description* explains design details, such as linings, topstitching and pockets, that may not be obvious from the illustration. It also includes information about how each view is different.

2—*Suggested fabric list* repeats the information that was printed on the catalog page. This is your guide to selecting the fabric that will give you the best results. See Chapter 3 for additional information.

3—*Yardage chart* tells you how much fabric to buy for the size and view you want to make. Note that different yardage amounts are listed, depending on the width of the fabric and whether it is with or without nap. If a garment is made from 45″ (115cm) wide fabric, it usually requires more yardage than if it is made from 60″ (153cm) wide fabric. If the fabric has a texture or design that must go in one direction on the finished garment (a "with nap" fabric), you'll need more yardage than you would for a fabric without a nap.

Yardage requirements for any lining, interfacing, elastic or trim are also included in the chart.

4—*Standard body measurements* were included on the catalog page to help you determine your correct pattern size. They're repeated on the envelope as a convenient reference guide for making pattern adjustments later on. For additional information, see Chapter 4.

5—*Notions* are all the extras, such as buttons, zippers, seam bindings and shoulder pads, that

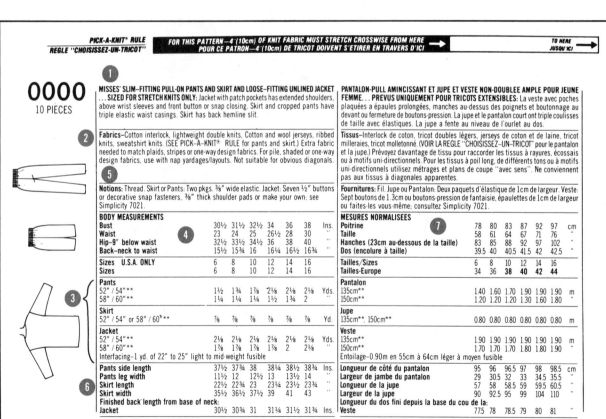

you'll need to complete the garment. To save time and to insure a close color match, you'll probably want to purchase these at the same time you buy your fabric.

6–*Finished garment measurements* are repeated on the back of the envelope. Like the standard body measurements, these are helpful if you need to make any pattern adjustments.

7–*Metric equivalents* for the standard body measurements and the finished garment measurements, as well as the yardage and notion requirements, are provided on a separate chart, opposite the Imperial chart.

INSIDE THE ENVELOPE

Your pattern envelope contains two things: the pattern instruction sheet and all the pattern pieces you need to make your garment.

THE PATTERN INSTRUCTION SHEET

The sheet of instructions inside the envelope guides your sewing every step of the way—from laying out and cutting the pattern to working at your sewing machine.

Before you purchase the pattern, you might want to pull out the instruction sheet and glance through it. Consider how many of the techniques are new to you . . . and how fast you want to complete this project. If you're sewing against a deadline, and the pattern has several new techniques, you might want to make another selection.

Once you get the pattern home, don't do any pinning or cutting until you've had time to carefully read through the instruction sheet. If there is more than one instruction sheet, each page is numbered so that you know what order to follow. Make sure you understand all the notations and that the sewing instructions make sense. Pay particular attention to any sewing technique that is new to you. Check out the index in the back of this book and review the sections that are pertinent to the technique.

On the left-hand side of the first page of the instruction sheet, you'll find:
(*Note:* Numbers correspond to the numbers on the sample sheet, shown on the next page.)

1–*Line drawings* are simplified sketches of all the views of versions that are included in the pattern. These sketches clearly show all the technical design details. In addition, because the layout and the sewing instructions may vary depending on the view, these drawings provide you with a convenient way to double-check which view you're following.

2–The *Select Pattern Pieces* section contains simplified diagrams of each pattern piece. Each diagram is identified by a letter. Look below the drawings to find out what each letter stands for, as well as what view(s) each pattern piece is used for. Put a check mark next to each piece you will need for the view you are making.

3–The section labeled *The Pattern* and *Cutting and Marking* is usually positioned across the top of the first page of the instruction sheet. This section explains the most common pattern symbols and how to make simple lengthen or shorten adjustments. It also includes tips to make your cutting and marking easier, along with an explanation of the special cutting notes that may be included in your *Cutting Layout.*

4–*Cutting Layouts* show you how to position the pattern pieces properly on your fabric with the least amount of waste. Layouts are given for different pattern sizes and various fabric widths. Find the diagram for your view, pattern size and fabric width, then draw a circle around it. If you are new to sewing, or if you are using a "With Nap" fabric, or if there is anything you don't understand about the cutting layout, it would be a good idea to review the section in Chapter 5 on The Cutting Layout.

5–*Sewing Information* explains some common sewing procedures. This section, which is usually located across the top of page 2 of the instruction sheet, includes the basic how-to's for ease-stitching or gathering, edge finishes, staystitching, understitching and applying interfacing. For a more detailed explanation of any of these topics, turn to Chapter 6.

6–*Sewing Directions*, starting on either the front or the back of the instruction sheet, take you step-by-step through the process of constructing the garment. The instructions are organized by garment section so that all the stitching and pressing is completed in one area, such as the bodice, before going on to another. This is the fastest, easiest system for most sewers to follow. However, as you become more experienced, you may find it faster to work on several sections simultaneously, sewing as far as you can on each one until you must stop and press. This method minimizes back-and-forth trips to the ironing board. If you are going to use this faster method, it's absolutely essential that you take the time to read through the sewing directions before you begin. Otherwise, in your enthusiasm, it's all too easy to sew too far or to skip a step.

Simplicity® 0000
page 1

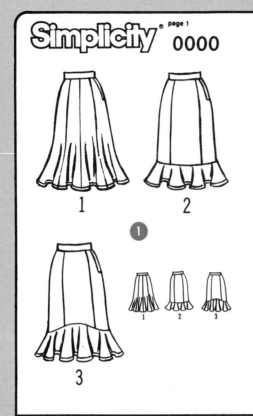

1 2

3

Select Pattern Pieces

15 pieces given

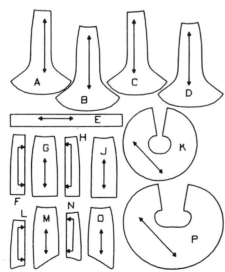

A-SKIRT FRONT V.1
B-SKIRT SIDE FRONT V.1
C-SKIRT BACK V.1
D-SKIRT SIDE BACK V.1
E-WAISTBAND
F-SKIRT FRONT V.2
G-SKIRT SIDE FRONT V.2
H-SKIRT BACK V.2

J-SKIRT SIDE BACK V.2
K-FLOUNCE V.2
L-SKIRT FRONT V.3
M-SKIRT SIDE FRONT V.3
N-SKIRT BACK V.3
O-SKIRT SIDE BACK V.3
P-FLOUNCE V.3

The Pattern

SYMBOLS	ADJUST IF NEEDED
GRAIN LINE Place on straight grain of fabric parallel to selvage.	Make adjustments before placing pattern on fabric.
PLACE BROKEN LINE on fold of fabric.	TO LENGTHEN: Cut pattern between lengthen or shorten lines. Spread pattern evenly, amount needed and tape to paper.
NOTCHES	
CUTTING LINE	TO SHORTEN: At lengthen or shorten lines, make an even pleat taking up amount needed. Tape in place.
SEAM LINE	

SEAM ALLOWANCE: 5/8" (1.5cm) unless otherwise stated.
On multi-size patterns, the seam allowance is included but not printed.
See chart on tissue pattern for other symbols.

When lengthen or shorten lines are not given, make adjustments at lower edge of pattern.

Cutting Layouts ★★ See SPECIAL

NOTE: Determine finished length before cutting.

V1 SKIRT

USE PIECES A B C D E

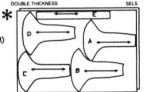

39"/40" (100/102 CM)
WITH NAP
ALL SIZES

CUT ONE E

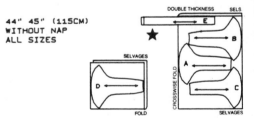

44" 45" (115CM)
WITHOUT NAP
ALL SIZES

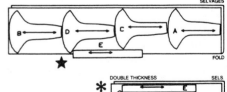

44" 45" (115CM) WITH NAP
SIZES 6 8 10 12 14 16

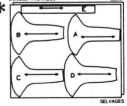

44" 45" (115CM)
WITH NAP
SIZES 18

CUT ONE E

Cutting And Marking

③

BEFORE CUTTING:

PRESS pattern pieces with a warm dry iron.

PRE-SHRINK fabric by pre-washing washables or steam pressing non-washables.

CIRCLE your layout.

PIN pattern to fabric as shown in layout.

- FOR DOUBLE THICKNESS: Fold fabric with RIGHT sides together.

- FOR SINGLE THICKNESS: Place fabric RIGHT side up.

- FOR PILE, SHADED OR ONE WAY DESIGN FABRICS: Use "with nap" layouts.

AFTER CUTTING:

Transfer markings to WRONG side of fabric before removing pattern. Use pin and chalk method or dressmaker's tracing paper and wheel.

To Quick Mark:

- Snip edge of fabric to mark notches, ends of fold lines and center lines.

- Pin mark dots.   ○ ○

SPECIAL CUTTING NOTES

If layout shows a piece extending past fold, cut out all pieces except piece that extends.

Open out fabric to single thickness. Cut extending piece on RIGHT side of fabric in position shown.

 Mark small arrows along both selvages indicating direction of nap or design. Fold fabric crosswise, with RIGHT sides together, and cut along fold (a).

Turn : e fabric layer around so arrows on both layers go in the same direction. Place RIGHT sides together (b).

CUTTING NOTES

KEY [   ] fabric   [▒▒] pattern printed side down   [   ] pattern printed side up

---

58" 60" (150CM) WITH NAP ALL SIZES

④

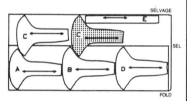

58" 60" (150CM) WITH NAP SIZES 16 18

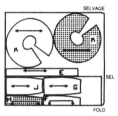

V2 SKIRT

USE PIECES E F G H J K

44" 45" (115CM) WITH OR WITHOUT NAP ALL SIZES

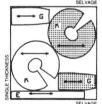

58" 60" (150CM) WITH NAP SIZE 6

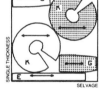

58" 60" (150CM) WITH NAP SIZES 8 10 12 14

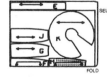

V3 SKIRT

USE PIECES E L M N O P

44" 45" (115CM) WITH OR WITHOUT NAP ALL SIZES

58" 60" (150CM) WITH NAP ALL SIZES

CUT ONE E

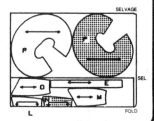

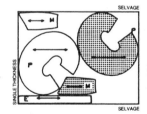

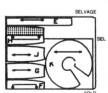

THE PATTERN PIECES

Each pattern piece contains written directions and symbols such as dots and arrows—a kind of shorthand that's easy to learn and speeds your sewing because it shows you which edges to match and where to position details.

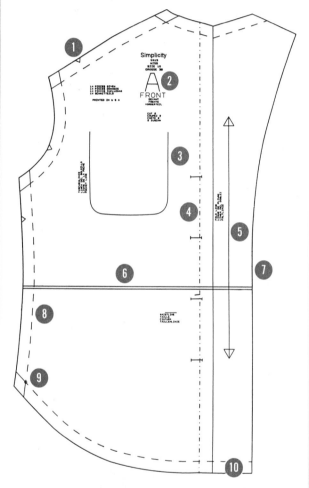

3–Solid lines* show where to position pockets, buttonholes, the waistline, or where to fold the fabric.

4–Center Line* is a broken line that appears on some pattern pieces.

5–Grainline arrow is used for positioning pattern piece on the correct fabric grain.

indicate pieces that must be placed parallel to the edge of your fabric.

Squared-off grainline arrows indicate pieces that are placed along folded fabric edges.

6–Lengthen or shorten here lines are two parallel lines which indicate where to make the pattern piece longer or shorter so the finished length will be right without distorting the garment shape.

7–Cutting lines are solid lines along the outer edge. Follow these lines when you cut your fabric.

8–Seamlines are broken lines, usually ⅝″ (1.5 cm) from the cutting line. When you sew a seam, you are actually stitching two layers of fabric together on the seamline. Multiple-size patterns do not have marked seamlines.

9–Dots* are circles which mark points to be matched before stitching and the placement of details, such as darts, tabs and belt loops.

10–Seam allowance is the area between the seamline and cutting line.

11–Darts* are shown as V-shaped broken lines with dots. To sew, match the dots, folding fabric with right sides together, and stitch along the broken line. Darts shape fabric to fit over your body curves—bust, hips, shoulders.

12–Hem tells you how much fabric to turn up for the hem.

1–Notches are triangular symbols extending from the cutting line *into* the seam allowance. To mark notches, cut triangles or snip into the seam allowances along notch lines. If you think you may have to let out a seam after stitching, mark notches by cutting triangular shapes that extend *out* from the cutting lines.

2–Letters are printed on each pattern piece so you can tell one from the other. The top of the letter always points to the top of the pattern piece.

Tucks* are shown as broken lines with double-headed arrows in between, near the end of each tuck. To sew, match the broken lines, folding the fabric with right sides together, and stitch along lines.

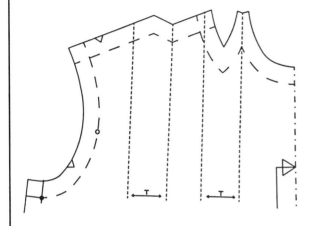

Pleats* are shown as broken and solid lines with directional arrows in between, at the end of each pleat. To make a pleat, fold your fabric on the solid line and bring the fold to the broken line. Press. Baste across top of pleat.

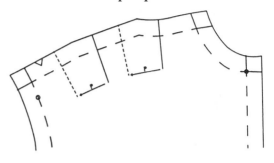

* The symbols with an asterisk (*) eventually get transferred onto your fabric; you'll learn more about this in Chapter 5.

TIP *Choosing the Right Pattern for You.*

Based on everything you've learned in Chapters 1 and 2, here's how to decide if the pattern you're contemplating is the one for you:

1. Consider your current sewing philosophy and evaluate how much time you have available to complete this project.

2. Mentally review what you learned from your wardrobe analysis. Does the design of the garment reflect what you learned about styles that flatter your figure?

3. Be realistic about what styles are compatible with your current sewing skills. Don't be afraid to choose an easy style. Some of the world's best fashion designers are celebrated for the simple lines of their clothes.

4. Analyze the information provided on the front and back of the pattern envelope.

5. Take out the instruction sheet and read it over BEFORE you purchase the pattern. If there are more new techniques than you have the time to learn right now, pick a simpler style.

CHAPTER 3

A BUYER'S GUIDE TO FABRICS AND NOTIONS

One of the most exciting things about sewing is being able to put fabric and pattern together to create a garment that is uniquely you . . . one that expresses your creativity, your wardrobe needs, your color preferences and your fashion style.

Many sewers, especially beginners, are so afraid of making a mistake that they spend hours looking for the exact fabric featured in the pattern catalog. If it's a fabric that suits your needs, that's fine. However, if you always let someone else's taste in fabrics dictate your selection, you're missing out on half the fun of sewing.

CLUES TO FABRIC SELECTION

Begin by studying the fashion photograph and fashion sketches on the catalog page and pattern envelope. Notice how the fabric falls in relation to the model's figure. It might be relaxed and flowing, gently accentuating the curves of the body. It might hug the figure closely, imitating the body's contours. It might be stiff and structured, creating a silhouette that is fuller or more architectural than the body that's underneath.

Next, read the list of fabric suggestions printed on the catalog page and on the back of the pattern envelope. Because there are so many fabric blends on the market today, the suggestion list often starts by indicating the type of fabric to look for, such as "silk types," "cotton types," or "wool types."

Some garments require soft, drapable fabrics such as jersey, crepe de chine, charmeuse, challis or handkerchief linen. Other garments call for crisper, more structured fabrics, such as corduroy, gabardine, suiting weight linens, taffeta, brocade or tweed. Sometimes the list of fabric suggestions may include fabrics that are crisp, such as taffeta, and fabrics that are soft, such as dotted swiss. Because the silhouette is versatile enough for either type of fabric, the choice depends on the fashion mood you desire.

WHEN ONLY A KNIT WILL DO

Many patterns are suitable both for wovens and for knits with a small amount of stretch, such as double knit or jersey.

TIP *You can tell a lot about a fabric just by handling it. Drape it over your arm. Does it lay smoothly against your skin or does it seem to have a shape of its own? Scrunch it up to create fullness. Does it fall into soft gathers or does it stand away from you? When you release the fabric, is it smooth or wrinkled?*

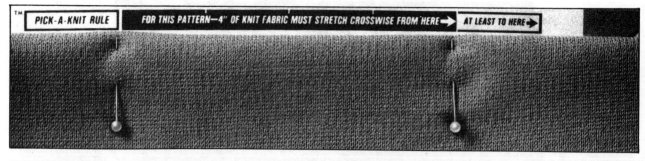

However, some patterns are designed exclusively for stretch knit fabrics. Most swimwear, sweatshirts and exercise wear, as well as many body-hugging silhouettes, are "knits only" fashions. If you tried to use a woven fabric or a knit that did not have enough stretch, the garment would be much too tight. In fact, since many of these garments are pull-on-over-the-head or pull-up-over-the-hips styles, you probably couldn't even get them on.

On Simplicity® patterns, these knits-only styles include a caution that says "Sized for Stretch Knits Only." Then, printed on the back of the pattern envelope, you'll find the "Pick-a-Knit Rule" that is designed to tell you if the knit you want to use has the right amount of stretch. To use this rule, fold the knit fabric crosswise and hold it against the left end of the rule. Pull on the knit to see if the indicated amount of fabric (usually 4″ or 10cm) will easily stretch to the end of the rule. Now let go of the fabric; it should relax to its original size and shape. If the fabric doesn't have

the proper stretch and recovery, it's not the right knit for that pattern.

A COLOR STRATEGY

Color is probably one of the first things that attracts you to a fabric. Of course, your goal is to select a color that looks as good on you as it does on the bolt.

One of the "hottest"—and smartest—trends in fashion these days is the growing awareness of how color affects the way we look and feel. Color systems, such as Carole Jackson's Color Me Beautiful®, show people how to find the colors that are personally the most flattering.

If you have not already done so, you might give serious thought to having your colors "done" by a professional color consultant. Through careful analy-

Color Me Beautiful® is a registered trademark of Color Me Beautiful, Inc.

sis of your hair, eye and skin tones, you can discover the color palettes that suit you best. Armed with this knowledge, you can build a completely coordinated—and flattering—wardrobe. You'll no longer be subject to the dictates of fashion. Suppose deep rose is one of your best colors, but the ready-to-wear departments are full of coral dresses. Sewing at home gives you the freedom to make the latest style in the color that suits you best.

Most color systems provide you with a set of colors that not only enhance your appearance but also coordinate with each other. If you stick to "your" palette when choosing fabric, your closet will start to bloom with color-coordinated clothes. The result: more outfits for less money.

THE EFFECTS OF TEXTURE AND SCALE

The next time you get a chance to people-watch, observe the fabrics they are wearing, paying careful attention to texture and scale. Note how your eye is automatically drawn to garments that feature:

■ lighter or brighter colors

■ bold or large-scale prints

■ bulky fabrics, such as tweed, mohair or fake fur

■ fabrics that cling, such as jersey and any fabric cut on the bias

■ fabrics that attract the light, such as satins and metallics.

Use what you learn from observing other people to select fabric for yourself. Your goal is to emphasize your good features, while minimizing your less-than-perfect ones. For example, if you're large busted, use eye-catching fabrics for a skirt or pants, not for a top or jacket.

GETTING THE BEST VALUE

There's no doubt about it: shopping for fabric is fun and exciting. But before you are dazzled by a particular fabric's color, texture or print, or even its great price, there are some other things you should think about before you part with your money.

Examine the information printed on the end of the cardboard bolt or on the attached hangtag. Besides telling you the width and the price per yard, it will also provide you with information about fiber content, special finishes and care requirements.

FIBER CONTENT

Fibers are divided into two categories. Natural fibers, such as cotton, linen, silk and wool, come from plants and animals. Synthetic fibers, such as acrylic, polyester and nylon, are man-made.

Fabrics made from 100 per-

cent natural fibers are generally more comfortable, more durable and more absorbent than those made from 100 percent synthetics. Natural fibers are easier to handle during sewing. Ripples and puckers are less of a problem. When they do occur, they can often be "erased" with the gentle touch of your steam iron.

On the other hand, synthetic fibers are usually much easier to care for—a particularly important factor for active sportswear and children's playclothes. Most can

be either hand or machine washed. Usually, they are wrinkle resistant. Once sewn, the garment rarely has to be pressed between cleanings. However, during sewing, this same characteristic sometimes makes it difficult to get synthetics to hold a crease or retain a sharp edge. You can't rely on your steam iron to do all the work. Instead, you must use topstitching or edgestitching to hold the edges flat.

Blends combine the best features of naturals and synthetics.

FIBER FACTS

FIBER AND TRADENAMES	COMMON FABRIC TYPES	SPECIAL PROPERTIES		TYPICAL CARE
		Advantages	Disadvantages	
NATURALS				
Cotton	batiste, broadcloth, corduroy, seersucker, terry, denim	absorbent, cool, strong	wrinkles and shrinks (unless treated), weakened by mildew and sunlight	machine wash, tumble dry, can be bleached, iron while damp
Linen	handkerchief, lawn, damask, fabrics with nubby textures	absorbent, cool, strong	wrinkles, shrinks, weakened by mildew	dry clean to retain crispness, or wash to soften, iron while damp
Silk	chiffon, crepe de chine, organza, broadcloth, linen, raw silk	absorbent, warm, lustrous, drapes beautifully	weakened by sunlight and perspiration	dry clean, though some can be hand washed; iron on wrong side at low temperature
Wool	flannel, tweed, melton, jersey, gabardine, crepe, challis	absorbent, warm, flame and wrinkle resistant, good insulation	shrinks, attracts moths, knits tend to stretch during wear	dry clean, though some can be machine washed; steam iron with a press cloth on the right side
SYNTHETICS				
Acetate Chromspun® Estron®	taffeta, satin, tricot, silklike fabrics	silk-like luster, drapes well, dries quickly, low in cost	fades, relatively weak, exhibits static cling, wrinkles	dry clean or gently machine wash, tumble dry (low), iron low temp
Acrylic Acrilan® Creslan® Orlon® Zefkrome® Zefran®	pile fabrics, double knits, fleece, wool-like fabrics	warm; resists wrinkles, mildew, moths and oily stains	sensitive to heat, pills, has static cling	machine wash, tumble dry, needs no ironing

As a rule, the fiber that is present in the highest percentage dominates the characteristics of the fabric. The chart above tells you what performance characteristics to expect from various types of fibers. To make this chart more meaningful to you, examine the labels in your favorite ready-to-wear garments. Note their fiber contents and care requirements. Which ones seem to dominate your wardrobe? These are the ones to keep in mind as you select your fabric.

FABRIC FINISHES

Fabrics are often treated with special finishes that improve or alter their basic characteristics. The following are some of the most common fabric finishes. If the fabric is treated with one of these, it will be mentioned on the hangtag.

Flame retardant: Resists spread of flames, required by law on children's sleepwear and home furnishings fabrics.

Permanent press: Sheds wrinkles after wearing or washing; needs little pressing. Cottons treated with a permanent press finish retain the look and feel of cotton without the wrinkling.

> **TIP** *SIZING is a starch or resin added to the fabric for extra body. Because it's usually a temporary finish, you won't find it mentioned on the fabric label. Unbranded, "bargain" fabrics may be sized to make them look and feel like their more costly counterparts. But, the first time these fabrics are washed, the sizing disappears, leaving you with a limp piece of goods—another excellent reason for pre-treating your fabric. Examine the fabric carefully: if the weave is loose, but the fabric feels firm and crisp, it's a result of the sizing.*

FIBER FACTS

	FIBER AND TRADENAMES	COMMON FABRIC TYPES	SPECIAL PROPERTIES		TYPICAL CARE
			Advantages	**Disadvantages**	
SYNTHETICS	**Nylon** Antron III® Cantrece® Crepeset® Vivana®	tricot, velvet, two-way stretch knits (swimwear), wet-look ciré	strong, warm, lightweight; resists moths, wrinkles and mildew	has static cling, pills, holds body heat	hand or machine wash, tumble dry, iron at low temperature
	Polyester Avlin® Ceylon™ Comfort Fiber® Dacron® Fortrel® Kodel® Trevira®	double and single knits, gabardine, jersey, crepe, cotton-, silk-, and wool-like fabrics	strong, warm, very wrinkle-resistant, holds shape and a pressed crease, resists moths and mildew	has static cling, pills, stains are hard to remove, holds body heat	machine wash, tumble dry, needs little or no ironing
	Rayon Avril® Coloray® Courcel Courtaulds Rayon Enka® Zantrel®	challis, matte jersey, linenlike fabrics	absorbent	relatively fragile, holds body heat, wrinkles, shrinks	dry clean or gently machine wash, iron at moderate temperature, can be bleached
	Triacetate Arnel®	velour, panné, fleece, suede types, novelty wovens	excellent drapability, good pleat and crease retention, easy care	poor elasticity, poor durability	machine wash & dry, no ironing needed
	Spandex Lycra®	two-way stretch knits (swimwear, leotards)	excellent stretch properties, good durability, no pilling or static	white spandex becomes yellow from prolonged exposure to air	wash or dry clean, iron quickly on low temperature setting
	Blends	combination of two or more fibers	meant to bring out the best properties of each fiber included		care determined by most sensitive fiber included

However, when you sew a permanent press cotton, it will handle like a synthetic. You won't be able to use your iron to steam out any puckers. Instead, you can keep the puckers away by carefully holding the fabric taut, with one hand in front and one hand behind the presser foot as you stitch.

Preshrunk or shrink resistant: Keeps later (residual) shrinkage to a minimum. However, have you ever noticed how some ready-to-wear garments labeled preshunk develop small puckers along the stitching lines after the first washing? Even a small amount of residual shrinkage can cause this. To keep it

from happening to the garments you sew, make it a practice to pretreat your fabrics according to their care labels, regardless of the finish. Chapter 5 includes more information on pretreating your fabric.

Wash and wear: Requires little or no ironing after laundering.

Waterproof: Fabric treated so no moisture or air can penetrate it. Garments made of waterproof fabric may keep you dry, but you'll feel clammy.

Water-repellent/water resistant: Resists absorption of liquids; they will bead on the surface. However, because air can penetrate the spaces between the

yarns, fabrics with this type of finish make very comfortable rainwear and running suits.

CARE REQUIREMENTS

Think before you buy! Now's the time to find out how to take care of that fabric. Otherwise, you might be in for some unpleasant surprises later on!

First, read the care label. Next, crush a corner of the fabric in your hand, release it and observe how much it wrinkles. If it wrinkles a lot, will you have the time to iron the garment before every wearing? If not, a knit or a wrinkle-resistant woven might be a better choice.

If the frequent dry-cleaning bills on a white silk blouse are more than your budget can bear, a silk-like polyester might be a better choice. Note that some silks can be washed. However, ironing freshly laundered silk can be extremely time-consuming, usually with less than satisfactory results, unless you've selected a simple pattern. A top or dress with minimal details, such as the patternless "T" in Part 3, would be an excellent choice if you want to be able to wash your silk garment.

QUALITY FACTORS

Before the salesperson cuts your fabric, ask him or her to un-roll it so you can examine the full length.

■ Be sure the color is even throughout the piece, with no streaks or faded spots.

■ If the fabric has a brushed sur-

face, make sure there are no pills. If it pills on the bolt, you can be sure the problem will get even worse on your body.

■ On knits, check for snags and pulls.

■ If the fabric was folded, then rolled onto the bolt, check the foldline to make sure there are no permanent signs of wear. This is a particular problem with knits. If necessary, purchase extra fabric so you can work around the fold as you lay out the pattern pieces.

NOTIONS

At the same time that you're shopping for fabric, you'll want to purchase the other supplies necessary to complete your project.

Review the information on the back of the pattern envelope. Look at the yardage requirements for your particular view. Note how many yards of interfacing, lining and/or trim you need to buy. Look at the Notions section. Note if, and how much, you'll need of items such as seam tape, elastic, shoulder pads, buttons, hooks and eyes, snaps, zippers, etc.

As you purchase these extras, keep your fashion fabric selection in mind . . . and check the labels for care requirements. Some cautions:

■ Don't buy a dry-clean-only trim for a garment that you intend to wash.

■ If you're buying elastic for a swimsuit, make sure it is labeled safe for swimwear. Some elastics lose their stretch when wet. Others lose their stretch or turn yellow when they come in contact with chlorine.

■ Check buttons for care requirements. Some are dry-clean only. A few very special ones may be too fragile to risk even dry cleaning. Are you willing to remove them every time the garment is cleaned?

■ Don't buy a trim that's too heavy for your fabric. For example, if you tried to trim a delicate chiffon with a heavy, beaded trim, puckers and a sagging hemline would be your reward.

■ Select an interfacing that's compatible in weight and care with your fashion fabric. For a review of interfacing types and techniques, see the section in Chapter 6 on Interfacings.

■ If your pattern calls for lining, make sure you're purchasing a fabric that's suitable. Since a lining is designed to protect the inside of a garment AND make it easier to get the garment on and off, the fabric should have a smooth, slippery surface. Silk types and satins are good lining choices. Because it is weakened by perspiration, 100 percent silk is a luxurious, but not necessarily practical, choice. If you can't find the right color match, don't despair. Linings don't have to match exactly. For a vivid effect, use a contrast color; for a more subtle effect, choose a neutral, such as gray, black, beige, white or navy, that blends with the fashion fabric.

NEEDLES AND THREAD

Needles and thread are an integral part of any project. The time to stock up is when you're in the store buying your fabric.

NEEDLES

Don't spend too much time belaboring what size machine needle to buy. The smartest sewers keep packets of several different sizes on hand so they'll always have the right size needle for their project.

How do you know if you're using the right size needle? If the needle breaks (and you didn't sew over a pin), it's too small. If the seam draws up, or if your machine skips stitches, the needle is too large.

Consult your sewing machine manual for its recommendations. It's also a good idea to check with your sewing machine dealer to see what brands he or she recommends. If a certain brand or type of needle isn't compatible with your machine, this knowledge will save you hours of frustration.

THREAD

The most important thing to remember when purchasing thread is to buy a quality thread. How do you recognize a quality thread? The next time you're shopping, pick up a spool of "promotional" thread (the type that's offered at a price too good to be true) and compare it to a spool of more expensive, branded thread. Notice the "fuzzies" on the cheaper thread. They're a sure sign that the thread is made inexpensively from short fibers. This type of thread will fray and break as you try to stitch with it. It will also deposit little bits of lint that will eventually clog up your sewing machine. Bargain threads are no bargain!

For universal use, **polyester** or **cotton-covered polyester thread** is recommended for all fabrics. It's a must if you're sewing on synthetics. Use regular for general sewing; extrafine for lightweight fabrics, such as chiffon,

organdy, organza and tricot knit, as well as for machine embroidery.

Mercerized cotton thread is used on fabrics with little or no stretch.

Silk thread is used on silk, wool and silklike synthetic fabrics. Because it is expensive, sometimes hard to find, and available in a limited color range, many sewers prefer to use polyester or cotton-covered polyester.

There are other special purpose or decorative threads, such as elastic thread, metallic threads and woolly nylon thread. In Chapter 6, you'll learn how to use these threads, as well as thicker "threads" such as yarn, crochet cotton or narrow knitting ribbon, to achieve special effects with your overlock and your conventional machine.

> **TIP** *If you can't find the right color thread, pick one that's a shade darker than the fabric. Thread usually looks lighter when sewn.*

A PLACE TO SEW

Everyone needs a place to sew. However, your workspace need not be as fancy or as elaborate as often pictured. The pictures are often that way in the hopes that you'll buy the products shown! And while it might be nice to dream about having a whole room devoted to sewing projects, where you can leave everything "in progress" and just close the door, it shouldn't hold you back from sewing if you don't have that kind of space.

All you really need to get started is a cleared-off surface for your sewing machine and a good light (an adjustable lamp is best). If possible, set up your iron and ironing board nearby. It cuts down on tedious trips back and forth between the sewing machine and the ironing board.

Your sewing notions should be stored somewhere in easy reach. Put them in a sewing box, in a wicker basket, in a rolling cart with wire baskets, or in a set of plastic-organizers. If your sewing area is permanent, hang the notions you use most often from a pegboard or mug rack above your sewing machine.

You'll also need a place to store all the pieces of your project between sewing sessions. Consider an empty drawer, a large wicker basket, a large dress box or an empty suitcase.

One final piece of equipment is a full-length mirror. If you can, put it in the same room as your sewing machine. You'll need it for the fit-as-you-go techniques you'll learn in the next chapter.

TOOLS
I MUST HAVE

Stitching Tools

- straight pins
- hand sewing needles
- machine sewing needles
- thread

Cutting Tools

- bent-handled shears
- seam ripper
- thread clippers or embroidery scissors

Measuring/Marking Tools

- tape measure
- yardstick or meter stick
- dressmakers' tracing paper and tracing wheel
- fabric marking pens (evaporating and water soluble)

Fitting Tools

- full-length mirror
- French curve
- see-through ruler
- tissue paper
- transparent tape
- pencil or nylon tip pen

Pressing Tools

- steam iron
- ironing board
- press cloths

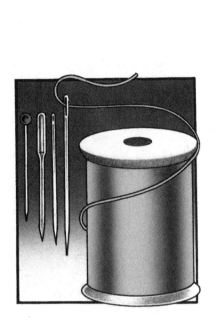

STITCHING TOOLS

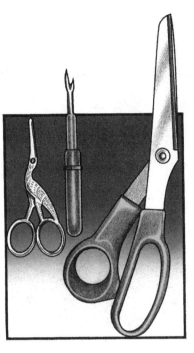

CUTTING TOOLS

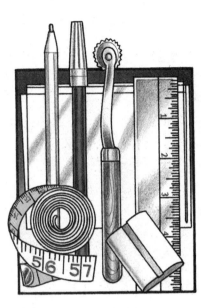

MEASURING/MARKING TOOLS

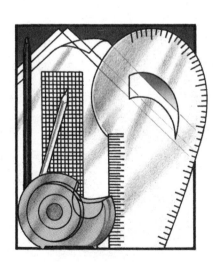

FITTING TOOLS

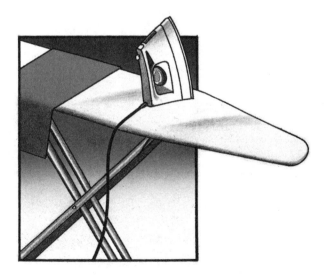

PRESSING TOOLS

CHAPTER 4

THE EASY WAY TO A PERFECT FIT

Somewhere in the history of sewing, people got the idea that there were only two ways to end up with a well-fitting garment: either start with a perfect body OR spend hours fussing with a fitting muslin, making complicated adjustments on the pattern tissue and attending every fitting seminar in town. Fortunately for today's sewer, this simply isn't true.

The path to a perfect fit is an easy one. It begins with something so basic you might think it's too obvious: the right size pattern. However, too many people purchase a pattern by their ready-to-wear size, without ever looking at or analyzing the measurements provided in the pattern catalog.

Most people think they know what size they are. Suppose you "know" you're a size 12. Think honestly about the last time you went shopping for clothes. Did EVERY size 12 dress, skirt or pair of pants fit you? Of course not! Every ready-to-wear manufacturer has its own set of standard measurements. That's why you might be a size 12 in some clothes, but a size smaller or larger in others.

To choose the right size pattern, you'll need to clear your head of any preconceived notions about what size you wear. Then, follow these three simple steps:

1. Take your measurements.
2. Determine your figure type.
3. Select the size within your figure type.

You will probably, BUT NOT NECESSARILY, end up with a pattern size that corresponds to your ready-to-wear size.

MEASURE YOUR BODY

You won't know where to begin to choose figure type and pattern size unless you have some body measurements to guide you. Using the accompanying Personal Measurement Chart, record your measurements in column 1.

Height and back waist length will be used to determine your correct figure type. Bust, waist and hips will be used to determine your correct pattern size. The other measurements will help you to fine-tune the fit of your pattern.

The procedures for determining figure type and pattern size are the same for everyone, male or female, adult or child. Basically, the same measurements are needed. The exceptions are the high bust and the shoulder-to-bust measurement (for females only) and the neck measurement (for males only). If you're sewing for a child, regardless of sex, these measurements are not necessary.

HOW TO MEASURE

■ Don't try to take your measurements by yourself. Only a contortionist can do it successfully! Enlist the aid of a friend.

■ For women and girls, take the measurements over undergarments or a leotard. For men and boys, take them over a T-shirt and shorts or unbelted, lightweight slacks.

■ Stand in a relaxed, normal position and look straight ahead.

■ To locate the natural waistline, tie a string snugly around the waist. If the waist is hard to find

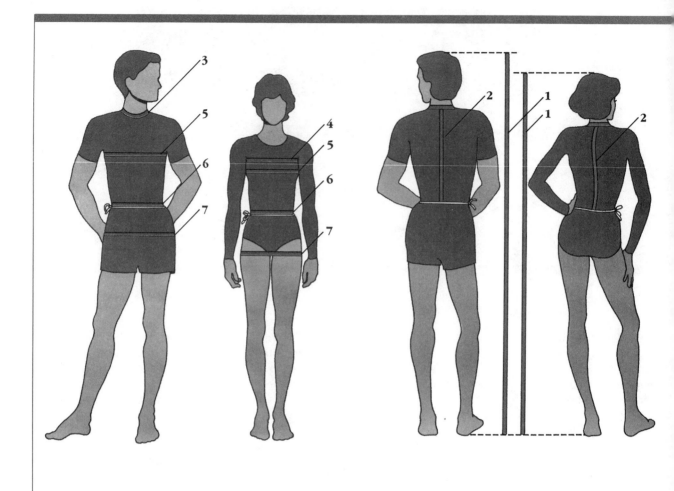

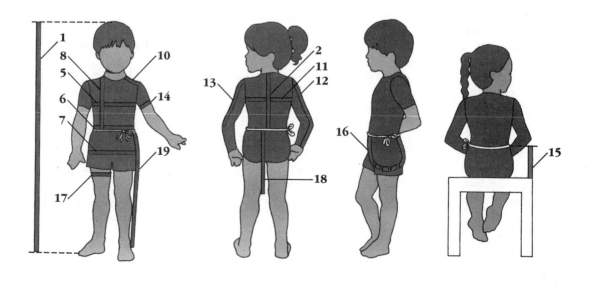

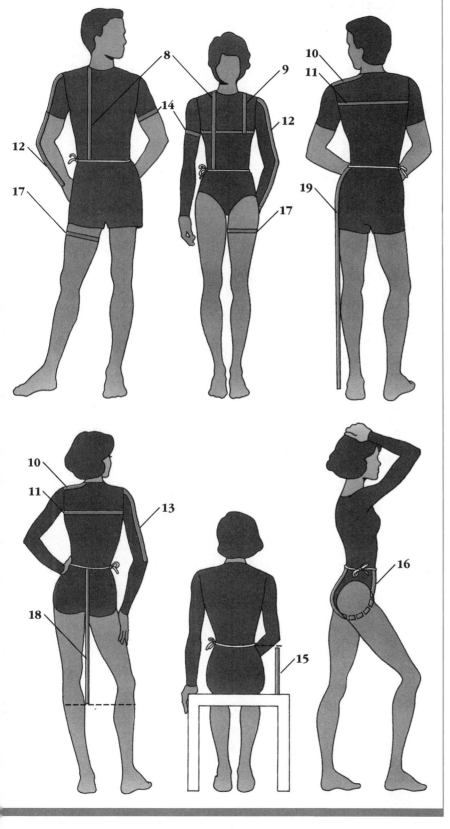

(a common problem on men and children), have them bend sideways. The crease that forms is at the natural waistline.

■ To find the shoulder point, raise the arm to shoulder level. A dimple will form at the shoulder bone—that's the shoulder point.

■ To find the back neck bone, bend the head forward so you can feel the first neck bone, or vertebra.

■ To locate the base of the neck in front, shrug your shoulders so that a hollow forms at the neck base.

■ For the "around" measurements, keep the tape measure parallel to the floor. The tape should be snug, but not tight, against your body.

■ Retake these measurements every six months, just in case your figure has changed enough to require a different size pattern or different adjustments. With rapidly growing children, you will probably need to remeasure more often.

DETERMINING YOUR FIGURE TYPE

Your height and back waist length (measurements #1 and #2), along with your body proportions, are the keys to determining your figure type.

To find your figure type, examine the FIGURE TYPE/PATTERN BODY MEASUREMENT charts on pages 54–61. Read the figure type descriptions, study the sketches and locate the back waist length measurements. If you find two figures with similar bust, waist and hip measurements, choose the one with the back waist length that is closest to your own.

PERSONAL MEASUREMENT CHART

WHAT TO MEASURE	BODY MEASUREMENTS		ADJUST-MENT
	Yours	Simplicity Standards (See charts on pages 00–00.)	(+ or −)
1. **HEIGHT** (without shoes)			
2. **BACK WAIST LENGTH** from prominent bone at back neck base to waist			
3. **NECK** (males only) at the Adam's apple. Add ½″ (1.3 cm) to neck body measurement. This measurement is now the same as ready-to-wear collar size.			
4. **HIGH BUST** (females only) directly under the arms, above the bust and around the back			
5. **BUST/CHEST** around the fullest part			
6. **WAIST** over the string			
7. **HIPS/SEAT*** around the fullest part See note (*) on opposite page for information pertinent to the various figure types.			
8. **FRONT WAIST LENGTH** from shoulder at neck base to waist (over bust point on females)			
9. **SHOULDER TO BUST** (females only) from shoulder at neck base to bust point			
10. **SHOULDER LENGTH** from neck base to shoulder bone			
11. **BACK WIDTH**** across the midback See note (**) on opposite page for information pertinent to the various figure types.			
12. **ARM LENGTH** from shoulder bone to wristbone over slightly bent elbow			
13. **SHOULDER TO ELBOW** (females only) from end of shoulder to middle of slightly bent elbow			

PERSONAL MEASUREMENT CHART (Continued)

WHAT TO MEASURE	BODY MEASUREMENTS		ADJUST-MENT
	Yours	Simplicity Standards (See charts on pages 00–00.)	(+ or −)
14. **UPPER ARM** around arm at fullest part between shoulder and elbow			
15. **CROTCH DEPTH** from side waist to chair. Sit on a hard, flat chair and use a straight ruler.			
16. **CROTCH LENGTH** from center back waist, between legs, to center front waist			
17. **THIGH** around the fullest part			
Garment measurements that are nice to have:			
18. **BACK SKIRT LENGTH** (females) from center back at waist to desired length			
19. **PANTS SIDE LENGTH** from side waistline to desired length along outside of leg			

* To determine the HIP measurement, measure around the body at these distances below the waist:
  MISSES, WOMEN & JUNIOR—9″ (23cm)
  MISS PETITE, JR. PETITE, TEEN-BOYS & HALF-SIZES—7″ (18cm)
  MEN—8″ (20.5cm)
  GIRLS—5½″ to 7″ (14cm to 18cm)
  BOYS—6″ (15cm)
  CHILDREN—4½″ to 5⅝″ (11.5cm to 14.3cm)
  TODDLERS—3½″ to 4½″ (9cm to 11.5cm)

** To determine the BACK WIDTH measurement, measure across the back at these distances below the neck base:
  MISS PETITE, JR. PETITES, MISSES, WOMEN & HALF-SIZES—5″ (12.5cm)
  MEN—6″ (15cm)
  TEEN-BOYS—4½″ (11.5cm)
  GIRLS & BOYS—4″ (10cm)
  CHILDREN—3″ (7.5cm)
  TODDLERS—2¾″ (7cm)

FEMALES: FIGURE TYPES AND PATTERN BODY MEASUREMENTS

JUNIOR PETITE

The short, well-developed figure about 5' to 5'1" (1.53 to 1.55 m) tall, with small body build and a shorter waist length than the Junior.

	INCHES						CENTIMETERS					
SIZE	3jp	5jp	7jp	9jp	11jp	13jp	3jp	5jp	7jp	9jp	11jp	13jp
Bust	30	31	32	33	34	35	76	79	81	84	87	89
Waist	22	23	24	25	26	27	56	58	61	64	66	69
Hip	31	32	33	34	35	36	79	81	84	87	89	92
Back Waist Length	14	14¼	14½	14¾	15	15¼	35.5	36	37	37.5	38	39
Front Waist Length	15¼	15⅝	16	16⅜	16¾	17⅛	38.7	39.7	40.7	41.5	42.5	43.5
Shoulder to Bust	8¼	8½	8¾	9	9¼	9½	21	21.5	22.3	23	23.5	24
Shoulder Length	4¼	4⅜	4½	4⅝	4¾	4⅞	10.7	11	11.5	11.7	12	12.3
Back Width	13¼	13½	13¾	14	14¼	14½	33.5	34.3	35	35.5	36	36.7
Arm Length	20⅝	20⅞	21⅛	21⅜	21⅝	21⅞	52.3	53	53.5	54.3	55	55.5
Shoulder to Elbow	12½	12⅝	12¾	12⅞	13	13⅛	31.7	32	32.3	32.7	33	33.3

JUNIOR

A well-developed figure, slightly shorter than a Miss, about 5'4" to 5'5" (1.63 to 1.65 m) tall, with shorter waist length than the Miss.

	INCHES						CENTIMETERS					
SIZE	5	7	9	11	13	15	5	7	9	11	13	15
Bust	30	31	32	33½	35	37	76	79	81	85	89	94
Waist	22½	23½	24½	25½	27	29	57	60	62	65	69	74
Hip	32	33	34	35½	37	39	81	84	87	90	94	99
Back Waist Length	15	15¼	15½	15¾	16	16¼	38	39	39.5	40	40.5	41.5
Front Waist Length	16	16⅜	16¾	17⅛	17½	17⅞	40.7	41.5	42.5	43.5	44.5	45.5
Shoulder to Bust	9½	9¾	10	10¼	10½	10¾	24	24.5	25.3	26	26.5	27.3
Shoulder Length	4½	4⅝	4¾	4⅞	5	5⅛	11.5	11.7	12	12.3	12.7	13
Back Width	13¾	13⅞	14	14¼	14⅝	15⅛	34	34.5	35.3	36	37	38.4
Arm Length	22	22¼	22½	22¾	23	23¼	56	56.5	57	57.7	58.3	59
Shoulder to Elbow	13¼	13⅜	13½	13⅝	13¾	13⅞	33.5	34	34.3	34.5	35	35.3

MISS PETITE

A short, well-proportioned and well-developed figure, about 5'2" to 5'4" (1.57 to 1.63 m) tall, with a shorter waist length and a slightly larger waist than the Miss.

	INCHES						CENTIMETERS					
SIZE	6mp	8mp	10mp	12mp	14mp	16mp	6mp	8mp	10mp	12mp	14mp	16mp
Bust	30½	31½	32½	34	36	38	78	80	83	87	92	97
Waist	23½	24½	25½	27	28½	30½	60	62	65	69	73	78
Hip	32½	33½	34½	36	38	40	83	85	88	92	97	102
Back Waist Length	14½	14¾	15	15¼	15½	15¾	37	37.5	38	39	39.5	40
Front Waist Length	15¾	16⅛	16½	16⅞	17¼	17⅝	40	41	42	43	43.7	44.7
Shoulder to Bust	9⅛	9⅜	9⅝	9⅞	10⅛	10⅜	23.3	23.7	24.3	25	25.5	26.3
Shoulder Length	4⅝	4¾	4⅞	5	5⅛	5¼	11.7	12	12.3	12.7	13	13.3
Back Width	13¾	14	14¼	14⅝	15⅛	15⅝	35	35.5	36	37	38.4	39.7
Arm Length	20½	20¾	21	21¼	21½	21¾	52	52.7	53.3	54	54.5	55.3
Shoulder to Elbow	12½	12⅝	12¾	12⅞	13	13⅛	31.7	32	32.3	32.7	33	33.3

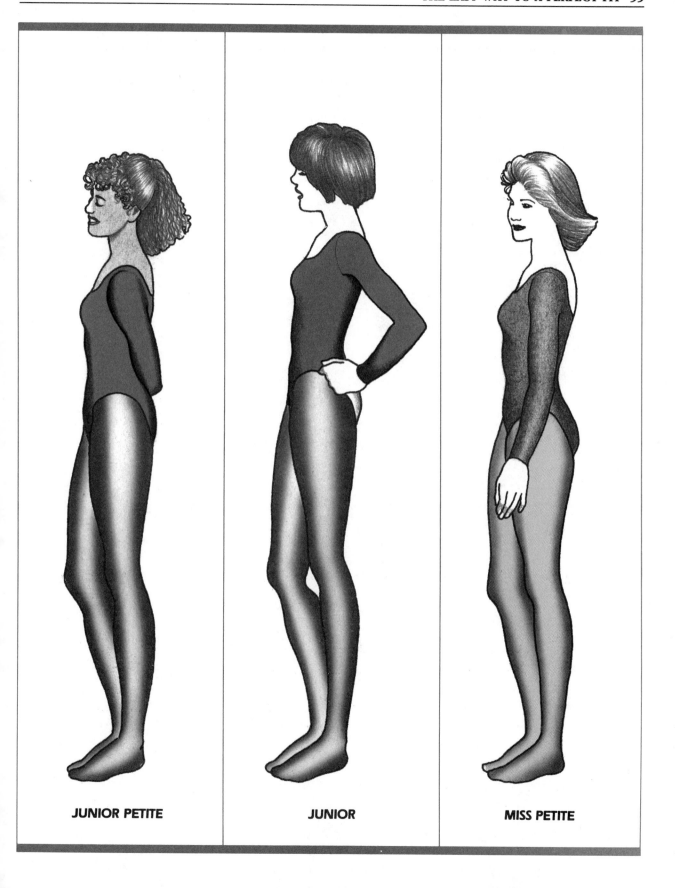

JUNIOR PETITE   JUNIOR   MISS PETITE

FEMALES: FIGURE TYPES AND PATTERN BODY MEASUREMENTS

MISSES

A figure that is well-proportioned and well-developed in all body areas. It is the tallest type, about 5′5″ to 5′6″ (1.65 to 1.68 m) tall, and could be considered the "average" figure

	INCHES									CENTIMETERS							
	6	8	10	12	14	16	18	20	SIZE	6	8	10	12	14	16	18	20
	30½	31½	32½	34	36	38	40	42	Bust	78	80	83	87	92	97	102	107
	23	24	25	26½	28	30	32	34	Waist	58	61	64	67	71	76	81	87
	32½	33½	34½	36	38	40	42	44	Hip	83	85	88	92	97	102	107	112
	15½	15¾	16	16¼	16½	16¾	17	17¼	Back Waist Length	39.5	40	40.5	41.5	42	42.5	43	44
	16⅝	17	17⅜	17¾	18⅛	18½	18⅞	19¼	Front Waist Length	42.3	43.3	44	45	46	47	48	49
	9⅞	10⅛	10⅜	10⅝	10⅞	11⅛	11⅜	11⅝	Shoulder to Bust	25	25.5	26.3	27	27.5	28.3	29	29.5
	4⅝	4¾	4⅞	5	5⅛	5¼	5⅜	5½	Shoulder Length	11.7	12	12.3	12.7	13	13.3	13.5	14
	13¾	14	14¼	14⅝	15⅛	15⅜	16⅛	16⅝	Back Width	35	35.5	36	37	38.4	39.7	41	42.3
	22¾	23	23¼	23½	23¾	24	24¼	24½	Arm Length	57.7	58.3	59	59.7	60.3	61	61.5	62.3
	13½	13⅝	13¾	13⅞	14	14⅛	14¼	14⅜	Shoulder to Elbow	34.3	34.5	35	35.3	35.5	35.7	36	36.5

HALF-SIZE

A fully-developed but shorter figure about 5′2″ to 5′3″ (1.58 to 1.60 m) tall, with narrower shoulders than the Miss Petite and with waist larger in proportion to bust than Woman.

	INCHES									CENTIMETERS							
	10½	12½	14½	16½	18½	20½	22½	24½	SIZE	10½	12½	14½	16½	18½	20½	22½	24½
	33	35	37	39	41	43	45	47	Bust	84	89	94	99	104	109	114	119
	27	29	31	33	35	37½	40	42½	Waist	69	74	79	84	89	96	102	108
	35	37	39	41	43	45½	48	50½	Hip	89	94	99	104	109	116	122	128
	15	15¼	15½	15¾	15⅞	16	16⅛	16¼	Back Waist Length	38	39	39.5	40	40.5	40.5	41	41.5
	17	17⅜	17¾	18⅛	18⅜	18⅝	18⅞	19⅛	From Waist Length	43.3	44	45	46	46.5	47.3	48	48.5
	10½	10¾	11	11¼	11½	11¾	12	12¼	Shoulder to Bust	26.5	27.3	28	28.5	29.3	30	30.5	31
	4½	4⅝	4¾	4⅞	5	5⅛	5¼	5⅝	Shoulder Length	11.5	11.7	12	12.3	12.7	13	13.3	13.5
	14½	15	15½	16	16½	17	17½	18	Back Width	36.7	38	39.3	40.7	42	43.3	44.5	45.7
	22¼	22½	22¾	23	23½	23¾	24	24¼	Arm Length	56.5	57	57.7	58.3	59	59.7	60.3	61
	14	14⅛	14¼	14⅜	14½	14⅝	14¾	14⅞	Shoulder to Elbow	35.5	35.7	36	36.5	36.7	37	37.5	37.7

WOMEN

A larger, more fully mature figure, the same height as the Miss, about 5′5″ to 5′6″ (1.65 to 1.68 m) tall. All measurements are proportionately larger.

	INCHES									CENTIMETERS							
	38	40	42	44	46	48	50	52	SIZE	38	40	42	44	46	48	50	52
	42	44	46	48	50	52	54	56	Bust	107	112	117	122	127	132	137	142
	35	37	39	41½	44	46½	49	51½	Waist	89	94	99	105	112	118	124	131
	44	46	48	50	52	54	56	58	Hip	112	117	122	127	132	137	142	147
	17¼	17⅜	17½	17⅝	17¾	17⅞	18	18⅛	Back Waist Length	44	44	44.5	45	45	45.5	46	46
	19⅝	19⅞	20⅛	20⅜	20⅝	20⅞	21⅛	21⅜	Front Waist Length	50	50.5	51	51.7	52.3	53	53.5	54.3
	12	12¼	12½	12¾	13	13¼	13½	13¾	Shoulder to Bust	30.5	31	31.7	32.3	33	33.5	34.3	35
	5	5	5⅛	5⅛	5¼	5¼	5⅜	5⅜	Shoulder Length	12.7	12.7	13	13	13.3	13.3	13.5	13.5
	16¼	16¾	17¼	17¾	18¼	18¾	19¼	19¾	Back Width	41.3	42.5	43.7	45	46.3	47.5	49	50.2
	23¾	24	24¼	24½	24¾	25	25¼	25½	Arm Length	60.3	61	61.5	62.3	63	63.5	64	64.7
	14⅜	14½	14⅝	14¾	14⅞	15	15⅛	15¼	Shoulder to Elbow	36.5	36.7	37	37.5	37.7	38	38.4	38.7

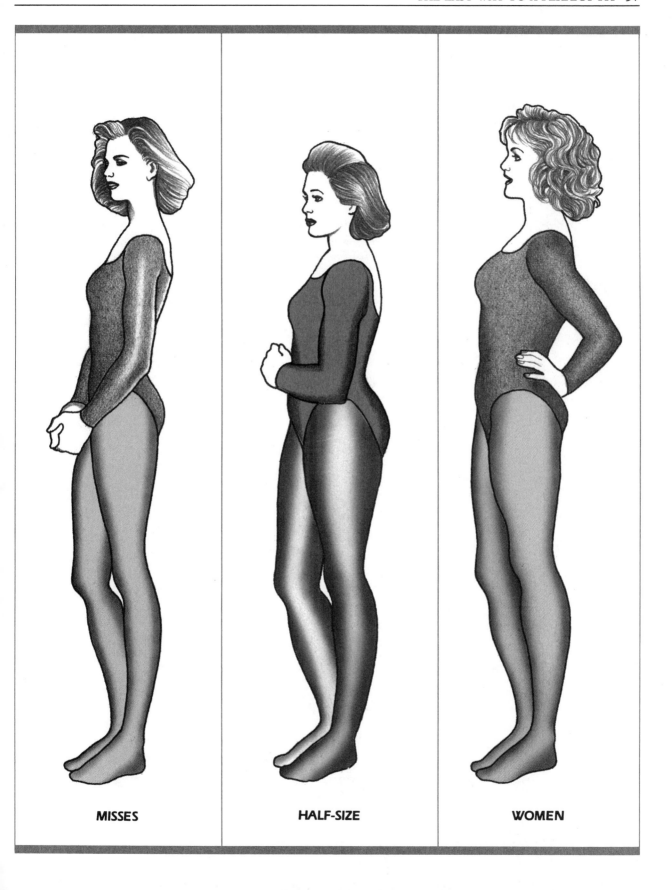

MISSES   HALF-SIZE   WOMEN

MALES: FIGURE TYPES AND PATTERN BODY MEASUREMENTS

BOYS

The just-developing figure, about 4′ to 4′10″ (1.22 to 1.47 m) tall, that is starting to mature.

INCHES 7	8	10	12	SIZE	CENTIMETERS 7	8	10	12
26	27	28	30	Chest	66	69	71	76
23	24	25	26	Waist	58	61	64	66
27	28	29½	31	Hip (Seat)	69	71	75	79
11⅜	11¾	12½	13¼	Back Waist Length	29	30	31.7	33.5
12⅜	12¾	13½	14¼	Front Waist Length	31.3	32.3	34.5	36
4	4⅛	4¼	4½	Shoulder Length	10.3	10.5	10.7	11.5
11½	11¾	12⅛	12¾	Back Width	29.3	30	30.7	32.3
16⅝	17¼	18½	19¾	Arm Length	42.2	43.8	47	50.2
11¼	11½	12	12½	Neck	28.5	29.3	30.5	31.7
11¾	12	12½	13	Neckband Size*	30	31	32	33
22⅜	23¼	25	26¾	Shirt Sleeve Size*	57	59	64	68

TEEN-BOYS

The young man figure that falls between Boys' and Men's sizes, about 5′1″ to 5′8″ (1.55 to 1.73 m) tall.

14	16	18	20	SIZE	14	16	18	20
32	33½	35	36½	Chest	81	85	89	93
27	28	29	30	Waist	69	71	74	76
32½	34	35½	37	Hip (Seat)	83	87	90	94
14	14¾	15½	16¼	Back Waist Length	35.5	37.5	39.3	41.3
14⅝	15⅜	16⅛	16⅞	Front Waist Length	37	39	41	43
4¾	5	5¼	5½	Shoulder Length	12	12.7	13.3	14
13⅞	14½	15⅛	15¾	Back Width	35.3	36.7	38.4	40
21⅞	22½	23⅛	23¾	Arm Length	55.5	57	58.7	60.3
13	13½	14	14½	Neck	33	34.3	35.5	36.7
13½	14	14½	15	Neckband Size*	34.5	35.5	37	38
29	30	31	32	Shirt Sleeve Size*	74	76	79	81

MEN

The man of average adult build, about 5′10″ (1.78 m) tall.

INCHES

SIZE	34	36	38	40	42	44	46	48	50	52	54	56
Chest	34	36	38	40	42	44	46	48	50	52	54	56
Waist	28	30	32	34	36	39	42	44	46	48	50	52
Hip (Seat)	35	37	39	41	43	45	47	49	51	53	55	57
Back Waist Length	17½	17¾	18	18¼	18½	18¾	19	19¼	19½	19¾	20	20¼
Front Waist Length	17¾	18	18¼	18½	18¾	19	19¼	19½	19¾	20	20¼	20½
Shoulder Length	6⅛	6¼	6⅜	6½	6⅝	6¾	6⅞	7	7⅛	7¼	7⅜	7½
Back Width	16	16½	17	17½	18	18½	19	19½	20	20½	21	21½
Arm Length	23⅝	23⅞	24⅛	24⅜	24⅝	24⅞	25⅛	25⅜	25⅝	25⅞	26⅛	26⅜
Neck	13½	14	14½	15	15½	16	16½	17	17½	18	18½	19
Neckband (Collar) Size*	14	14½	15	15½	16	16½	17	17½	18	18½	19	19½
Shirt Sleeve Size*	32	32	33	33	34	34	35	35	36	36	37	37

CENTIMETERS

SIZE	34	36	38	40	42	44	46	48	50	52	54	56
Chest	87	92	97	102	107	112	117	122	127	132	137	142
Waist	71	76	81	87	92	99	107	112	117	122	127	132
Hip (Seat)	89	94	99	104	109	114	119	124	129.5	134.5	139.5	145
Back Waist Length	44.5	45	45.7	46.3	47	47.5	48.3	49	49.5	50.3	50.7	51.3
Front Waist Length	45	45.7	46.3	47	47.5	48.3	49	49.5	50.3	50.7	51.3	52
Shoulder Length	15.5	15.7	16	16.5	16.7	17	17.5	17.7	18	18.5	18.7	19
Back Width	40.7	42	43.3	44.5	45.7	47	48.3	49.5	50.7	52	53.3	54.5
Arm Length	60	60.7	61.3	62	62.5	63.3	63.7	64.3	65	65.7	66.3	67
Neck	34.3	35.5	36.7	38	39.3	40.7	42	43.3	44.5	45.7	47	48.3
Neckband Size*	35.5	37	38	39.5	40.5	42	43	44.5	46	47	48	49.5
Shirt Sleeve Size*	81	81	84	84	87	87	89	89	91	91	94	94

* a ready-to-wear measurement used for reference.

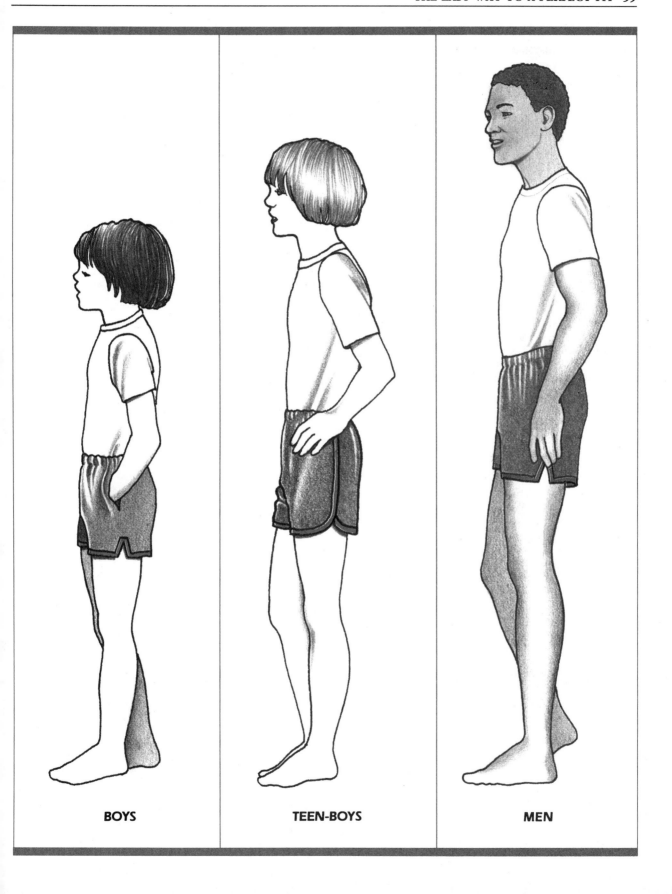

BOYS   **TEEN-BOYS**   **MEN**

CHILDREN: FIGURE TYPES AND PATTERN BODY MEASUREMENTS

TODDLER

The figure that is taller than a baby but shorter than a child. Toddler patterns have a diaper allowance and often apply to both boys and girls.

INCHES					SIZE	CENTIMETERS				
½	1	2	3	4		½	1	2	3	4
19	20	21	22	23	Chest	48	51	53	56	58
19	19½	20	20½	21	Waist	48	50	51	52	53
20	21	22	23	24	Hip	50.7	53.3	56	58.3	61
7½	8	8½	9	9½	Back Waist Length	19	20.3	21.5	23	24
8⅜	8⅞	9⅜	9⅞	10⅜	Front Waist Length	21.3	22.5	23.7	25	26.3
2⅜	2½	2⅝	2¾	2⅞	Shoulder Length	6	6.3	6.5	7	7.3
7¾	8	8¼	8½	8¾	Back Width	19.7	20.3	21	21.5	22.3
10	10¾	11½	12¼	13	Arm Length	25.3	27.3	29.3	31	33
6½	6⅞	7¼	7⅝	8	Shoulder to Elbow	16.5	17.5	18.5	19.3	20.3
28	31	34	37	40	Approximate Height	71	79	87	94	102

CHILDREN

The child with the same chest and waist measurements as Toddler but taller, with wider shoulders and back. In many instances designs are suitable for both boys and girls.

INCHES						SIZE	CENTIMETERS					
2	3	4	5	6	6x		2	3	4	5	6	6x
21	22	23	24	25	25½	Chest	53	56	58	61	64	65
20	20½	21	21½	22	22½	Waist	51	52	53	55	56	57
22	23	24	25	26	26½	Hip	56	58.3	61	64	66	67
8½	9	9½	10	10½	10¾	Back Waist Length	21.5	23	24	25.5	27	27.5
9⅜	9⅞	10⅜	10⅞	11⅜	11⅝	Front Waist Length	23.7	25	26.3	27.5	28.9	29.5
2⅞	3	3⅛	3¼	3⅜	3½	Shoulder Length	7.3	7.5	8	8.3	8.5	9
9½	9¾	10	10¼	10½	10⅝	Back Width	24	24.5	25.3	26	26.5	27
12¾	13½	14¼	15	15¾	16⅛	Arm Length	32.3	34.3	36	38	40	41
7¾	8⅛	8⅝	9	9½	9⅞	Shoulder to Elbow	19.7	20.7	22	23	24	25
35	38	41	44	47	48	Approximate Height	89	97	104	112	119	122

GIRLS

The young figure, about 4'2" to 5'1" (1.27 to 1.55 m) tall, without bust development.

INCHES					SIZE	CENTIMETERS				
7	8	10	12	14		7	8	10	12	14
26	27	28½	30	32	Chest	66	69	73	76	81
23	23½	24½	25½	26½	Waist	58	60	62	65	67
27	28	30	32	34	Hip	69	71	76	81	87
11½	12	12¾	13½	14¼	Back Waist Length	29.5	31	32.5	34.5	36
12⅜	13	13⅞	14¾	15⅝	Front Waist Length	31.3	33	35.3	37.5	39.7
6¾	6⅞	7¼	7⅝	8	Shoulder to Chest	17	17.5	18.5	19.3	20.3
3⅝	3¾	4	4¼	4⅜	Shoulder Length	9.3	9.5	10.3	10.7	11
11¾	12	12½	13	13½	Back Width	30	30.5	31.7	33	34.3
17⅞	18½	19¾	21	21½	Arm Length	45.4	47	50.3	53.3	54.6
10⅝	11	11⅝	12¼	12⅜	Shoulder to Elbow	27	28	29.5	31.1	31.4
50	52	56	58½	61	Approximate Height	127	132	142	149	155

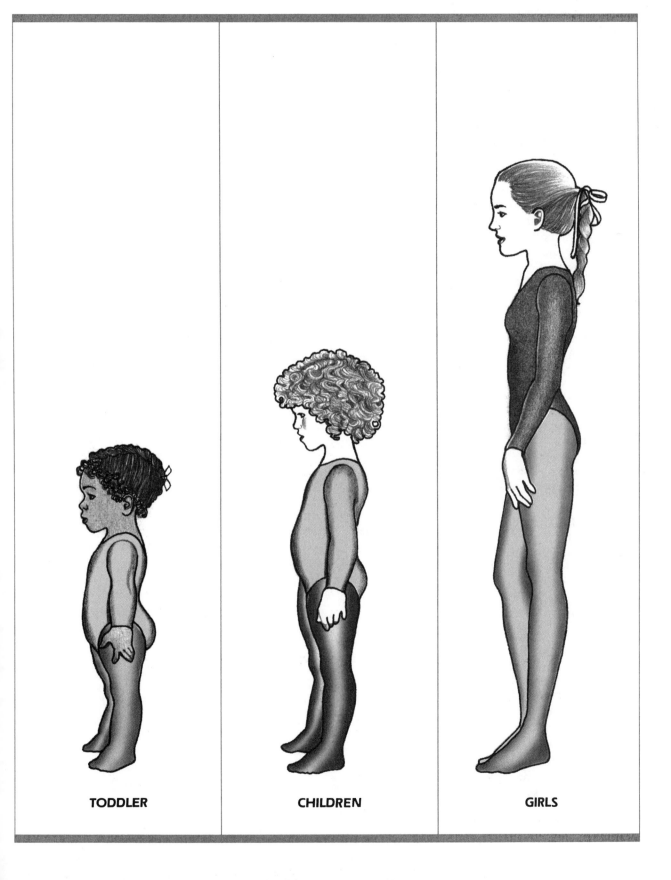

TODDLER **CHILDREN** **GIRLS**

SELECT THE PROPER SIZE

Compare your bust, waist and hip measurements to the ones listed for your figure type. If you're a perfect match, lucky you! You can always buy the same size pattern, regardless of what you're making. However, if you're like most people, you're not an exact match. Therefore, when you select your pattern size, you may need to consider the type of garment. By varying the size according to the type of garment, you'll be able to achieve the best possible fit with the fewest possible adjustments or alterations.

SOME COMMON QUESTIONS ABOUT PATTERN SIZE

Q: How do I know what size maternity pattern to buy?
A: Purchase the same size as before pregnancy or use your bust measurement. Don't buy a larger size—maternity patterns already include the required additional ease.

Q: What if I fall between sizes?
A: Choose the smaller size if you're small-boned, want a closer fit or are using a knit. Choose the larger size if you're large-boned, want a looser fit or are using a woven fabric.

Q: Why do you recommend buying most patterns by the bust size?
A: Sewing should be easy—and pattern adjustments are much easier to make in the waist and hip areas.

Q: Are there any shortcuts to adjusting a pattern if I'm a different size on top and on the bottom?
A: Look for multi-size patterns, such as Simplicity's® ADJUST-TO-FIT patterns. Because these are printed with several sizes on the same pattern tissue, you can use one set of cutting lines for the upper portion of your garment and another set for the lower portion. To make the cutting lines easy to follow, stitching lines are not printed on these patterns.

Q: What size bra cup are patterns designed for . . . and why do I need to take my high bust measurement?
A: Patterns are designed for the B-cup figure. If you are a B cup, the difference between your bust and your high bust measurement should be 2″ (5cm). If it's 3″ (7.5cm), you're a C cup; if it's 4″ (10cm), you're a D cup. If the difference is more than 2″ (5cm), buy the pattern closest to your high bust measurement. The result will be a better fit in the neck and shoulder areas. Then follow the directions starting on page 66 to adjust the cup size.

Q: I'm confused about the difference between Toddler's and Children's sizes. How do I know what figure type to look at when sewing for little ones?
A: Toddler's patterns include a built-in "diaper allowance;" Children's patterns do not. The Children's figure type is also slightly taller than the Toddler's.

Q: If I'm a Miss Petite, why can't I use a Misses' pattern and just shorten the garment at the hemline?
A: Miss Petite sizes have a shorter back waist length and a slightly larger waist than Misses' sizes. Look for Misses' patterns that have the ADJUSTABLE FOR MISS PETITE logo. These have special, easy-to-follow cutting lines and instructions for adjusting the pattern to a Miss Petite size.

Q: I know from years of being dissatisfied with the way ready-to-wear fits me that I have some special fitting problems. Do you have any guidelines for me about pattern selection?

TYPE OF GARMENT	KEY MEASUREMENT TO USE FOR PATTERN SELECTION
Dress, blouse, shirt, jumpsuit, coordinated separates pattern	BUST for adult females. However, if there's 2″ (5cm) or more difference between your bust and high bust, use your HIGH BUST measurement. BREAST for young females. CHEST or ready-to-wear NECKBAND (collar) size for males.
Suits, coats and jackets	Use the same guidelines as for dress, blouse, shirt and jumpsuit. These patterns are designed with enough ease to fit over other garments.
Skirts, pants, overalls, shorts	WAIST. However, if your hips measure two sizes larger, or if you're making hip-huggers, or pull-on pants with an elasticized waistline, use your HIP measurement.

A: Look for specially designed patterns that include adjustment information. Simplicity® PERSONAL FIT™ patterns have fitting adjustments for bust, hip, derriere and height printed on the pattern tissue. Simplicity® FUSS-FREE FIT® patterns include lines that indicate the location of bust, waist, hip and back width. In addition, a 1" (2.5cm) seam allowance in key areas gives you the flexibility to make alterations after you've cut out the garment.

DETERMINING ADJUSTMENTS

Once upon a sewing time, making a muslin fitting shell was the recommended—and time-consuming—way to find out if you needed to make any pattern adjustments. Today's smart sewer can say good-bye to that tedious method and turn to her tape measure instead.

The "basic five" measurements (bust, waist, hip, height and back waist length) are used to determine your figure type and pattern size. However, if you take a careful look at the FIGURE TYPE/PATTERN BODY MEASUREMENT charts on pages 54–61, you'll note that they include additional measurements. These extra Pattern Fitting Measurements are the ones you need to fine-tune your fit.

Using these charts, locate the

> **TIP** *Don't be confused by the terms "adjustments" and "alterations." Adjustments refer to changes made on the pattern tissue before the garment is cut out; alterations refer to changes made on the actual garment itself.*

Simplicity® standard measurements for your pattern size. Record these standards in column 2 of the Personal Measurement Chart. To determine if you will need any adjustments, compare your personal measurements (column 1) with the Simplicity® standard (column 2). Record any differences in column 3.

PATTERN EASE

Don't make the mistake of thinking it's easier and more efficient to determine adjustments by comparing your measurements with the actual pattern pieces. Sewers who do that may find themselves in big trouble because of something called ease.

Ease, or the fullness included in a pattern design, determines how the fashion will fit and look. Patterns are designed with two types of ease—wearing ease and design ease, as shown on the next page.

Wearing ease is the amount of "wiggle room" built into a garment. Without it, your garment would be skin-tight. Because this extra width is added to the standard body measurements when the pattern is designed, the actual pattern pieces will measure more than the standard body measurements. All garments, except swimwear and some exercise wear, contain some wearing ease. Patterns designed for knits only include less wearing ease because the fabric itself stretches to provide the necessary fit, comfort and mobility.

Design ease is fashion ease; it's the extra fullness, over and above wearing ease, that determines the garment's silhouette. In today's fashion world, there is no one contemporary silhouette. Garments that hug the body are just as fashionable as those that are loose and billowy.

Closely fitted garments have

minimal wearing ease but no design ease. Bridal gowns, sundresses and evening wear with close-fitting bodices are good examples of this type of silhouette.

Semifitted garments have wearing ease, plus some design ease. Feminine blouses, A-line skirts, blouson dresses and body-skimming chemises are all popular semifitted garments.

Loosely fitted garments have wearing ease plus a great deal of design ease. Gathered skirts, full-cut jump suits and oversized jackets and coats are good representatives of this silhouette.

STOP AND THINK: IS THIS ADJUSTMENT REALLY NECESSARY?

As you review the entries you made in Column 3 of the PERSONAL MEASUREMENT CHART, (pages 52–53), don't get discouraged if it looks like everything needs to be adjusted. That's highly unlikely! In fact, many people have a tendency to overfit.

To analyze whether or not the adjustment is necessary, keep three things in mind:

■ the amount of the adjustment
■ its location on the garment
■ the style of the garment

Lengthwise measurements are critical to the fit and proportion of a garment.

■ *Crotch depth and crotch length:* If either of these vary ⅛" (3mm) or more from the standard measurement, you should ALWAYS make the adjustment (see page 69 for how tos.)

■ *Back waist length and front waist length:* Examine the silhouette and analyze the amount of the adjustment. If it is ⅛" (3mm) or less, and the garment has no waistline seam and no design features below the waist, you can omit the adjustment and sim-

ments of ½" (1.3cm) or less can usually be accommodated for by simply stitching a narrower seam allowance.

On long-sleeved garments, arm length is critical. On fitted garments with set-in sleeves, shoulder length is also important. If your shoulders are narrow, an alternative to pattern adjustment is to add, or use thicker, shoulder pads. If you have broad shoulders, you might want to avoid the issue altogether by choosing patterns with dropped or extended shoulders, or raglan- or kimono-style sleeves.

ADJUSTING FOR LENGTH

Special lines printed on the pattern piece indicate where to shorten or lengthen it. Sometimes you can also change the length at the lower edge.

To Shorten

Along the shorten/lengthen line:

■ Measure up from the printed shorten/lengthen line the amount needed: draw a new line straight across the pattern at that point.

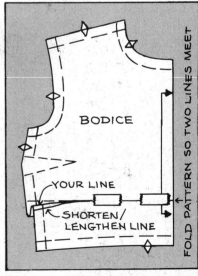

SHORTEN

ply cut the hem a little bit longer. However, if the garment has any type of defined waistline, and the difference in the back waist length measurement is more than ⅛" (3mm), you'll need to adjust the pattern (see how tos, at right.)

The basic circumference adjustments—bust, waist and hip—may or may not be necessary, depending on the amount of the difference and the silhouette of the garment. Loose-fitting silhouettes will require fewer adjustments than close-fitting ones. Adjust-

In today's sewing world, there's an ever-expanding collection of notions designed to make sewing faster, easier and more enjoyable than ever before.

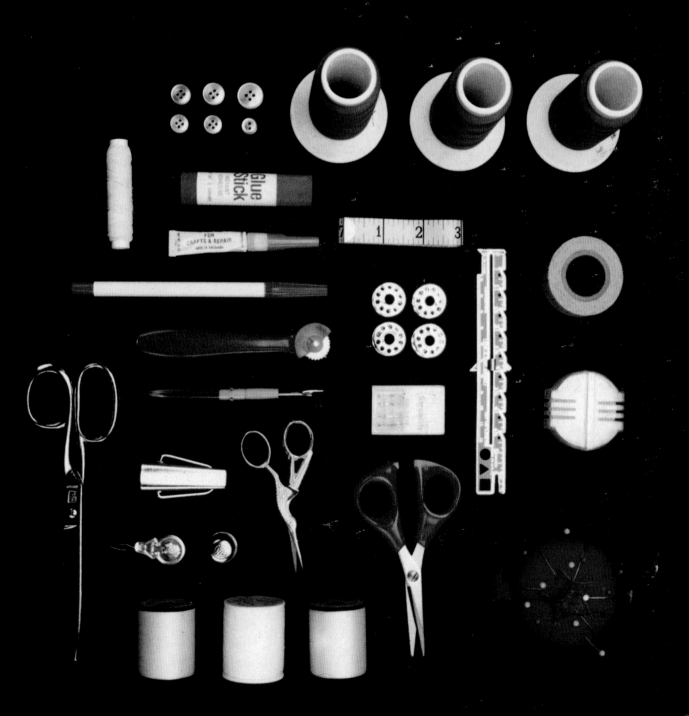

Ribbon trim adds that personal touch.

Twin needle topstitching gives ribbing a ready-to-wear finish.

For elastic casings that NEVER curl, stitch in the ditch.

Flexible knits need flexible seams.

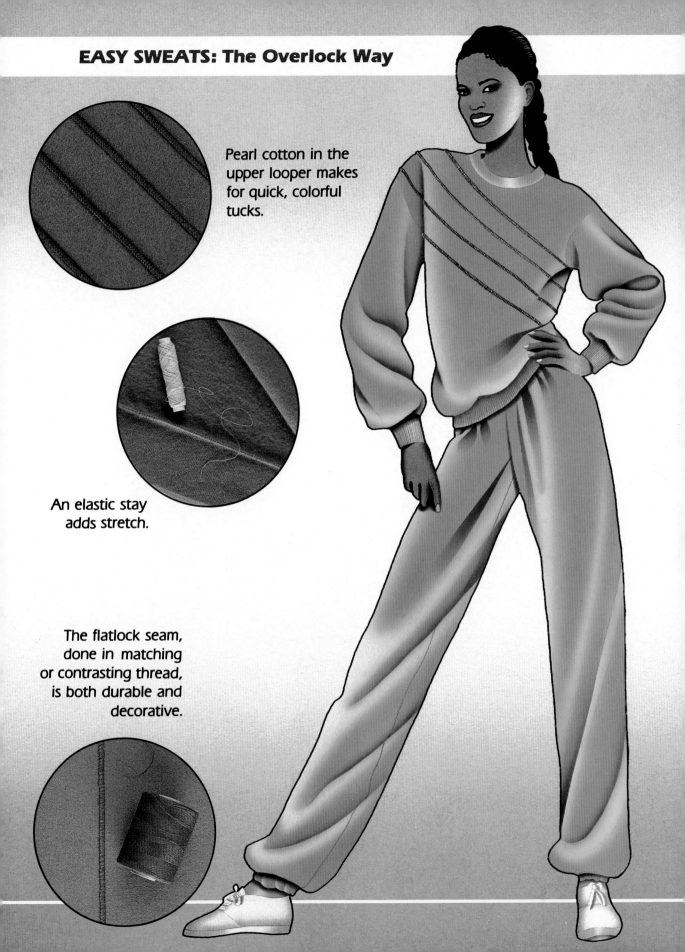

EASY SWEATS: The Overlock Way

Pearl cotton in the upper looper makes for quick, colorful tucks.

An elastic stay adds stretch.

The flatlock seam, done in matching or contrasting thread, is both durable and decorative.

TAILORED TOUCHES: The Conventional Way

To quick-finish a facing, fuse the interfacing in place, then stitch-and-pink the edge.

For fast, even gathers, with no broken threads, machine zig-zag over cording, then pull up on the cord.

The stitch-in-the-ditch method puts an end to waistband bulk.

The wide topstitched hem is a timesaver that looks great, too.

TAILORED TOUCHES: The Overlock Way

A serged edge is the easy overlock alternative to the stitched-and-pinked finish.

Gathering on the overlock builds in fullness as you serge.

The overlock method is a quick way to attach a waistband and finish the raw edges in one step.

For soft fabrics, a simple narrow hem provides the finishing touch.

ELEGANT EVENINGS: The Conventional Way

For neat, narrow spaghetti straps that are easy to turn, a piece of string is the magic notion.

Ribbons make wonderful sashes and ties. To keep the ends from fraying, apply a touch of seam sealant.

SEAM SEALANT

The machine rolled hem is the modern way to narrow-hem even the most elegant of fabrics.

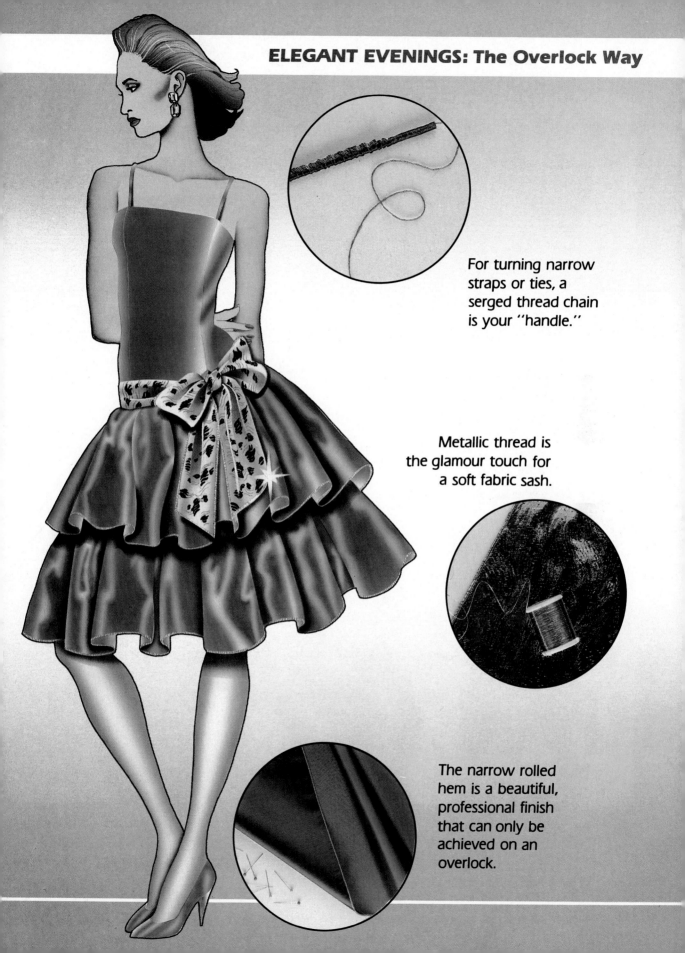

ELEGANT EVENINGS: The Overlock Way

For turning narrow straps or ties, a serged thread chain is your "handle."

Metallic thread is the glamour touch for a soft fabric sash.

The narrow rolled hem is a beautiful, professional finish that can only be achieved on an overlock.

SIMPLY THE BEST SEWING MACHINE

A well-cared-for conventional machine—whether it's a simple zigzag version or a sophisticated electronic model—makes today's sewing a pleasure.

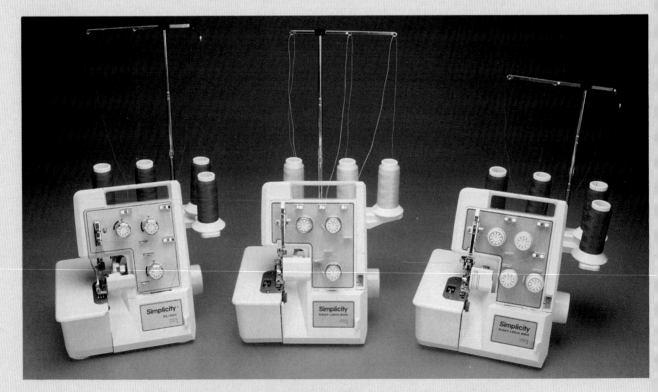

The overlock machine adds new dimensions to home sewing. Learn to use it side by side with your conventional machine. You'll soon be able to duplicate the finest commercial techniques.

■ Fold the pattern along the printed line, bring the fold to the drawn line, and pin or tape the fold in place.

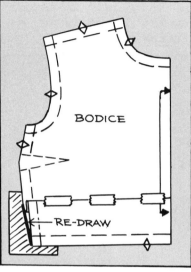

SHORTEN

■ Redraw the affected cutting and stitching lines, including any darts.

At the lower edge:
Measure and mark the change, then cut off the excess pattern tissue.

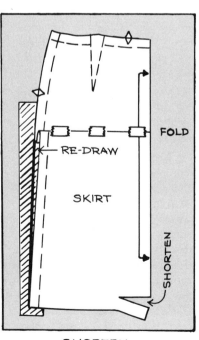

SHORTEN

To Lengthen

Along the shorten/lengthen line:

■ Cut the pattern piece apart on the printed shorten/lengthen line.

■ Place one portion of the pattern piece on top of a piece of paper and pin or tape in place along the printed line.

■ Measure down from the printed line the amount needed; draw a line straight across the paper at that point.

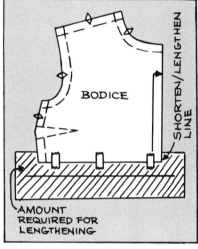

LENGTHEN

■ Using a ruler to keep the grainline or foldline aligned, position the printed line on the remaining pattern piece along the drawn line; pin or tape in place to the paper.

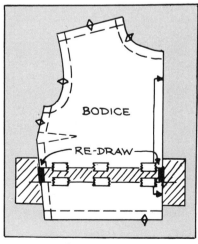

LENGTHEN

■ Connect the affected cutting and stitching lines, including any darts.

At the lower edge:

■ Pin or tape paper in place underneath the pattern.

■ Extend the cutting lines evenly and redraw the lower edge.

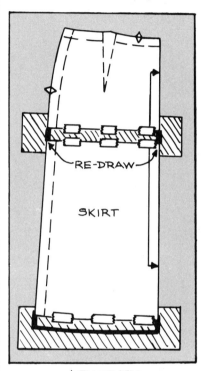

LENGTHEN

ADJUSTING FOR WIDTH

When you're adding to the pattern, you may need to pin or tape extra paper underneath the pieces.

Waist and Hip Adjustments

To adjust up to 2″ (5cm), add or subtract ¼ of the total amount at

> **TIP** *Remember to make adjustments on all corresponding pattern pieces. For example, if you adjusted the waistline on a skirt, you must also adjust the waistband a corresponding amount.*

the side waist (for a waist adjustment) or the side seam (for a hip adjustment). Do this on both the front and back pattern pieces. Taper the new cutting line back to meet the original cutting line.

If you need to adjust more than 2″ (5cm), do one of the following:
■ Check your pattern size again—you may need a larger or smaller size.

■ Analyze the style of the garment. Adding more than 2″ (5cm) at the sides may distort the design lines. If this is the case, you will be better off adjusting the pattern by slashing and spreading the front and back pattern piece ¼ of the total amount.

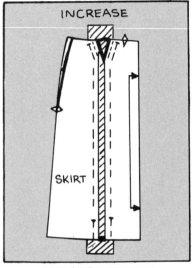

HIP ADJUSTMENT
[MORE THAN 2″(5cm)]

Bust Adjustments

To increase or decrease up to 1″ (2.5cm) in the bust area:

■ Mark ½ of the amount of increase or decrease at the side seam along the bustline. (For an increase, place paper under the side edges.)

■ Draw a new cutting line, tapering up to the original line at the armhole and down to the original line at the waistline.

If the required adjustment is 1″ (2.5cm) or more, it indicates that you are larger or smaller than the B-cup size the pattern was designed for. Since adding or subtracting 1″ (2.5cm) or more from the side seams will distort the fit of the garment, some other remedies are required. Consider purchasing patterns with the PERSONAL FIT™ logo that include bust adjustments or utilize the method given below.

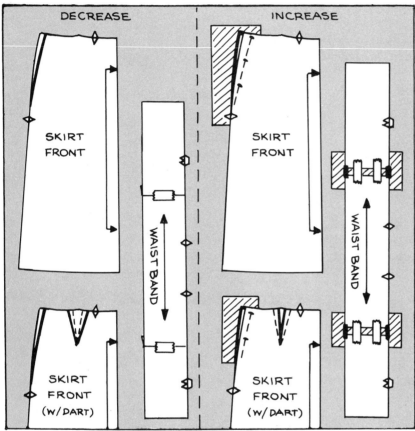

WAIST ADJUSTMENTS [LESS THAN 2″(5cm)]

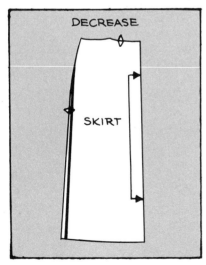

HIP ADJUSTMENT [LESS THAN 2″(5cm)]

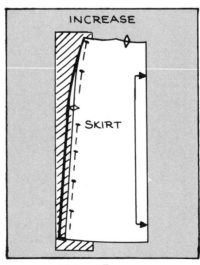

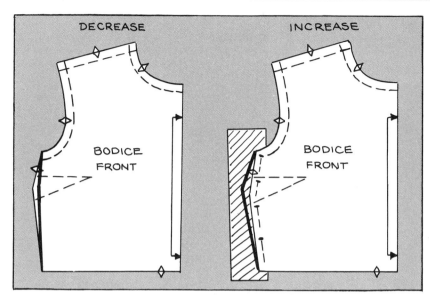

DECREASE   INCREASE

BODICE FRONT BODICE FRONT

BUST ADJUSTMENT ~ UP TO 1" (2.5 cm)

If you require a large cup (C or D), your clothes may pull across the front and perhaps across the back too. They may ride up at the front waistline where more length is needed. If you require a smaller cup (A or AA), your garments may fall into vertical folds in front. If the front waist length is too long, they will also droop at the waistline.

The first step when increasing or decreasing the cup size is to locate the bustline on your pattern. To do this:

■ Subtract your shoulder to bust measurement (#9) from your front waist length measurement (#8). Measure up that distance from the waistline marking and make a mark.

■ Draw a horizontal line that intersects the mark and is at a right angle to the grainline or center front foldline.

■ Draw a vertical line that extends from the midpoint of the shoulder to the waistline. It should be perpendicular to the horizontal line.

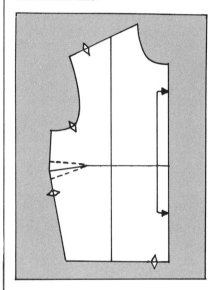

To increase the cup size:

■ Place paper under the pattern. Keeping the center front aligned, slash the pattern along the horizontal line and spread it the amount needed for the front waist length adjustment. Pin or tape the pattern in place.

■ Slash along the vertical line, just to, but not through, the cutting lines at the shoulder seam and waistline or hemline.

■ Spread each of the vertical cut edges half the amount needed for the bust adjustment, tapering to nothing at the shoulder seam and waistline or hemline. Pin or tape the cut edges in place.

DECREASE BUST AREA IF FABRIC PUCKERS.

INCREASE BUST AREA IF FABRIC PULLS.

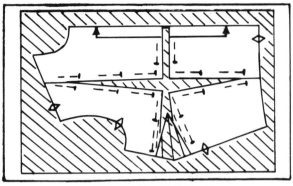

INCREASE CUP SIZE

TIP *If you have narrow or uneven shoulders, or a large bust, adding shoulder pads to your garment may eliminate the need for any pattern adjustments. See SHOULDER PADS, pages 185-188.*

Shoulder Length

To adjust up to ¼″ (6mm), mark the amount inside (to shorten) or outside (to lengthen) the shoulder seam at the armhole. Draw a

■ Because you have lengthened the garment in the bust area (where you need it) and at the side seam (where you don't) you'll have to add or redraw the side seam bust dart as shown. This will get rid of the extra length at the side seam.

To decrease cup size:

■ Reverse the steps for increasing the cup size, lapping the pattern instead of spreading it.

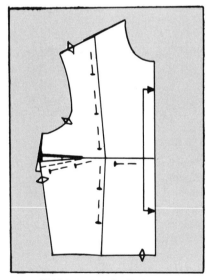

DECREASE CUP SIZE

■ Because you have shortened the garment in the bust area (where you need it) and at the side seam (where you don't), you'll have to redraw the existing dart or add the necessary length to the lower edge of the garment at the side seam.

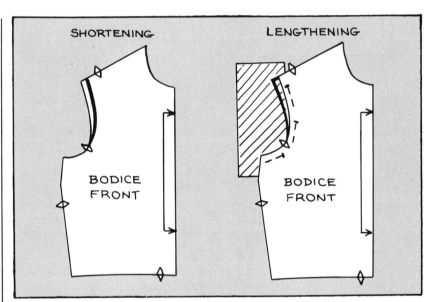

SHOULDER LENGTH

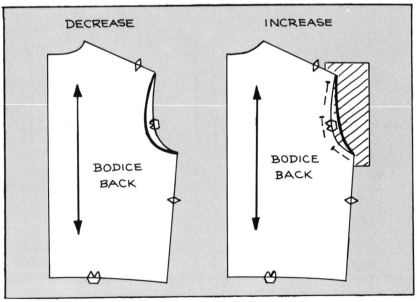

BACK WIDTH UP TO 1″ (2.5cm)

new cutting line, tapering to the original line at the armhole notch. Do this on both the front and back pattern pieces as shown below.

Because this adjustment may affect the way the sleeve hangs on the finished garment, baste the sleeve in place first and try on the garment. If necessary, pull out the basting stitches and reposition the sleeve until it hangs properly, then permanently stitch it in place.

Back Width

To adjust up to 1″ (2.5cm), mark ½ the amount needed inside (to decrease) or outside (to increase) the armhole cutting line. Do this above the notch on the back pattern piece only. DO NOT adjust the front. Draw a new cutting line, starting at the mark and tapering up to the shoulder and down to the underarm, as shown at right.

This adjustment may affect the hang of the sleeve. Be sure to baste in the sleeve and try on the garment before permanently stitching the sleeve in place.

SOME PANTS ADJUSTMENTS

Pants should fit smoothly and comfortably with enough room to move, bend and sit easily. The crotch depth and crotch length must be the correct ones for your body or else the pants will bind or sag.

The way your ready-to-wear pants fit provide clues to the type of adjustments you may have to make. If yours smile when you're standing—meaning that there are wrinkles that point up from the crotch area—they're too tight in the crotch area. If they frown, they're too loose. Smiles or frowns can occur in the front or the back, depending on your figure.

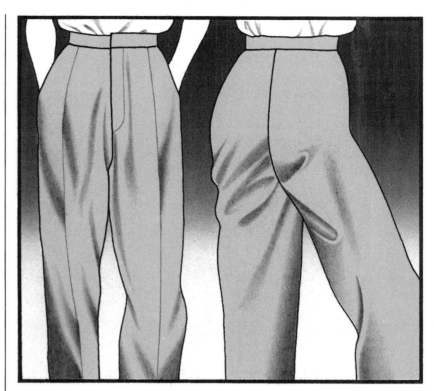

WHEN WRINKLES POINT DOWN, CROTCH AREA IS TOO LOOSE.

WHEN WRINKLES POINT UP, CROTCH AREA IS TOO TIGHT.

Take another look at the FIG-URE TYPE/PATTERN BODY MEASUREMENT charts. Note that the stardards for crotch depth and length are NOT included. Now, remember the earlier rule about never measuring the actual pattern pieces? Well, here's the exception: for an accurate fit, you MUST compare your body measurements with the actual pattern pieces.

Crotch Depth

IMPORTANT: Check and adjust the crotch depth first, BEFORE checking or adjusting the crotch length. Otherwise, it's a sure bet that your pants won't fit properly!

To check the crotch depth on your pattern, measure from the

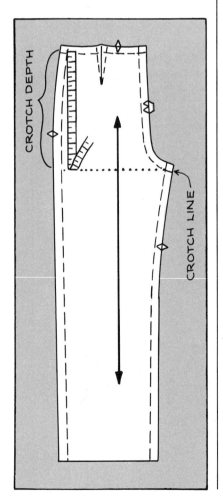

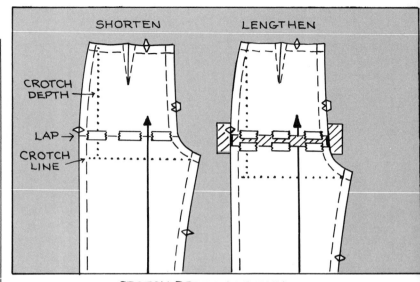

CROTCH DEPTH ADJUSTMENT

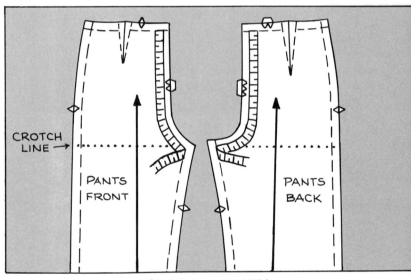

CROTCH LENGTH

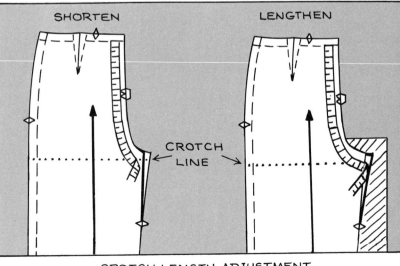

CROTCH LENGTH ADJUSTMENT

crotch line up to the waistline seam. Your measurement line should be close to the side seam, but parallel to the grainline, as shown at right. This measurement should be equal to your crotch depth (#15, plus ½" or 1.3cm) of ease for hips up to 36" (91.5cm) wide. Larger sizes may need to include up to 1¼" (3.2cm) of ease.

To lengthen or shorten the crotch depth, use the shorten/lengthen line on the pattern piece. Follow the procedures described under ADJUSTING FOR LENGTH (page 65), slashing and spreading the pattern pieces to lengthen, lapping them to shorten.

Crotch Length

Once you've checked and made any changes in the crotch depth, stand a tape measure or flexible ruler on end and measure along the stitching line of the center front and center back seam of your pants pattern. Measure from the waistline seam to the inner leg seam on both the front and back pattern pieces. Add these two measurements together to get the pattern's crotch length.

The pattern's crotch length should be equal to your crotch length measurement (#16) plus 1½"–2" (3.8cm–5cm). This extra amount is the ease you need to be able to sit down.

Before you make any adjustments on the pattern tissue, stand sideways and take a look at your figure in the mirror. You can divide the difference in half and make an equal adjustment on the front and the back of the pants. However, depending on your shape, you can also divide it unevenly between the front and back. In fact, if you're round in the front and flat in the back, you might want to add the entire amount to the front; if you're "normal" in front, but have a very flat derriere, you might want to subtract the entire amount from the back. Experience, and your own good judgment, are your best guides.

Lengthen or shorten the crotch by adding or subtracting half the adjustment amount at the inner leg seam, as shown.

FITTING AS YOU GO

Because fabric is not the same as tissue paper, you can't be guaranteed of a good fit simply by making the indicated adjustments on your pattern tissue.

As you sew, stop at least twice and try the garment on. The best time for the first fitting is right after the major garment seams are sewn. Be sure to wear the undergarments that you plan to wear with the finished product. Otherwise, you might be unpleasantly surprised at how a change of bra can alter the fit of a garment. If the pattern calls for shoulder pads, be sure to have a set available for your fitting. In fact, have several sets in different thicknesses. The right thickness of shoulder pad can solve many a fitting dilemma!

If the garment is a fitted or semifitted style, it might be a good idea to try it on with the major garment seams only basted together. Then, if alterations are required, you won't have to rip out any permanent stitching.

If you anticipate fitting problems in the sleeve area, baste them in first. Try the garment on a second time before permanently setting in the sleeves.

Your final fitting should be to check the length before the garment is hemmed. Be sure to wear the same height heel, if not the same shoes, as you plan to wear with the finished garment. It's the smartest way to insure pleasing lengthwise proportions.

PART TWO

SIMPLY THE BEST SEWING RESOURCE

If you're overwhelmed at the idea of mastering sewing skills and techniques, don't be. Too many people are intimidated because they look only at the end results. "Oh, but I could never sew that!" they say, unaware of the easy, step-by-step process involved.

In this part of the book, Simplicity® shares with you the secret for success that all sewing experts share: to approach each new skill or technique in a one-step-at-a-time manner and to understand there is no one "right" way of doing it. The fabric you choose, the type of machine (overlock or conventional) you use, the effect you want to create all influence your choice of sewing techniques. Proceed with the method that makes you the most comfortable. You'll be surprised with the beautiful, confident results you can achieve.

You'll find yourself referring to the next two chapters again and again as you sew—first for the "universal basics" required for every sewing project you undertake; then for the specific techniques you'll need for the project in hand.

CHAPTER 5

THE UNIVERSAL BASICS

No matter what style pattern you choose, what fabric catches your eye, or what your level of sewing skill, there are certain "universal basics" that are common to almost any project you make.

Much of what you'll learn in the following two chapters will challenge some of traditional sewing's hard and fast rules. Fortunately, today's sewer can have it both ways—easy techniques AND professional results—by combining serger sewing with conventional sewing.

So, dust off your conventional sewing machine, take your overlock out of the box, and get ready to break some of the rules!

FABRIC PRELIMINARIES

Have you ever purchased a ready-to-wear garment that turned into a total disaster after its first laundering or dry cleaning? When you sew, it's easy to prevent these unpleasant (and expensive!) surprises.

TIP *If you're a fabric collector, get into the habit of preshrinking your yardage before you put it away. Then it's always "needle ready"!*

PRESHRINKING

The first step, before you even think about cutting out your garment, is to preshrink the fabric.

The simplest preshrinking method is to put washable fabrics in the washing machine and to take dry-clean-only fabrics to the dry cleaner's. Pay attention to the manufacturer's recommendations for water temperatue, drying cycle or dry cleaning solvents.

If the fabric is marked "sponged," "preshrunk," or the label says it will shrink less than 1 percent, you may be tempted to omit this step. However, shrink-age control is not the only reason you should pretreat your fabric. By preshrinking it, you can discover the fabric's true character.

■ Some fabrics contain special finishes or sizings that dissolve the first time the fabric is cleaned. Consequently, your once-crisp garment may come out soft and limp.

■ Some knits contain sizings that will cause your sewing machine to skip stitches. Preshrinking removes these sizings—eliminating the problem before it ever starts.

A GLOSSARY OF FABRIC TERMS

Selvage: One of two finished lengthwise edges on a piece of fabric. These edges are usually a little stiffer and firmer than the crosswise, cut edge of the fabric and will not ravel.

TIP *Notions, such as tapes, braids, zippers, linings and interfacings, may require preshrinking too. Read the labels and check the fiber content. Trims, braids and zipper tape made from 100 percent polyester do NOT need to be preshrunk. Although most interfacings should be preshrunk, many fusibles do not require it. Check the manufacturer's information.*

Straight or lengthwise grain:
Refers to the threads (in a
woven) or the ribs (in a knit)
that are parallel to the selvages.
Pattern pieces are usually laid out
along the lengthwise grain
because it has the least stretch
and is the most stable.

Crosswise grain: Refers to the
threads that run across the fabric
between the two selvages,
perpendicular to the lengthwise
threads or ribs. Fabric stretches
more on the crosswise than on
the lengthwise grain.

Bias: Any diagonal direction.

True bias: The diagonal edge
formed when fabric is folded so
that the lengthwise and crosswise
grains match. Fabric has the
greatest amount of stretch along
the true bias.

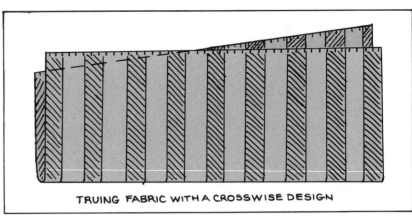

TRUING FABRIC WITH A CROSSWISE DESIGN

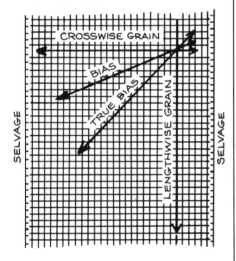

STRAIGHTENING

The ideal fabric is "on-grain,"
with lengthwise and crosswise
yarns that are exactly perpendicular to one another.

One of the recurring myths of
sewing is that EVERY fabric
should be straightened so that it
is perfectly on-grain before the
pattern pieces are cut out. Otherwise, the theory goes, the finished
garment will have out-of-kilter
seams and a drooping hem—the

result of yarn's natural tendency
to hang perpendicular to the
floor. This was true before the ad-
vent of knits, modern synthetics,
and wonder finishes. When many
of these newest fabrics are pulled
off-grain during the manufactur-
ing process, the fabric acquires a
permanent memory that can't be
altered no matter how hard you
try.

Truing the Fabric
Truing the fabric is today's smart
substitute for straightening.

■ *If the fabric has a crosswise
design:* fold it so that the design
matches across the width of the
fabric (see above).

■ *If the fabric does NOT have
a crosswise design:* draw a line
at one end of the fabric that is at
right angles to a selvage edge.
This crosswise line will function
as your crosswise grainline. Fold
the fabric so that this crosswise
line matches at the selvage.

It's possible that the selvages
won't match along the length of
the fabric. If this is the case, use
the lengthwise fold, not the selvage edge, as your reference
point when you lay out the pattern pieces.

Straightening with Steam
A few fabrics, particularly those
made of 100 percent natural fi-

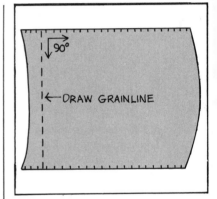

DRAW GRAINLINE

bers such as cotton, wool or
linen, do not have a permanent
memory. These fabrics, usually
can and should be straightened.

Begin by raveling a few crosswise threads until you can pull
one thread off across the entire
width of the fabric, as shown at
the top of the next page. Trim off

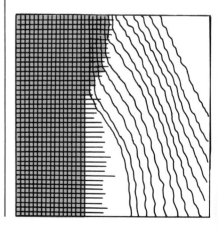

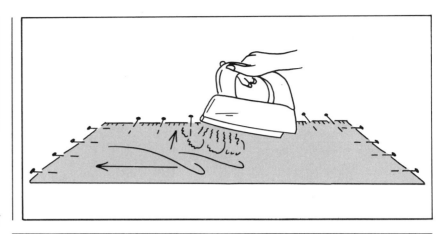

the resulting fringe. Repeat at the other end of the fabric.

Spread the fabric out on a large flat surface and fold it in half lengthwise, matching the selvages and the cut, crosswise end. If the fabric bubbles, or if it ripples along the lengthwise fold, it is off-grain.

To straighten, steam press until the bubbles or ripples disappear. As you press, move the iron in the lengthwise and crosswise directions only. Never move it diagonally as this will further distort the fabric. (See above).

Don't attempt to pull or force any fabric into shape. Fabrics that require more than a gentle steam treatment are probably permanently and forever off-grain. If this is the case, use the truing method described earlier.

THE CUTTING LAYOUT

Open up your pattern envelope and pull out the instruction sheet. On the first page you'll find a variety of *cutting diagrams*, or *layouts.* To locate the one you need, look for:

■ the pattern view you're making;
■ the fabric width which is the same as yours;
■ your pattern size.

Once you've found the right layout, circle it so it's easy to locate as you refer back and forth from instruction sheet to fabric.

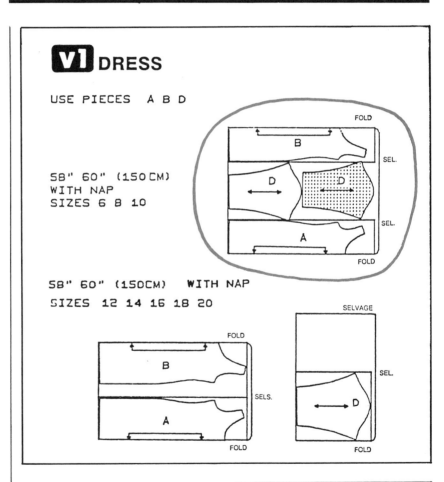

V1 DRESS

USE PIECES   A B D

58" 60" (150 CM)
WITH NAP
SIZES 6 8 10

58" 60" (150CM)   WITH NAP
SIZES   12 14 16 18 20

FOLD THE FABRIC

Make careful note of how the fabric is folded in your chosen layout. The most common way of folding fabric for cutting is *in half lengthwise, with the selvage edges matching* (A).

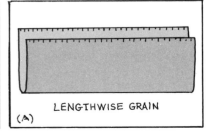

LENGTHWISE GRAIN

(A)

However, because pattern layouts are designed to make the most efficient use of the fabric, this is not the only way the fabric can be folded. Other layouts include:

■ *a crosswise fold* (B). This is used only for fabrics that do not have a nap or a one-way design.

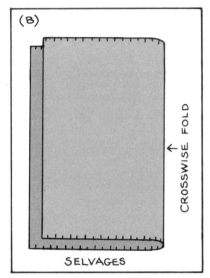

(B)

CROSSWISE FOLD

SELVAGES

■ *a crosswise cut* (C). This type of "fold" is used for fabrics that have a nap, such as velvet or corduroy, and for fabrics that have a one-way design. The fabric is folded in half along the crosswise grain, then cut along the fold. Next, the top layer is turned around so that the nap is running in the same direction on both layers.

■ *single thickness* (D). Fabric is placed right side up.

■ *a combination of lengthwise fold and single thickness* (E). The fabric is folded along a lengthwise grain so that the selvages are parallel to each other but not matching.

■ *two lengthwise folds* (F). The fabric is folded so that the selvages meet in the center.

Although fabric can be folded with either the right or the

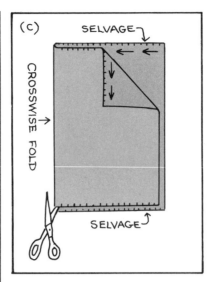

(C)

SELVAGE

CROSSWISE FOLD

SELVAGE

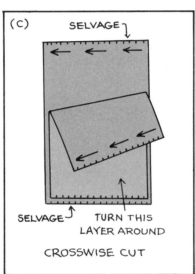

(C)

SELVAGE

SELVAGE TURN THIS LAYER AROUND

CROSSWISE CUT

wrong sides together, most sewers prefer to fold it right sides together because:

■ It makes it easier to transfer the pattern markings to the fabric.
■ Center seams are automatically

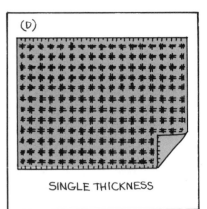

(D)

SINGLE THICKNESS

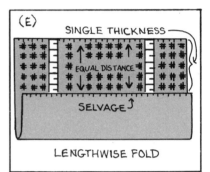

(E)

SINGLE THICKNESS

EQUAL DISTANCE

SELVAGE

LENGTHWISE FOLD

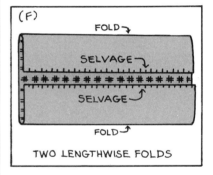

(F)

FOLD

SELVAGE

SELVAGE

FOLD

TWO LENGTHWISE FOLDS

matched and ready to sew once the pattern tissue is removed.

However, if your fabric has a bold design or one that requires matching, it's easier to fold it wrong sides together so you can

TIP *To make sure you don't miss any important information as you lay out and cut your pattern pieces, look over the pattern instruction sheet before you begin. Start at the upper left-hand corner and, reading each section completely, work your way from left to right. Although this may sound too obvious to have to mention, you'd be surprised at how many people just let their eyes wander over the instruction sheet, reading sections at random. Then they wonder why their garment doesn't turn out right!*

readily see the design as you pin and cut. If the fabric has a thick nap, you may prefer to cut it out single thickness. Otherwise, the layers might shift as you pin and cut. For additional information, refer to the section on "Special Layouts" (page 80).

SECURE THE SELVAGES

Your pattern layout will be more accurate if you pin the selvages in place. This keeps the fabric from shifting as you pin and cut. Depending on how your fabric is folded, pin the two selvages together or pin one selvage in place along the length of the fabric.

LAY OUT THE PATTERN PIECES

Check to make sure you have all the pattern pieces you need for the view you are making. You'll find them listed at the beginning of each view's cutting layout. If you followed the guidelines in Chapter 4, you've already adjusted these pattern pieces to give you the best possible fit.

Before laying out your pattern, it's a good idea to press the pieces with a warm, dry iron to remove any creases or wrinkles. This will help make sure that your garment sections are accurate in size and shape.

The cutting layout not only

TIP *As your sewing skills progress, you may want to invest in a cutting board. This heavy-duty cardboard surface opens up to 36" × 68" (91.5cm × 173cm) and accordion folds for easy storage. It's marked with a 1" (2.5cm) grid, as well as special markings to aid you in cutting circles, scallops and bias strips.*

TIP *Examine your cutting layout carefully for any special notations:*

■ *A shading key tells you how to place the pattern:*

☐ *indicates "Pattern Printed Side Up"*

▨ *indicates "Pattern Printed Side Down"*

☐ *indicates "Fabric"*

and ★ tells you to look for special instructions printed elsewhere on the instruction sheet.

■ *If your pattern includes interfacings or linings, these cutting layouts are usually grouped with the fabric layouts for each view.*

shows you how to fold your fabric, it also shows you where to place the pattern pieces.

■ Position the larger pieces first, beginning with those that should be placed on the fabric fold.

■ Position all other pattern pieces so that the grainline arrow is parallel to the selvages or to the lengthwise fold. To be sure each piece is parallel, measure from each tip of the grainline marking to the selvage or the fold. Both measurements should be the same. If they don't match, shift the pattern piece a bit until the measurements are equal.

TIP *If you're using a cutting board, align the selvage edges with one of the lines on the board. Use pushpins to hold the selvages in place.*

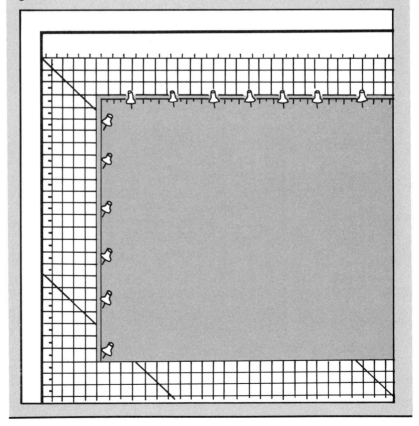

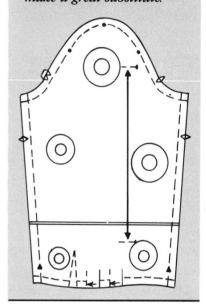

■ Once a pattern piece is properly positioned, pin it in place at each end of the arrow so it doesn't shift off-grain.

■ As you work, don't let the fabric hang over the edge of the table or it might stretch out of shape. Instead, loosely roll up the excess fabric and leave it on the end of the table. Unroll it as you work your way along the cutting layout.

PINNING

Pin through all the layers of pattern and fabric. First, position the pattern piece on-grain, an-choring it with pins at both ends of the grainline arrow. Next, pin diagonally at the corners, smoothing the pattern out from the grainline arrow as you go. Then add pins around the edge of the pattern. These pins should be placed parallel to the cutting line, at 2"–3" (5cm–7.5cm) intervals. Don't let the pins extend beyond the cutting line.

Depending on the size of your cutting surface, you may want to position all the pattern pieces on-grain first. Once they are all positioned, you can go back and finish pinning each piece. If your cutting surface is small, you may have to work in sections. As you pin, check to make sure none of your cutting lines overlap. And, unless you're following a special layout or your layout requires several different folds, don't do any cutting until ALL your pattern pieces are in place. Cutting as you go means any miscalculations in your layout are permanent.

SPECIAL LAYOUTS

With most fabrics, you can confidently follow the layouts printed on the Pattern Instruction Sheet. However, there are a few fabrics that require some special planning. Some need to be laid out so all the pattern pieces run in the same direction; others must be laid out so that the design either

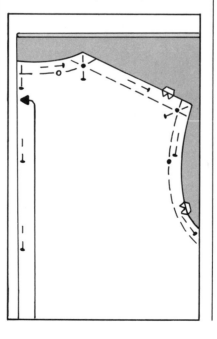

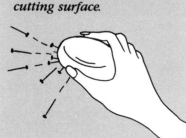

matches at the seamlines or is attractively spaced on the body.

If your fabric requires a special layout, it will be easier to plan if you choose a simple pattern with a limited number of seams.

"WITH NAP" LAYOUT

Some fabrics will change the way they look depending on which way you hold them. Sometimes, the difference is very obvious, as in the case of one-way designs. At other times, the difference might be a very subtle variation in color. For layout purposes, these are called "With Nap" fabrics and include:

■ *Pile fabrics*, such as velvet, velveteen, velour and corduroy. If you hold the fabric with the nap going down, it feels smoother and the color is lighter. If the nap runs up, the color is darker. For deeper color, the nap should go up; for better wear, the nap should go down.

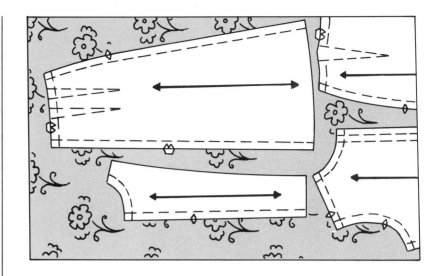

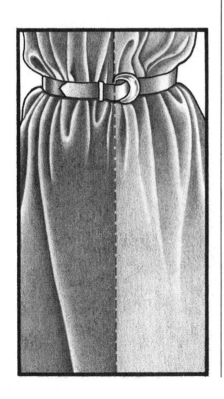

■ *Fuzzy-surfaced fabrics*, such as brushed flannel and fake fur. Cut with the nap running down.

■ *Shiny fabrics*, such as satin and damask and KNITS. These reflect the light differently, depending on which way you hold them. It doesn't matter which direction you choose, as long as all the pattern pieces run in the same direction.

■ *Plaids and stripes with an uneven repeat.* In addition to following the "With Nap" layout, you'll need to plan the placement of the pattern pieces so that the color bars match.

■ *Printed or woven motifs with a "this end up" look.* For example, all the flowers should "grow" in the same direction on every part of your garment, as shown above.

Take another look at your Instruction Sheet and at the example on pages 34–35. Note that the words "With Nap" or "Without Nap" are printed next to each cutting layout. If your fabric falls into one of the categories listed above, or if you are unsure about whether it has a nap, follow the "With Nap" layout.

Sometimes, because of space limitations, the pattern doesn't include a "With Nap" layout. In that case, you'll need to develop your own. Use the "Without Nap" layout as a guide, reversing the position of the pattern pieces as necessary so that the tops of all the pattern pieces are pointed in the same direction. To accommodate this new layout, you'll probably need to purchase more fabric than the pattern envelope recommends.

DESIGNS THAT MUST BE MATCHED

Garments made from plaids, bold stripes, big and medium-sized checks, border prints or large design motifs must match at the seams. To accomplish this, you'll have to make some adjustments to the cutting layout provided on your instruction sheet. In general, you'll find it easier to work with the fabric folded right side out or on a single thickness with the right side facing up.

Extra yardage is required to accommodate for this matching. How much extra depends on the size of the motif and the frequency of the repeat. Small, even plaids and stripes require about ¼–½ yard (.25m–.50m) extra;

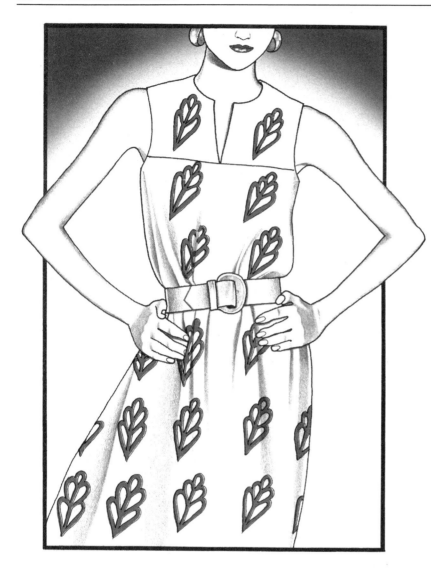

■ Dominant horizontal bars fall at straight or slightly curved hemlines. As you do this, observe what will happen on the rest of the garment—you may not want a repeat of the dominant bar or motif to fall at the fullest part of the bust, abdomen or hips.

■ In the case of a border print or large motif, the hemline should fall just below the lower edge of the design.

■ Where possible, motifs should not be chopped off at the seamlines, creating an unattractive effect.

■ The design matches vertically, as well as horizontally—i.e., center back of collar to center back of garment.

As you lay out the first piece, be sure the grainline arrow is parallel to the selvages or to the bars of the design. Then position the remaining pattern pieces so that the adjoining pieces match at the seams. To match adjoining pieces:

■ Trace the design of the fabric onto the pattern at the notch and indicate colors.

■ Place the pattern piece to be joined on top of the first piece,

large, even designs require about ½–1 yard (.50m–.95m) extra.

Positioning Bars or Motifs

Think about where you want the most prominent bar or motif to fall on your body. Beginning with the main front section, position the pattern pieces on the fabric (as shown) so that:

■ Prominent vertical bars and large squares or motifs fall at the center front and back of the garment, and at the center of sleeves, yokes and collars.

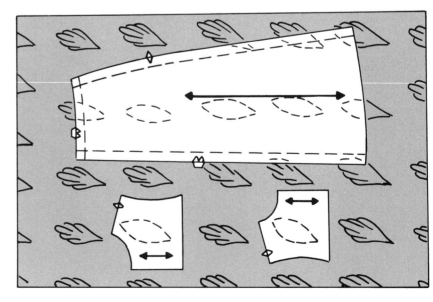

lapping seamlines and matching notches.

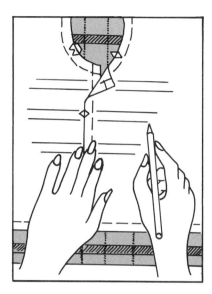

■ Trace the design onto the second piece, then place it on the fabric so that the traced design matches the fabric.

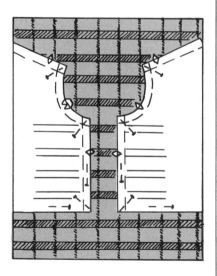

Some details can't be matched, no matter how hard you try. These include raglan seams, shoulder seams, darts, the area above a bust dart on princess seams, the back of the armhole seam, gathered or eased seams and circle skirts. Half-circle skirts will chevron at the seams.

MORE ABOUT PLAIDS AND STRIPES

How you lay out a plaid or a stripe depends on whether the design is even or uneven. In an even plaid or stripe, the arrangement of bars (stripes) is the same on both sides of the main bar. The result is a perfectly balanced design repeat that is easy to match.

In an uneven plaid or stripe, the arrangement or color of bars is different on either side of the main bar.

To see what your fabric is, fold it on the center of a main lengthwise bar. See if the design and colors repeat evenly on either side of it. Do the same for the main crosswise bar. If all the bars on both fabric layers match, the fabric is even; if not, it's uneven.

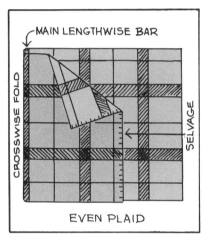

EVEN PLAID

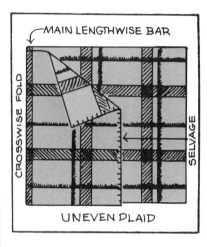

UNEVEN PLAID

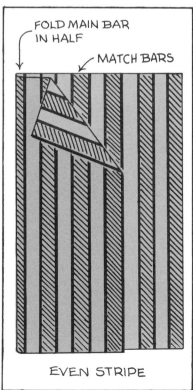

EVEN STRIPE

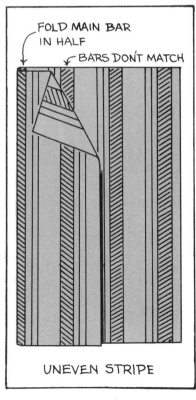

UNEVEN STRIPE

pieces that must be cut on the fold. Then cut the remaining pieces from a single layer of fabric. For fly-front openings, place the foldline on the center of a main bar. Be sure to place sleeves so that the plaid moves in the same direction on both sleeves.

For a mirror-image effect, the pattern must have a center front and back seam or closure. Work with a single layer of fabric. The main pieces (garment front and back) must be cut once, then reversed and turned upside down before they are cut again. Place center seams or center front lines along the center of a main bar or group of bars. Position the center of the sleeve along a main bar and cut it out. Then, to cut out the second sleeve, reverse and turn the pattern piece. Match the direction of the plaid on the right sleeve to the right side of the bodice front; on the left sleeve to the left side of the bodice front.

For even plaids and stripes, you may use a "Without Nap" layout unless the fabric surface is brushed or napped. In that case, use the "With Nap" (the "this end up") layout. Although cutting a single fabric layer is more accurate, you can use a double layer if you align the bars first. Pin the fabric together along several of the bars to keep it from shifting.

For uneven plaids and stripes, use a "With Nap" layout. An uneven plaid can be made to go around the figure in one direction or in opposite (mirror-image) directions from the center.

To lay out the plaid so it goes around the figure, fold fabric at the center of a main bar or group of bars. Position the pattern

TIP *Now that you've matched the fabric motifs in the cutting stage, you'll want to keep it matched as you sew. Use basting tape or glue stick (see "Basting," pages 94–95), or use this slip basting technique:*

■ *Press one seam allowance under along the seamline. Lap it over the adjoining section, matching seamlines and fabric design. Pin at right angles.*

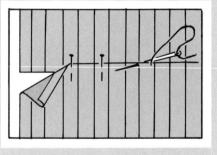

Bring the needle through to the right side at the folded edge, through all three layers.

■ *Insert the needle just opposite the fold, through the single layer of fabric, and bring it back up through the fold, about ³/₈" (1cm) to the left of the previous stitch.*

■ *Continue to slip baste the seam in place.*

■ *To sew the seam, remove the pins, open out the fabric, and machine stitch along the basting line.*

TIP *To eliminate some of the matching—and add visual interest to your garment—cut small detail areas, such as collars, cuffs, pockets and yokes, on the bias.*

TIP *One of the best things about sewing on the overlock machine is that the fabric won't shift or crawl as you serge. As a result, keeping your plaids and stripes matched is a snap. The trick is in the pinning:*

■ *With right sides together, pin the fabric layers together, pinning at right angles to the seamline and matching the motifs as you go. Alternate each pin so that one is pinned from left to right, the next from right to left, etc. Space the pins about 2″ (5cm) apart, making sure that the layers are pinned together at the dominant points of the repeat.*

■ *Serge the seam slowly, removing the pins just before the serger knives reach them.*

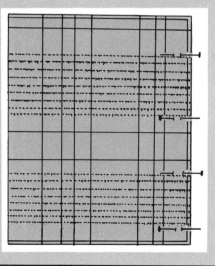

CUTTING

Use a pair of sharp, bent-handled dressmaking shears. The ones with the 7″ or 8″ (18cm or 20.5cm) blades are the most popular. Use your free hand to hold the edge of the pattern flat as you cut.

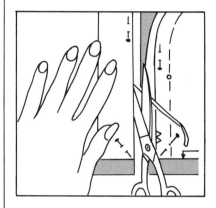

DO NOT use pinking shears to cut out your garment. They won't give you the sharp, straight cutting line that is the necessary guideline for accurate stitching. Pinking shears are meant to be used for finishing seams (see page 99).

When you come to the notches, either cut around them with the tips of your scissors or cut right through them and snip-mark later on when you transfer the other markings.

MARKING

As you learned in Chapter 2, a variety of notations, or symbols, are printed on the pattern tissue. Many of these symbols serve as guidelines for matching up garment sections and for sewing details such as darts, pleats, zippers and tucks. In addition to the notches (which you may have already marked as you cut out your

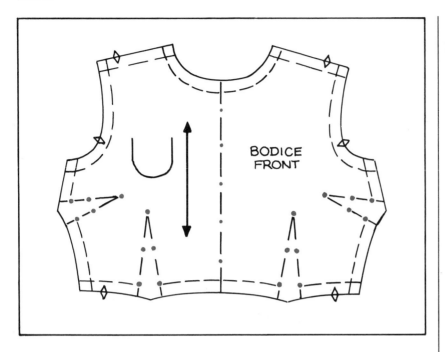

BODICE
FRONT

pattern), ALWAYS mark the following:

■ *Dots*, including those that indicate dart stitching lines.

■ *Solid lines* that indicate foldlines, as well as position lines for details such as pockets and buttonholes. Do not mark the solid line that indicates the grainline arrow.

■ *Center front* and *center back*, as indicated by a broken line or a foldline, unless these are located on seamlines.

■ *Stitching lines* that occur within the body of the garment section, such as for pleats, tucks or fly-front zipper openings.

MARKING METHODS

Use the method, or combination of methods, that suit your needs and your fabric.

Fabric marking pens are one of the fastest and easiest ways to mark. These pens contain a disappearing ink that makes it possible to mark on either the right or wrong side of the fabric.

There are two types of disappearing pens:

■ Water-soluble marking pens contain a blue ink that disappears when the marks are treated with plain water.

■ Evaporating or air-soluble marking pens contain a purple ink that simply evaporates from the fabric, usually in less than 48 hours. To guarantee that your markings will still be visible when you need them, don't use these pens until just before you're ready to sew.

No matter which type of marking pen you choose, be sure to test for removability on a scrap

> **TIP** *If you've used an evaporating marking pen and your sewing gets interrupted, put your work in a large Ziploc® bag, squeeze out the air and seal it. The markings will remain until you reopen the bag.*

of your fashion fabric. If your fabric water-spots or is "dry clean only," then the water-soluble pen is not a good choice. If the evaporating ink leaves an oily residue on the fabric, it's not a good choice either.

To mark with either of these pens, stick pins straight through the pattern tissue and both fabric layers at all marking points.

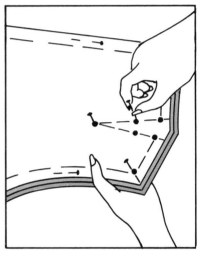

Starting from the outside edges of the pattern piece, carefully separate the layers of tissue and fabric just enough to place an ink dot where the pin is inserted. Mark both layers of fabric, then remove the pin. As you work your way from the outer cut edges of the pattern to the center or the center fold, continue separating and marking the layers.

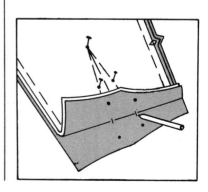

Dressmaker's Marking Pencils are available in two styles. The first contains a leadlike substance that can be washed out of the garment. The second contains a soft, chalklike substance. The chalk pencils have a stiff brush on one end to "erase" the markings once the garment is completed. Test first on a scrap of your fabric to determine if you can use the chalk on the right side of the fabric. Mark as for the disappearing pens, using straight pins to locate the position of the symbols. Mark on the right or the wrong side of the fashion fabric, as appropriate.

Tracing Paper (sometimes called dressmaker's carbon) *and A Tracing Wheel* are a good choice for marking smooth, flat-surfaced fabrics. On textured or bulky fabrics, the markings may be hard to see.

Traditionally, tracing paper markings were permanent. This meant that you couldn't use this method for sheers or for marking on the right side of the fabric. The introduction of "disappearing" tracing paper has changed all that. The markings can be sponged off with clear water. If you use one of these new tracing papers, read the manufacturer's directions carefully. Test first on a scrap of your fashion fabric. The heat of your iron may permanently set some of these formulas. If this is the case, sponge off the markings before you press that area of the garment.

You can usually save time by marking two layers at once. How-ever, heavyweight fabrics must be marked one layer at a time or the markings won't be clearly visible.

Because the tracing wheel has teeth, you may need to protect your work surface by marking on top of your cutting board or by slipping a magazine or a piece of cardboard underneath the fabric and pattern.

To mark, remove any pins that are in your way and position the tracing paper between the layers of fabric and pattern. For standard tracing paper, the carbon sides should face the wrong sides of the fabric; for disappearing tracing paper, the carbon can face either the right or the wrong sides of the fabric. Roll the tracing wheel over any symbols to be marked. Use a ruler as a guide

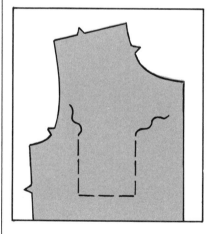

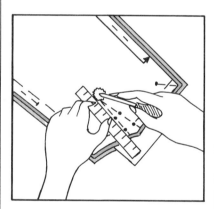

when tracing straight lines. Mark dots with an "X" so that one of the bars of the "X" is on the stitching line, as shown at bottom left.

Hand- or Machine-Basting is a way to transfer markings from the wrong side to the right side of the fabric. It's particularly useful for indicating placement lines, such as those for pockets or buttonholes, for marking center front and center back along the full length of the pattern piece, or for marking pleat foldlines and placement lines.

Use any appropriate method to mark on the wrong side of the fabric. Then separate the layers of fabric and hand- or machine-baste along the marking points. Now the markings are visible on the inside and the outside of the garment.

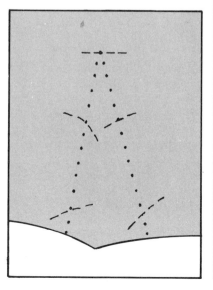

Snip Marking is a fast way to mark the ends of darts, foldlines, pleats and tucks, as well as center fronts and center backs. It's also an alternative way to mark notches. Just make a small clip (⅛″ or 3mm deep) in the seam allowance at the marking point.

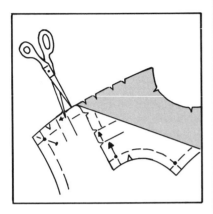

Press Marking is used in conjunction with snip marking to mark foldlines for details such as extended facings, folded casings, pleats and tucks.

■ Make a tiny clip in the seam allowance at each end of the foldline. If pleats or tucks do not extend the length of the pattern piece, use one of the methods described earlier to mark the end of the foldline.

■ Unpin and remove the pattern tissue so you can press mark each fabric layer separately.

■ Fold the fabric wrong sides together, using the clip marks as guides, and press the fold.

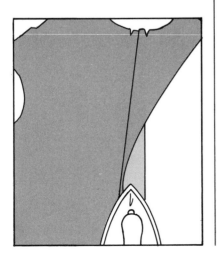

CONVENTIONAL MACHINE STITCHING

Whether your conventional sewing machine is a basic straight stitch variety, or a space-age computerized model, or something in between, it's the most valuable and useful piece of sewing equipment you own.

Because features and capabilities vary among models and manufacturers, the best advice anyone can give you is to study the manual that comes with your sewing machine. Among other things, you'll learn important information about how to keep the machine in good working order, including:

■ how to keep it clean and lint-free;

■ whether or not it requires oiling and lubricating—and how often this should be done;

■ recommended types and sizes of needles;

■ instructions for adjusting tension, pressure and stitch length—in short, all the things that contribute to good quality stitching.

If you've misplaced the manual, write to the manufacturer and ask for a new one. Be sure to include the model number of your machine. You'll find it printed on a small metal plate attached to the machine. On a free-arm machine, the plate is located on the back of the machine; on a flatbed machine, it's located on the front. If you don't understand how to operate some of the attachments or special features, stop in at a local dealer and ask about a few lessons. It will be time well spent!

THE PERFECT STITCH

If you follow the recommendations in the manual and keep your sewing machine in good working order, you can expect it to reward you with good quality stitching. Then you'll be able to make the simple adjustments that fine-tune the stitch quality to match your fabric.

Before you sew even one seam on your garment, test-stitch on scraps of your fashion fabric.

Thread Tension

Tension refers to the amount of drag or tautness exerted on both the needle thread and the bobbin thread as they move through the sewing machine. When the tension is correctly set, the stitches should be perfectly balanced: the two threads interlock in the center of the fabric so that the stitches look the same on both sides of the fabric.

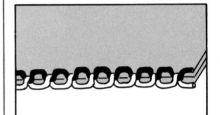

If the tension is not balanced, your manual will tell you how to correct it by adjusting the dial or button that controls the needle tension. Most tension problems can be solved by adjusting the needle tension to match the bobbin tension. Although some machines have a screw on the bobbin case that controls the bobbin tension, most manufacturers do not recommend adjusting this screw. If a bobbin adjustment is required, you'll be better off leaving that to a skilled repairperson.

To test for balanced tension, take a scrap of the fashion fabric and fold it along the bias. Put a row of stitching about ½″ (1.3cm) from the fold. Then, pull the fabric until a thread breaks.

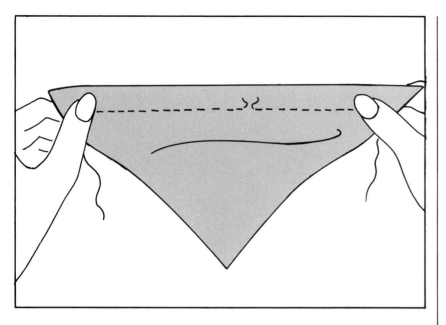

■ If both the bobbin and the needle thread break, then the tension is fine.

■ If only the bobbin thread breaks, that means that the bobbin tension is tighter than the needle tension. Solution: Tighten the needle tension to match the bobbin.

■ If only the needle thread breaks, that means that the needle tension is tighter than the bobbin tension. Solution: Loosen the needle tension to match the bobbin.

Presser Foot Pressure

Pressure refers to the force the presser foot exerts on the fabric as it moves between the presser foot and the feed dog. The amount of pressure needed can be affected by the fabric's weight, bulk, texture or finishes. If the pressure is correctly set for the fabric, both layers will move through the machine at the same rate.

On most machines, the amount of pressure is regulated by a knob or a dial. Check your manual to be sure. Your manual will also suggest suitable settings for various fabrics and sewing situations.

Stitch Length

Depending on the make and model of your machine, you will be able to adjust the stitch length by pushing a button or moving a lever or a dial. These will all have numbers that correspond to various stitch lengths. On some machines, these numbers represent the number of stitches per inch; on other machines, they indicate, in millimeters, the length of each individual stitch. Consult your manual for information.

The following is a guide to the most commonly used stitch lengths:

■ REGULATION—10 to 15 stitches per inch (per 2.5cm) or 2mm to 2½mm long is the length used for most general sewing, including stitching seams.

■ BASTING—the longest stitch on your machine, usually 6 to 8 stitches per inch (per 2.5cm) or 3mm to 4mm long. Since this is temporary stitching, the longer stitch is easier to remove.

■ REINFORCING—the shortest stitch length, usually 18 to 20 stitches per inch (per 2.5cm) or 1mm to 1½mm long.

■ EASING or GATHERING—8 to 10 stitches per inch (per 2.5cm) or 2½mm to 3mm long.

STITCHING TECHNIQUES

The guidelines for good stitching are so easy to follow that they soon become automatic.

1. Get a good start.

This technique guarantees that your beginning stitches will be smooth and the thread won't get jammed up in the throat plate hole!

■ Grasp the needle and bobbin threads with one hand and pull them under, then behind or to the side of, the presser foot, as shown on the next page.

■ Place the fabric under the presser foot so that the right edge is aligned with the desired marking on the throat plate. The bulk of the fabric should be to the left of the presser foot.

■ Turn the wheel to lower the needle into the fabric near the beginning of the seamline.

■ While still holding the thread tails, lower the presser foot and begin stitching with a slow, even speed. Continue to hold onto the thread tails until you have stitched for about 1″ (2.5cm).

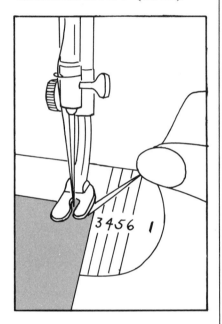

■ Release the thread tails and continue stitching.

2. *Guide the fabric.*

Rest one hand on the fabric in front of the presser foot and the other hand behind the presser

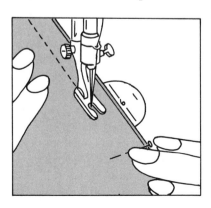

foot. Use both hands to gently guide the fabric through the machine as you stitch. At the same time, keep your eye on the cut edge of the fabric, rather than on the needle. This helps you keep the stitching straight.

3. *Keep it accurate.*

The easiest way to maintain accurate stitching is to align the right edge of the fabric with one of the following stitching guides:

■ The lines permanently etched on the throat plate of many sewing machines. These are placed at ⅛″ (3mm) intervals.

■ A piece of tape placed on the throat plate the desired distance from the needle hole.

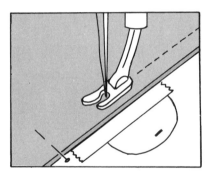

■ A screw-on or magnetic seam guide placed the desired distance from the needle hole. Place it parallel to the presser foot for straight edges or at an angle for curves.

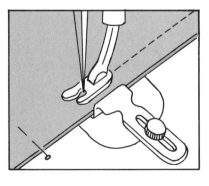

■ A quilting foot attachment. This is particularly useful for curved

edges and edges up to 2″ (5cm) away from the needle.

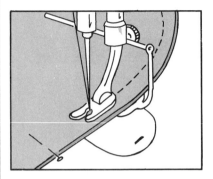

■ The toe of the presser foot. This is particularly useful when stitching close to an edge or ¼″ (6mm) away from it.

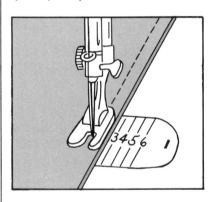

4. *Prevent slipping and shifting.*
If you're working with more than one layer of fabric, you'll want to pin or baste them together to keep them from slipping as you sew.

Match seam edges, markings and notches, then baste together

> **TIP** *If your fabric is still being swallowed up into the throat plate opening at the beginning of each seam, try using a smaller size needle. If the problem still remains, use a scrap of nonwoven, tear-away backing material, such as Stitch-n-Tear™ or Trace Erase™, as a "seam starter."*

TIP *If the seamline or stitching line will ultimately be intersected by another row of stitching, there's no need to secure the ends. The second row of stitching will "lock" the first row in place.*

using one of the techniques described on pages 94–95. As you become more proficient, you may find that simple, straight seams will require only one or two pins unless the fabric is very slippery.

5. *Secure the thread ends.*
To prevent the stitching from coming undone at the beginning and end of the seam, use one of these techniques:

■ Backstitch. Insert the needle a little bit in from the start of the seam, set the machine to stitch in reverse and backstitch (a). Set the machine to stitch forward and complete the seam (b). Slow down near the end of the seam and backstitch again (c).

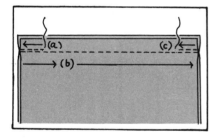

■ Tie the threads. This technique is useful if the line of stitching ends before you reach the edge of the fabric, such as on a patch pocket, or if your machine doesn't stitch in reverse. Leave at least 4″ (10cm) long thread tails at the beginning and end of the stitching.

Before tying the threads, it may be necessary to bring both tails of thread to the same side of the fabric. To do this, tug gently on one thread until the loop of the other thread appears, then in-

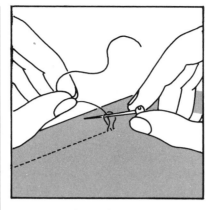

sert a pin through the loop and draw it up. (See above.)

To tie the threads, hold the threads in the left hand and form a loop. With the right hand, bring the tails through the loop. Then insert a pin into the loop so that the tip of the pin is at the end of the line of stitching. Pull the

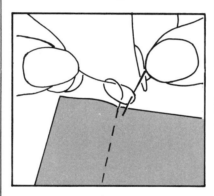

thread ends until the loop forms a knot at the tip of the pin. Remove the pin and clip the thread tails.

GLOSSARY OF STITCHING TERMS

Easestitching

This technique is used when you are joining a longer garment edge

TIP *If only a small amount of easing is required, try EASE-PLUS STITCHING—a quick method that crowds the fabric, distributing the fullness. Using a regulation stitch length, stitch between the ease markings. As you do this, press your index finger against the back of the presser foot crowding the fabric. Stitch for several inches (centimeters), letting the fabric pile up between your finger and the presser foot. Release the fabric and repeat.*

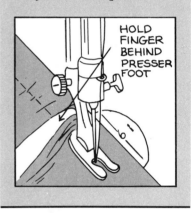

HOLD FINGER BEHIND PRESSER FOOT

to a slightly shorter one. Although the technique is similar to one used for gathering, there shouldn't be any folds or gathers visible on the outside of the garment once the seam is stitched.

■ Loosen the needle tension slightly and adjust the machine to sew with a longer (3mm or 8 to 10 stitches per inch) stitch.

■ Stitch just next to the seamline, within the seam allowance, as shown below. Stitch slightly beyond the markings on your pat-

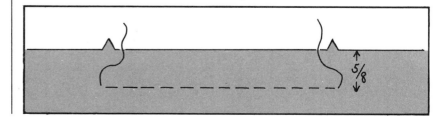

$\frac{5}{8}$

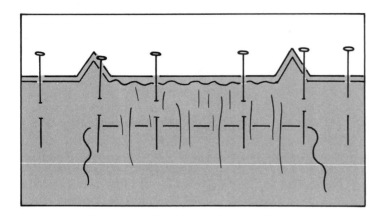

tern tissue that indicate the area to be eased.

■ Pin the eased section to the adjoining section, matching notches and markings. Draw the fabric up along the bobbin thread and distribute the fullness evenly. Stitch with the eased section up.

Edgestitching

This extra row of regulation-length stitches appears on the outside of a garment. It's placed approximately ⅛″ (3mm) or less away from a seamline or a fold-line, or close to a finished edge. Although it is similar to topstitching (on opposite page), edgestitching is less noticeable be-

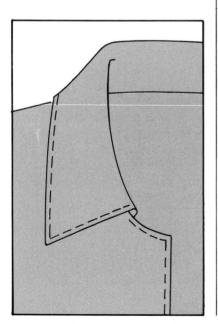

cause it is closer to the edge and it is always done in matching thread.

Reinforcement Stitching

This technique strengthens the stitching in areas that will be closely trimmed, such as corners, or along deep curves that will be clipped or notched at frequent intervals. The basic premise is simple—just sew with a shorter stitch length.

At inside and outside corners, reduce the stitch length for about 1″ (2.5cm) on either side of the corner.

When joining an inside corner to an outside corner, first rein-

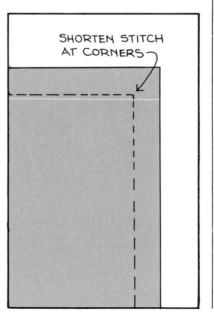

force the inside corner with small stitches, then clip just to the stitching.

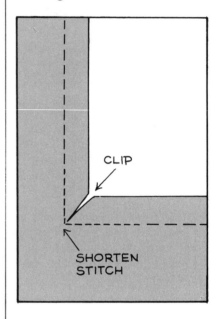

Staystitching

This line of regulation-length stitching prevents curved or bias edges, such as necklines, shoulders and waistlines, from stretching out of shape as they are handled. If your garment section requires it, staystitching should be the very first type of stitching you do.

To staystitch, stitch with a regulation-length stitch ½″ (1.3cm) from the cut edge of the fabric. On deep curves, shorten the stitch length so the staystitching doubles as reinforcement stitching. (See opposite page, at top.)

To keep the edge of the fabric from stretching as you staystitch, stitch in the same direction as the fabric grain. As a guideline, you may find arrows printed on the instruction sheet illustrations or along the seamline on the pattern tissue. If there are no arrows to direct you, you can determine which way to stitch by "stroking the cat." Run your finger along the cut edge of the fabric. The

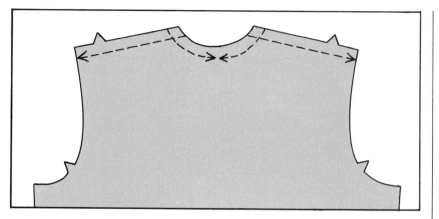

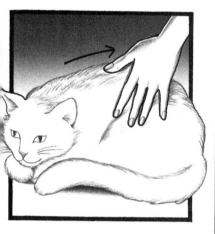

yarns will curl smoothly in one direction, just the way a cat's fur does. Stitch in that direction.

Stitch-in-the-Ditch

This technique is a quick way to hold layers of fabric in place at the seams. It's an effective way to secure neckline, armhole or waistband facings, as well as fold-up cuffs.

On the outside of the garment, stitch in the groove formed by the seam. Be sure to catch all the underneath layers in your stitching.

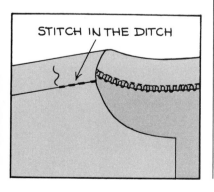

Topstitching

This is an extra row of stitching on the outside of the garment along or near a finished edge. Although topstitching is usually added as decoration, it can also be functional. For example, it can be used to attach a patch pocket or to help keep seam allowances flat on hard-to-press fabrics.

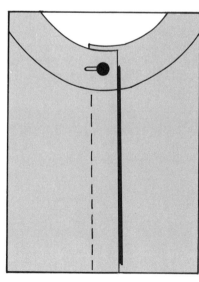

■ Use a matching or contrasting color thread, depending on how noticeable you want the stitching to be.

■ Stitch with a slightly longer stitch (3mm or 8 to 10 stitches per inch).

■ To keep your stitching straight, use one of the stitching guides as described on page 90.

■ Before topstitching on your garment, test-stitch using the same number of layers (fashion fabric, interfacing, facing, lining, seam allowances, etc.) as your garment has. To make each stitch more pronounced, you may want to slightly loosen the needle thread tension. You may also need to adjust the presser foot pressure to accommodate the extra layers

Understitching

This row of stitching prevents an inside layer of fabric, usually a facing, from rolling to the outside of the garment.

Understitching is done after the seam allowances are trimmed, graded and clipped or notched. (See Sewing with Your Scissors, page 100.) Then:

■ Press the seam allowances toward the facing.

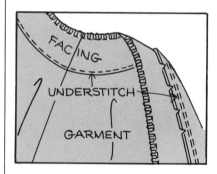

■ On the right side of the garment, stitch ⅛" (3mm) from the seamline, through the facing and seam allowances only.

BASTING

Basting refers to any of several methods that can be used to temporarily join layers of fabric until they're permanently stitched on the machine.

Pin basting is the most common method. Place pins perpendicular to the seamline, 1″–3″ (2.5cm–7.5cm) apart. Insert the pins so you take small bites of fabric right at the seamline. The heads should be to the right of the presser foot so they can be efficiently removed as you stitch.

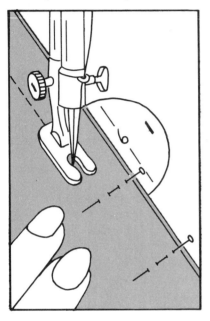

If your machine has a hinged presser foot, it IS possible to sew right over the pins but ONLY if

TIP *Fasten a strip of magnetic tape to the bed of your sewing machine or keep a magnetic pincushion (see page 80) close by. Use it to catch the pins as you remove them.*

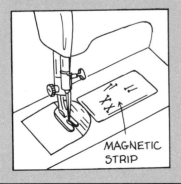

MAGNETIC STRIP

your manual describes this feature. Otherwise, don't experiment. The sad result will be a damaged sewing machine needle that can cause all sorts of stitching problems.

Paper clips are a quick substitute for pins on bulky, hard-to-pin fabrics, such as fake fur. They're also useful for fabrics where pins would leave permanent holes, such as leather and vinyl. Never, never try to stitch over a paper clip!

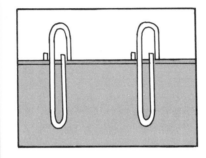

Fuse basting is a fast way to hold fabric layers in place for hand finishing or topstitching. Cut a strip of fusible web the desired length. Sandwich it between the two fabric layers and fuse, holding the iron in place for only a few seconds. Follow the manufacturer's recommendations for heat and steam.

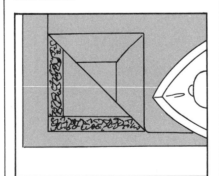

Machine basting is most often used to temporarily sew a garment together in order to check the fit.

■ Pin-baste the fabric layers together, matching the markings.

TIP *If you're doing a lot of machine basting, use different color threads in the bobbin and the needle. Later on, it will be easy to know which thread to clip and which one to pull.*

■ Loosen the needle thread tension, adjust the stitch setting to the longest length, and stitch. Don't bother to secure the stitching at the ends of the seams.

To remove the basting easily, clip the needle thread every inch (2.5cm) or so, then pull out the bobbin thread.

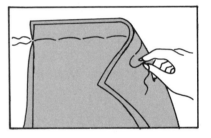

Hand basting is a very secure method of basting. It is frequently used in detail areas where pin basting would not be accurate enough or secure enough and machine basting would be difficult to do. It can also be used on sheer or very slippery fabrics.

For the firmest holding power, weave the needle in and out of the fabric so that the stitches and the spaces between them are all the same size—approximately ¼″ (6mm) long.

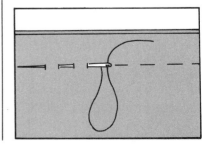

TIP *Machine basting and hand basting are also ways to transfer markings to the right side of the fabric. See page 87 for more information.*

For areas that don't need to be as secure, make the stitches ¼″ (6mm) long and the spaces between them ½″ to ¾″ (1.3cm to 2cm) long.

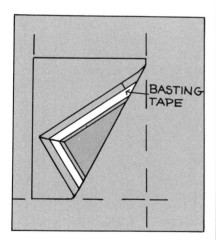

Double-faced basting tape is a valuable aid when you need to be sure that stripes or plaids match at the seamline, or for positioning detail areas such as zippers and pockets.

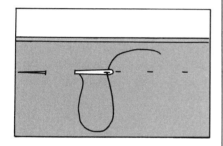

To match a stripe or plaid along a seamline:

■ Press one seam allowance under at the seamline.

■ Position the basting tape so that the sticky side is against the right side of the seam allowance, about ⅛″ (3mm) from the fold.

■ Remove the protective covering from the tape. Lap the pressed seam allowance over the unpressed one, matching both the seamline and the fabric design.

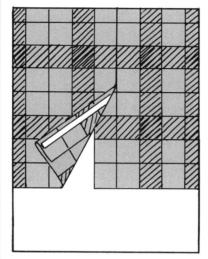

■ Turn the garment sections to the wrong side, open out the folded seam allowance and stitch along the creaseline. DO NOT stitch through the tape as it will gum up your needle.

Glue stick can be used instead of basting tape. Unlike basting tape, you can stitch right through the glue without harming your needle. Just be sure you've allowed a few minutes for the glue to dry thoroughly before stitching.

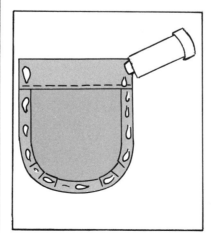

SEAMS AND SEAM FINISHES

Seams are the backbone of your sewing. Happily, there's nothing to learn about seams that's difficult to grasp. Once you know the techniques, you're on your way to wonderful sewing results.

A seam is basically a line of stitching that joins two or more layers of fabric. Seams are stitched on the seamline. The seam allowance is the distance between the seamline and the cut edge. Unless your pattern instructions tell you otherwise, the standard seam allowance is ⅝″ (1.5cm) wide.

SEAM TECHNIQUES

Some seams require special handling. Here are some terms and techniques you should be familiar with.

Directional Stitching

This means to stitch the way the arrows on the pattern point, in the direction of the fabric grain. Directional stitching helps keep fabrics, especially knits and napped fabrics, from stretching out of shape or curling. ALWAYS use directional stitching when you staystitch. For more information, see Staystitching, page 92.

Many sewing books will tell you to use directional stitching throughout your garment. In theory, this is a great idea. In fact, it isn't always practical when stitching seams. With some techniques and situations, you may not be able to clearly see what you're doing or you may end up with too much fabric in the smaller working space that's to the right of the machine needle. So . . . use directional stitching wherever it's practical.

Intersecting Seams

When one seam or dart will be crossed by another—for example, side seams crossed by a waist seam or the inside corners of a waistband—diagonally trim the ends of the first seam allowance or dart to reduce bulk.

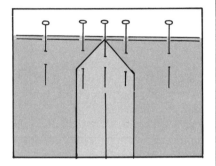

Trimming and Grading

Enclosed seams, those that end up sandwiched in between two layers of fabric, must be trimmed and graded to reduce bulk or thickness. Enclosed seams are frequently found at the outer edges of collars and cuffs, as well as along any faced edges. See Sewing with Your Scissors, page 100, for more about trimming and grading techniques.

Gathered or Eased Seams

ALWAYS stitch with the gathered side up. (This is a good example of where directional stitching may not be possible!) Guide the fabric with your hands to prevent unwanted tucks or puckers from forming.

Bias Seams

To join two bias edges—such as the side seam of a bias-cut skirt—hold the fabric in front and in back of the presser foot and stretch it gently as you stitch. Although this allows the seam to "give" as you stitch, it will also relax into a smooth seam when you are finished.

Corners

To strengthen seams at corners, shorten the stitch length for about 1″ (2.5cm) on either side of the corner. This reinforcement stitching helps prevent the corner from fraying after it is trimmed and turned right side out.

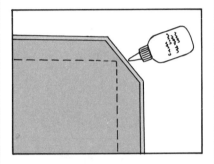

> **TIP** *If your fabric frays a lot, seal the corner with a dot of liquid seam sealant after you've trimmed it.*

For outward corners, trim diagonally.

For sharp outward corners, for example, on a collar point, take one or two diagonal stitches across it instead of stitching right up to the point. Trim across the point first, then trim diagonally on either side.

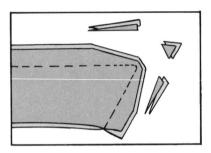

For inward corners, clip almost to the stitching.

To join an inward corner to an outward corner—for example, on a yoke—do the following:

■ Reinforce the inward corner with small stitches and clip just to the stitching.

■ Pin the two sections together, matching seamlines and markings, with the clipped section on top.

■ Stitch to the corner. Leave the needle in the fabric, raise the

> **TIP** *The trick to perfect corners is knowing just where to pivot the fabric. The easiest way to do this is to make a mark, using chalk or a disappearing marking pencil, at the point the two seamlines intersect.*
>
> ■ *Stop the machine when you come within a few stitches of this mark. Then, use the hand wheel to form the next few stitches until the needle is exactly at the mark.*
>
> ■ *With the needle still in the fabric, raise the presser foot. Pivot the fabric to bring it into the correct position for stitching the seam on the second side of the corner, lower the presser foot and continue stitching.*

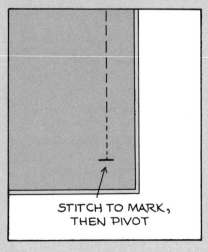

STITCH TO MARK, THEN PIVOT

presser foot and pivot the fabric so that the clipped edge spreads apart and the cut edges of the fabric match.

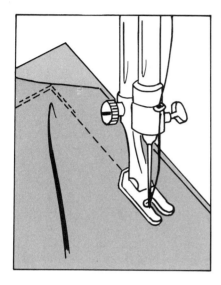

■ Lower the presser foot and continue stitching.

TYPES OF SEAMS

Although the plain seam is the one that you'll use most often, there are other choices. You might want a specific decorative look or you might be using a fabric that requires some special handling. The plain seam usually requires a seam finish. However, many of the other seams highlighted here incorporate the seam finish into the seam technique.

Remember: your pattern instructions will probably utilize a plain seam but you have the option of changing that. Consult Fabrics, pages 39–43, for some suggestions. Be sure to make a sample seam in some scraps of your fabric before you begin.

Plain Seam

■ With right sides together, stitch along the seamline, which is usually ⅝" (1.5cm) from the cut edge, with a regulation-length

stitch. For knits, stretch the fabric slightly as you sew.

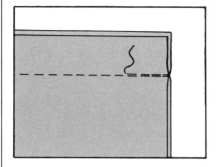

■ Press the seam flat, then open, and finish the seam allowances with the appropriate finish.

Double-stitched Seam

This is a combination seam and edge finish that creates a narrow seam especially good for sheers and knits. To prevent the fabric from raveling, it's stitched twice.

■ Stitch a plain seam.
■ Stitch again, ⅛" (3mm) away, within the seam allowance, using a straight or zigzag stitch.
■ Trim close to the second row of stitching.

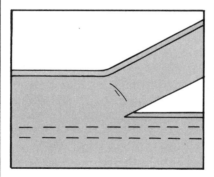

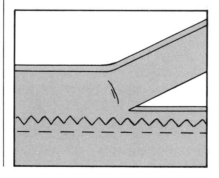

TIP *If you're using a machine zigzag, overcast, or overlock stitch to finish your plain seams, plan ahead. Finish all the seam allowances at one time, before stitching the seams.*

■ Press the seam flat to set the stitches, then to one side.

Stretch Knit Seams

Stretch knits need seams that are supple enough to "give" with the fabric. You can sew them with straight stitches, zigzag stitches, one of the stretch stitches built in to many conventional machines, or on your overlock machine.

Here are some variations, utilizing the straight stitch and the zigzag stitch:

■ Stitch a plain seam, stretching the fabric slightly as you sew.
■ For extra strength, stitch a double-stitched seam.
■ For even greater strength, straight-stitch along the seamline or use a narrow, medium-length zigzag stitch. Then zigzag ¼" (6mm) away, within the seam allowance, and trim close to the last stitching.

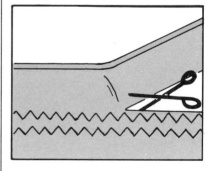

If your machine has a built-in stretch stitch, consult your owner's manual for instructions. Usually, the seam allowance must be trimmed before stitching.

Stabilizing Knit Seams

Seams at the neckline, shoulders and waistlines should NOT stretch or the knit garment will lose its shape. Stabilize them by stitching seam binding or twill tape into the seams.

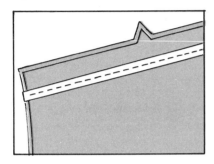

Flat-felled Seam

The flat-felled seam is frequently used on sportswear, menswear and reversible garments.

■ With WRONG sides of the fabric together, stitch a plain seam and press the seam allowances to one side.

■ Trim the underneath seam allowance to ⅛″ (3mm).

■ Turn under ¼″ (6mm) of the top seam allowance and baste it in place over the trimmed edge. (For quick sewing, use pins or glue stick.)

■ Edgestitch close to the fold.

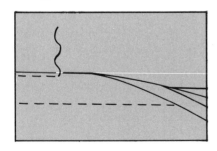

French Seam

This seam adds a couture look to the inside of garments made from sheers and lightweight silks. The finished seam, which should be very narrow, completely encloses the raw edges of the seam allowances.

■ With the WRONG sides together, stitch a ⅜″ (1cm) seam.

■ Trim the seam allowances to a scant ⅛″ (3mm), then press them open.

■ Fold the fabric right sides together along the stitching line; press.

■ Stitch ¼″ (6mm) from the fold. Press the seam allowances flat, then to one side.

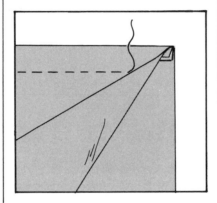

Lapped Seam

This type of seam is frequently used on nonwoven fabrics, such as synthetic suede and leather, as well as real suede and leather, because their edges do not fray.

■ Trim away the seam allowance on the upper (overlap) section.

■ Lap the edge over the underneath section, placing the trimmed edge along the seamline; hold it in place with double-faced basting tape, glue stick or fuse basting.

■ Edgestitch along the trimmed edge. Topstitch on the overlap, ¼″ (6mm) away from the first stitching.

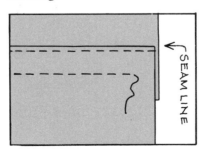

Topstitched Seam

This treatment accents the seamlines. It also helps keep the seam allowances flat—a great benefit when you're working with crease-resistant fabrics.

■ Stitch a plain seam and press it open.

■ Working on the outside of the garment, topstitch on both sides of the seam, ⅛″–¼″ (3mm–6mm) from the seamline.

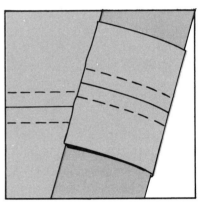

As an alternative, stitch a plain seam, press the seam allowances to one side and topstitch ⅛″–¼″ (3mm–6mm) from the seam, through all layers.

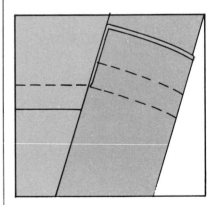

Welt Seam

This type of seam is a good way to reduce bulk and hold seam allowances flat on heavyweight fabrics. From the outside, it looks like a topstitched seam; the double-welt version looks like a flat-felled seam.

■ Stitch a plain seam and press the seam allowances to one side.

■ Trim the underneath seam allowance to a scant ¼″ (6mm).

■ On the outside, topstitch ¼″ (6mm) from the seam, catching the untrimmed seam allowance.

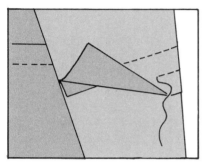

■ For a double-welt seam, also edgestitch close to the seamline.

SEAM FINISHES

To prevent raveling and add durability, plain seams usually require some type of seam finish. If the garment is going to be lined, or if the fabric is very tightly woven, no seam finish is required.

Here are some easy-to-do seam finishes. They can also be used as an edge finish on facings and hems.

Stitch and Pink

This is the quickest method for finishing fabrics that do not ravel easily.

■ Stitch ¼″ (6mm) from each seam allowance edge.

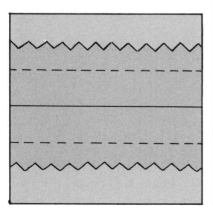

■ Trim close to the stitching with pinking shears.

Zigzag

This is a good choice for most fabrics, including heavyweight ones that ravel. Experiment with the stitch width, using a smaller stitch width for lightweight fabrics and a larger one for heavyweights.

■ Zigzag over, or as close as possible to, each raw edge.

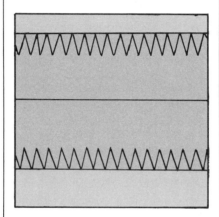

■ If your machine has an overcast stitch, you can use it in place of the zigzag stitch.

Straight-stitch

Use this finish on knits that curl, including swimwear fabrics, jersey and stretch terry. To minimize curling, finish the seams *before* stitching them.

■ Stitch ¼″ (6mm) from the raw edges.

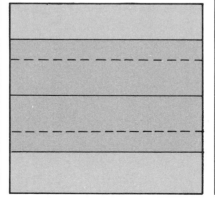

TIP *Don't use pinking shears on knit fabrics. It's unnecessary work—and may cause the fabric to curl.*

Tricot Bound

This is a custom finish that's suitable for any fabric. However, if the fabric ravels a great deal, bind the seam allowances before stitching the seams. Use a sheer, lightweight tricot seam binding, such as Seams Great® or Seams Saver™. To make sure you are applying it so the tape automatically curls around the seam allowance, hold the tricot up and tug on the ends.

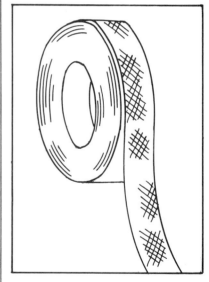

■ Position the tape so it curls around the seam allowance and secure it at the start with a pin.

■ Take one or two machine stitches, remove the pin and con-

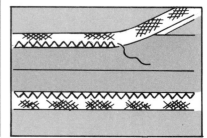

tinue to stitch, gently stretching the tape so it encases the fabric. As you stitch, you'll be sewing through both edges of tape at once. You can use a straight stitch, but for best results, particularly on fabrics that ravel, use a narrow zigzag stitch.

SEWING WITH YOUR SCISSORS

Not all good sewing techniques are centered around the sewing machine. Your scissors are an invaluable aid to professional results. Thanks to them, your garment can have crisper corners, flatter edges, and smoother curves and seams.

Trimming simply means to cut away some of the seam allowance. Do this:

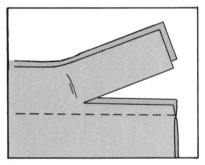

■ in areas such as the underarm section of an armhole seam, where the wider seam allowance would interfere with the fit.

■ when a special seam technique, such as French seams or welt seams, requires it.

■ on enclosed seams as a preliminary step to grading.

■ to eliminate excess fabric at the seam allowances of corners and points. That way, they will be smooth and flat once they're turned right side out.

Grading refers to the process of trimming each seam allowance to a different width so that the lay-

ers won't create ridges on the outside of the garment. This technique is most commonly used on enclosed seams, such as those sometimes found along collar, cuff, pocket and faced edges. If the fabric is lightweight, grading is usually not necessary—trimming is enough. However, if the fabric is medium to heavy weight,

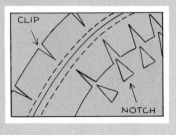

TIP *For a stronger seam, or when joining an inward curve to an outward curve, staystitch each curve a scant 1/8" (3mm) inside the seamline. Pin or baste the garment sections together and stitch the seam. Then, being careful not to cut through the staystitching, clip one seam allowance to release the fabric and notch the other to eliminate excess fullness.*

all enclosed seams must be trimmed AND graded. Corners require special treatment: see page 96.

To grade, trim the seam allowance that will end up closest to the inside of the garment to 1/8" (3mm); trim the seam allowance that will be closest to the outside of the garment to 1/4" (6mm). The wider seam allowance acts as a cushion for the narrower one.

Clipping and notching are techniques used to make curved seams lie flat.

■ On inside, or concave, curves, make little clips, or snips, in the seam allowance just to, but not through, the stitching.

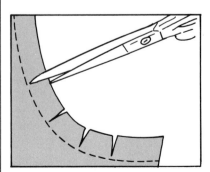

■ On outward, or convex, curves, cut wedge-shaped notches from the seam allowance to eliminate excess fullness when the seam is pressed open.

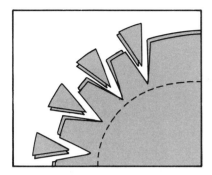

SEWING WITH AN OVERLOCK MACHINE

Overlock . . . serger . . . merrowing machine—these are all synonymous for a sewing machine that stitches the seam, trims off the excess fabric, and overcasts the raw edges, all at the same time. Seams on the overlock come out so narrow they don't need to be trimmed and graded; shallow curves lay flat without any notching or clipping.

To get the most out of your overlock machine, you'll want to use it hand-in-hand with your conventional machine. You can't entirely replace one machine with the other . . . but together there is almost no commercial sewing technique that you can't duplicate.

Like the other general sewing information included in this chapter, what follows here are the basics you need to know about operating your overlock. Chapter 6 will show you how overlock techniques can be used in place of conventional techniques. In addition, it will show you how to combine overlock techniques with conventional techniques so you get the best of both sewing worlds.

Discover the fabulous world of OVERLOCK/SERGER sewing

- **FAST** . . . Sew a seam or finish an edge at twice the speed of the fastest conventional home sewing machine.
- **EFFICIENT** . . . stitch, trim and overcast a seam in one simple step.
- **PROFESSIONAL** . . . provides a true ready-to-wear look.
- **DECORATIVE** . . . an easy way to create special effects on seams and edges.
- **FLEXIBLE** . . . from sportswear to evening wear, perfect for knits, silks, synthetics, heavy coatings and actionwear fabrics.
- **VERSATILE** . . . the best of all sewing worlds; use the overlock serger alone or as a supplement to your conventional machine.

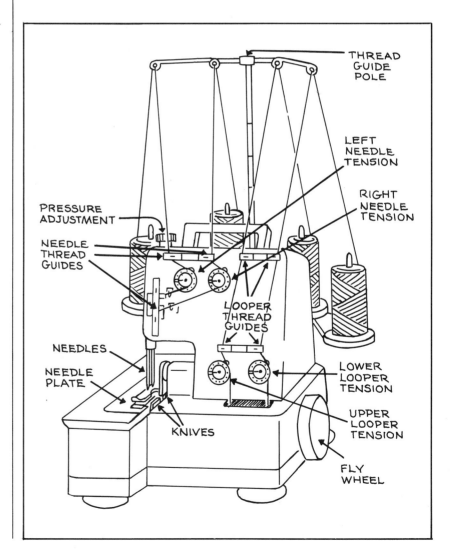

TYPES OF OVERLOCKS

As you explore the world of serger sewing, you'll have to learn some new terminology. Take a look at the illustration on the previous page that identifies the various parts of an overlock machine. Note that:

■ Instead of bobbins, there are loopers. The two threads that come up from underneath the needle plate are called the lower looper thread and the upper looper thread. Each looper has its own tension adjustment dial.

■ Each needle thread has its own tension adjustment dial.

■ On the right of the needle there are knives that cut off the excess fabric.

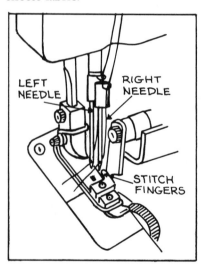

Not all overlock machines can create every type of overlock stitch. Some machines perform only one or two functions, or stitch configurations, while others can perform several. You'll hear them described as two-thread, three-thread, three/four-thread, four-thread, four-thread mock safety and even five-thread machines.

The key is to understand what each stitch function can do, then select the overlock model that offers the functions that are most important to you.

Two-Thread Function

The two-thread overlock stitch uses one needle and one looper. The two threads interlock at the fabric edge. On the underside of the fabric, the needle thread forms a "V."

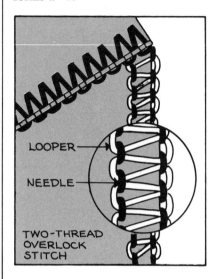

Because the two-thread overlock stitch uses less thread than the other stitches, it creates a flat, economical stitch that's ideal for a seam finish. It also creates a stitch called a flatlock that can be used for decorative outside seaming and to reduce bulk in specialty fabrics such as fake fur and sweater knits. The flatlock stitch can be done so that the "ladders" appear on the inside or the outside of the garment.

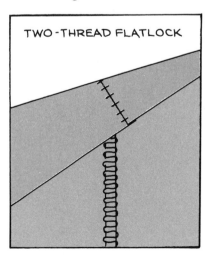

This function can also be used to create a flat blind hem.

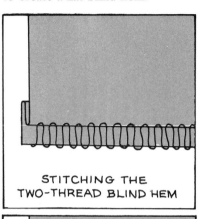

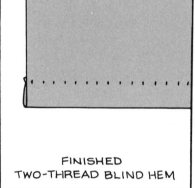

Three-Thread Function

The three-thread overlock stitch uses one needle and two loopers. All three threads interlock at the fabric edge.

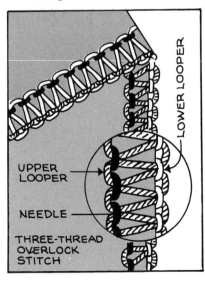

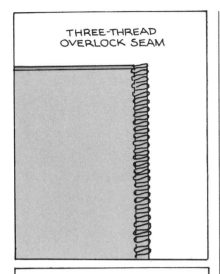

THREE-THREAD
OVERLOCK SEAM

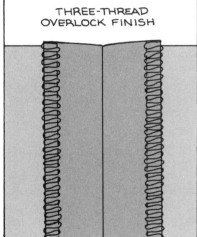

THREE-THREAD
OVERLOCK FINISH

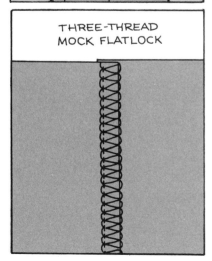

THREE-THREAD
MOCK FLATLOCK

A three-thread overlock can be used by itself to join and overcast a seam or as an edge finish for a seam stitched on a conven-

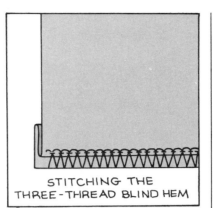

STITCHING THE
THREE-THREAD BLIND HEM

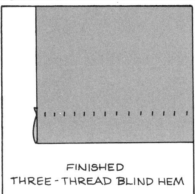

FINISHED
THREE-THREAD BLIND HEM

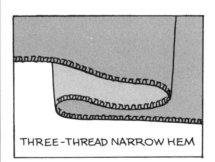

THREE-THREAD NARROW HEM

tional machine. It can also be used to create a mock flatlock seam, a blind hem (although not as nice a one as the two-thread function) and a narrow hem. In addition, the three-thread overlock stitch is the most popular choice for decorative work.

Four-Thread Functions

There are three types of four-thread overlock stitches.

The FOUR-THREAD SAFETY STITCH is a combination chain stitch and two-thread overlock

stitch. It uses two needles and two loopers. One needle and one looper create a two-thread safety chain stitch; the remaining needle and looper create a two-thread overlock stitch.

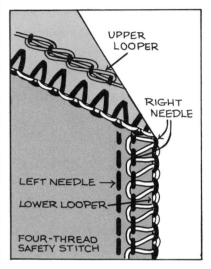

UPPER
LOOPER

RIGHT
NEEDLE

LEFT NEEDLE →

LOWER LOOPER

FOUR-THREAD
SAFETY STITCH

This stitch is suitable for stable or woven fabrics. Because the chain isn't a flexible, stretchable stitch, this stitch is not recommended for knits. The chain will "pop" when the fabric is stretched.

On machines that have this function, you can use the overlock and chain stitches together or separately. The two-thread

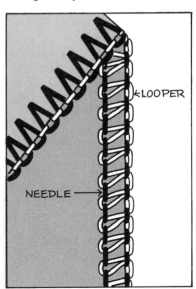

LOOPER

NEEDLE →

TWO-THREAD OVERLOCK STITCH

chain stitch can be used alone for seaming. On many of these machines, the cutter can be removed or disengaged so that the chain stitch can be used for top-stitching along an edge of your garment.

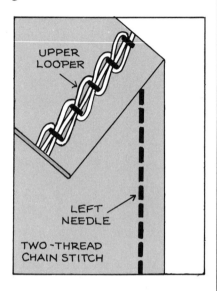

UPPER LOOPER

LEFT NEEDLE

TWO-THREAD CHAIN STITCH

The FOUR-THREAD OVER-LOCK STITCH and the FOUR-THREAD MOCK SAFETY STITCH use two needles and two loopers. The looper threads interlock with the needle threads at the left and with one another at the fabric

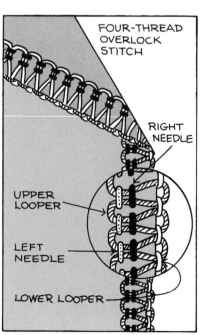

FOUR-THREAD OVERLOCK STITCH

RIGHT NEEDLE

UPPER LOOPER

LEFT NEEDLE

LOWER LOOPER

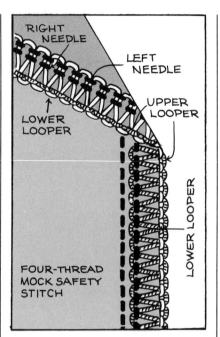

RIGHT NEEDLE

LEFT NEEDLE

UPPER LOOPER

LOWER LOOPER

FOUR-THREAD MOCK SAFETY STITCH

edges. Although these functions were designed specifically with knits in mind, they can also be used on wovens. The extra row of straight stitching that runs down the middle of the overlock stitch configuration adds stability.

Narrow-Rolled Edge Function

This is a variation of the three-thread stitch. It's used to create a fine edge finish on a wide variety of items, such as ruffles, scarves, napkins, tablecloths and garment hems.

The narrow-rolled hem uses one needle and two loopers. The lower looper tension is tightened so that the upper looper thread rolls the fabric edge and encases it.

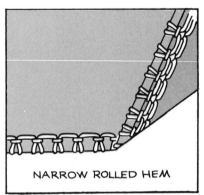

NARROW ROLLED HEM

No matter what type of over-lock machine you choose, the best advice anyone can give you is to read the manual carefully and familiarize yourself with the machine. Overlocks are extremely easy to operate. Once you've learned how to thread the machine, and which tension dials control which thread, you've just about learned it all!

As you sew, the cutting action will create a great deal of lint. For good performance, it's important to keep your overlock machine clean. Make it a practice to clean out the lint every time you sit down to sew. Open the front and

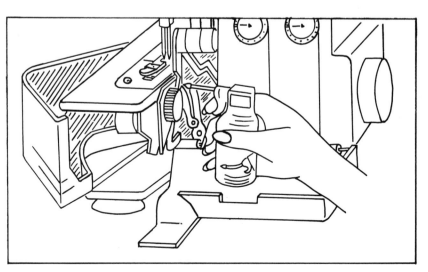

> **TIP** *Here's a quick way to learn which thread forms which part of the stitch. Use a different color thread for each looper and needle. Make some practice seams, changing the tensions. Observe what happens to the stitch formation. If you forget which way to turn the dials to tighten or loosen the tension, just remember this catchy rhyme: "righty, tighty; lefty, loosey."*

> **TIP** *Although woolly nylon thread can be used through the needle(s) and loopers, its texture makes threading difficult. Use it in the upper looper only. Use cotton-wrapped polyester, 100 percent polyester or nylon thread in the lower looper and needles. It will be easier to thread your machine, but your finished seams will still have some stretch.*

side covers to expose the loopers. Using the small brush that comes with your machine, get rid of all the lint that has accumulated. To keep it super-clean, apply a few squirts of compressed air.

SELECTING THE RIGHT THREAD

Whether you're choosing thread for your overlock or your conventional machine, you'll have better stitch quality and fewer problems with thread breakage if you select a good quality thread, one that is made from long, continuous fibers. One way to tell if it's a quality thread is to examine it carefully for the "fuzzies." These indicate that the thread is made up of lots of short fibers, resulting in a weaker thread that will break easily. The fuzzier the thread, the poorer the quality.

Because the overlock sews fast—from 1200–1800 stitches per minute—the thread should be strong enough to withstand the speed, yet fine enough to create a soft, supple seam finish. One of the best all-purpose threads for conventional sewing is cotton thread with a polyester core. Although it is possible to use this same thread in your overlock machine, you'll be happier with the results if you use a thread especially designed for the overlock machine.

Cotton-wrapped or 100 Percent Polyester Serger Thread

These threads are similar to, but finer than, conventional sewing threads. They're available on large (1,000 yards or more) cones.

Nylon Serger Thread

This is very strong and is recommended for knitted swimwear, lingerie and active sportswear, including leotards or other clothing made with Lycra® or elasticized fabric. It also works well for rolled hems when threaded through the upper looper (see Chapter 6, page 169).

Woolly Nylon Thread

This thread comes in either a "kinked" or a smooth "flossy" configuration. As with nylon serger thread, it is recommended for knitted swimwear, lingerie, leotards and Lycra® or elasticized fabric. Because these garments have seams that come in direct contact with the body, you may prefer woolly nylon over 100 percent nylon serger thread because it's softer and it lays flatter than many other threads.

100 Percent Silk Thread

This is the same silk thread that you use in your conventional machine. It has a luster, shine and color range difficult to find in other threads. However, it is expensive and may not be readily available. Save your silk thread and use it where it has the greatest value—for rolled hems. Because silk is very resilient and very lustrous, it will create a tighter, richer-looking edge.

100 Percent Cotton Serger Thread

This type of thread isn't quite as strong as the other threads. Use it

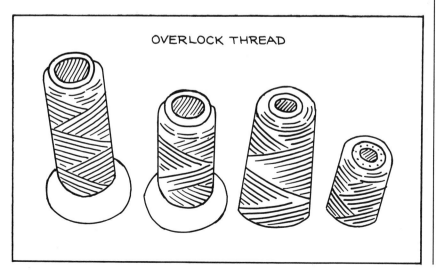

OVERLOCK THREAD

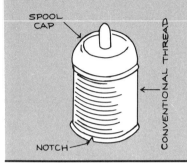

TIP *If you're using conventional thread, place it on the spool pin with the notched end down and use a spool cap. This way, as the thread rapidly unwinds, it won't get caught in the spool's rough edges.*

SPOOL CAP

CONVENTIONAL THREAD

NOTCH

only on woven fabrics . . . or use it in the loopers, with polyester or nylon thread in the needle(s).

Conventional Sewing Thread

Sometimes this is the only thread you can find in the color you want. If this is the case, use the matching conventional thread in the needle(s) and use serger thread in the loopers. The serger thread should be in a color that "blends" with your fashion fabric. For example, try gray for medium to dark fabrics, white or ecru on pastels, brown on rust, navy on purple, etc.

Decorative Threads

Because its loopers have large eyes that can accommodate heavier threads, you can use a wider range of decorative threads on the overlock than on the conventional sewing machine. Experiment! You'll probably prefer to use the decorative threads in the loopers only. Try baby yarn, metallic or silk thread, #8 pearl cotton, 1⁄16″ (2mm) wide silk or rayon ribbon, machine embroidery thread, shiny rayon thread, candlewicking thread, crochet cotton, even embroidery floss

(two, three or six strands). Some ideas:

■ Thread the upper looper with baby yarn and serge the edges of a placemat, a coat or a jacket. It's a great substitute for foldover braid or bias tape. (See Chapter 6, pages 135–136.)

■ Use metallic or silk thread in the upper looper for beautiful rolled hems. (See Chapter 6, page 169.)

■ Use variegated #8 pearl cotton in the looper and flatlock your seams, using the two-thread stitch configuration. With a three-thread stitch configuration, try a mock flatlock seam, wih the pearl cotton in the upper looper. (See Chapter 6, page 189.)

SOLVING YOUR STITCH PROBLEMS

Your overlock manual provides information on how to adjust your tension dials to achieve

a well-balanced stitch. Sometimes, however, you may have stitching problems that no amount of fiddling with the tension dials will correct. For causes and solutions to these problems, see pages 108–109.

PINNING AND BASTING

Safety First, Then Serge

Did you ever break a pin by sewing over it? Even if your conventional machine is designed to sew over pins, it's a bad habit to get into—particularly if you're joining the enthusiastic ranks of those who use an overlock machine.

Overlock machines have both stationary and moveable cutters, or knives. As you serge, they are constantly moving, cutting off the excess seam allowances or ragged fabric edges. If a pin happens to be in the way, the knives will cut the pin off, dulling the blades and sending pin fragments through

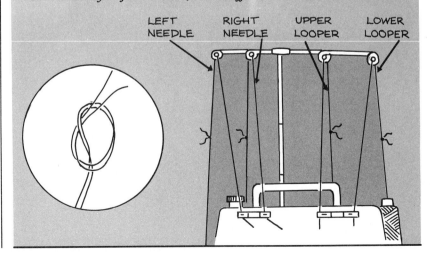

TIP *Instead of rethreading the machine manually each time you change colors, try this:*

■ *Cut off the old thread just above the spool.*

■ *Replace the old spool with the new thread and tie the ends together in a knot.*

■ *Pull the threads through the machine in the following sequence— lower looper, upper looper, right needle, left needle. When the knot reaches the eye of the needle, cut it off and rethread the needle.*

LEFT NEEDLE   RIGHT NEEDLE   UPPER LOOPER   LOWER LOOPER

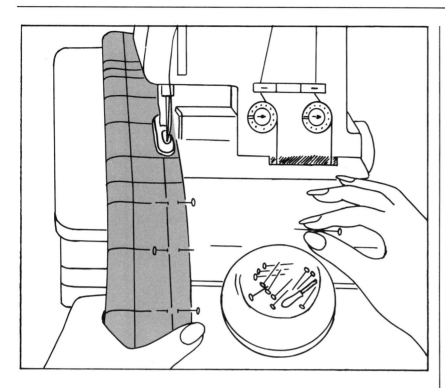

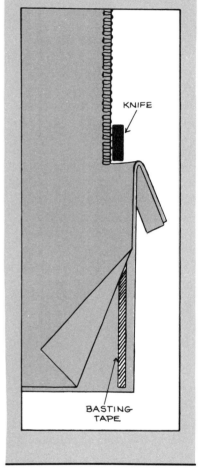

TIP *As a substitute for pin-basting, try glue stick or double-faced basting tape. Place the tape next to the cut edge of the fabric so you don't gum up your machine by stitching or cutting through it.*

KNIFE

BASTING TAPE

the air. *Flying pins can cut your face or damage your eyes.* If they miss you and get into the inner workings of your machine, the result is a serviceman's nightmare!

This doesn't mean you have to forego pin basting altogether.

■ Pull out the pins before the knife reaches them. A Grabbit® pincushion next to your machine provides the pins with a nice home.

■ Place the pins at least 1″ (2.5cm) from the cut edge, paral-

lel to the seamline. This method is good for long seams but not for small detail areas.

GETTING STARTED

With a conventional sewing machine, you must ALWAYS re-

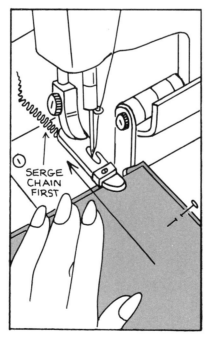

SERGE CHAIN FIRST

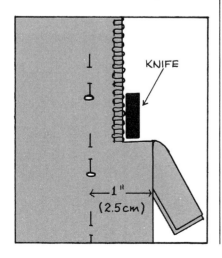

KNIFE

←——1″——→
(2.5cm)

member to lower the presser foot before stitching and raise it again when you're finished—or else your machine won't form the stitches properly. With an overlock, you can leave the presser foot in the "down" position all the time. For a smooth start, serge a 2″–3″ (5cm–7.5cm) thread chain, then gently feed the fabric under the foot. If you're sewing on very thick fabric, or through many layers, you may want to serge a chain, then use your thumb to lift the front of the foot onto the fabric.

FINISHING UP

If you're using your overlock to finish the seams, or if the seam will be intersected by another seam, you don't need to bother securing the thread ends. To simply end your stitching, here's what to do:

1. Serge off the fabric for about 5"–6" (12.5cm–15cm).

2. Without raising the presser foot, bring the chain and the fabric around so the chain crosses in front of the knife. Stitch for a few more seconds so that the knives automatically cut the thread chain off for you.

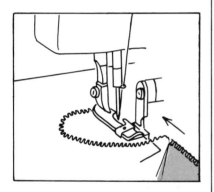

This method cuts the thread but doesn't secure the ends. To do that, use one of the following methods.

"Backstitching"

Your conventional machine usually has a backstitch button or knob that allows you to sew two or three stitches back over themselves. Although this isn't possible with an overlock, it is possible to stitch back over a serged seam or thread chain.

At the beginning of the seam:

■ Serge a 2" (5cm) thread chain.

■ Lift the tip of the presser foot with your thumb, place the garment underneath and take four or

PROBLEM: Skipped Stitches	
POSSIBLE CAUSE:	**SOLUTION:**
Needle may be too heavy for the fabric.	Change to a finer needle.
The upper looper tension may be too tight.	Loosen it slightly.
The needle may be dull or bent.	Change to a new needle.
The machine may be threaded incorrectly.	Rethread and check all the threading points.
The needle may not be the right type.	Use a sharp point needle—size 11 or 14, designed for YOUR overlock. (Not all serger needles can be used with all machines. Check the needle package and your manual.)

PROBLEM: Stitches pull through to the right side of the fabric.	
POSSIBLE CAUSE:	**SOLUTION:**
Needle tension may be too loose.	Tighten it slightly.
Incorrect needle plate or wrong stitch width for weight of fabric.	Use a 3mm–4mm needle plate or the widest stitch width.
The thread is not fully lodged between the tension disks.	Hold the thread securely above the tension dial and pull the thread firmly below the knob, sliding it between the disks.
Thread has slipped out of thread guides.	Same as above.
Needle is dull, bent or burred.	Change the needle.
Knife is not set correctly.	Consult the instruction manual or your dealer.

PROBLEM: Threads break.	
POSSIBLE CAUSE:	**SOLUTION:**
Incorrect threading.	Rethread machine from right to left (i.e., lower looper, upper looper, right needle, left needle). Check the manual—you may need to loosen tensions to "0" before rethreading.
Incorrect threading sequence.	If looper thread is breaking, remove the thread(s) from the eye of the needle(s) before rethreading the loopers.

PROBLEM: Threads break.	
POSSIBLE CAUSE:	**SOLUTION:**
Thread pole isn't completely extended.	Check and correct.
Tension is too tight.	Reduce the tension slightly on the looper or needle thread that is breaking.
Thread is caught on spool or wrapped around spool pin.	Check and correct.
Needle is dull, bent or burred.	Change the needle. You'll need a new one every 60–100 hours of sewing time.
Thread is old, brittle or coarse.	Try a different thread.

PROBLEM: Loops form at the edge of the fabric.	
POSSIBLE CAUSE:	**SOLUTION:**
Thread is not lodged fully between tension disks.	Check to see that the thread is laying inside the tension disks.
Looper threads are too loose.	Increase tension on upper and lower loopers.
Thread has slipped out of take-up lever or thread guides.	Recheck threading points.
Knife is cutting too much fabric.	Check that the blade is aligned evenly with the needle plate. Consult the instruction manual or your dealer.

PROBLEM: Machine is jamming.	
POSSIBLE CAUSE:	**SOLUTION:**
Presser foot pressure is too heavy for your fabric.	Consult the instruction manual to decrease pressure.
Fabric has been inserted behind the knife.	Insert fabric from the front of the machine. Since the knife is in front of the needle, the fabric must be trimmed BEFORE it reaches the needle.
Thread is caught under the presser foot.	After completing a row of stitching, continue stitching so that you "chain off" a 2″–3″ (5cm–7.5cm) tail behind the presser foot.

five stitches, leaving the needle in the fabric.

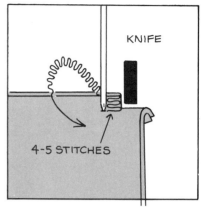

■ Raise the presser foot. Swinging the chain around to the front from the left of the needle, place it on the seam allowance, between the needle and the knife.

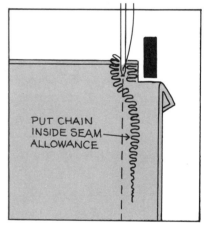

■ Lower the presser foot and serge, encasing the thread chain in the seam allowance.

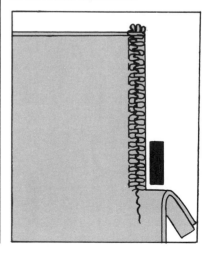

At the end of a seam:

■ Serge to the end of the seam, one stitch past the edge of the fabric. Stop with the needle up, out of the fabric.

■ Raise the presser foot. Then, gently pull on the needle thread to create slack.

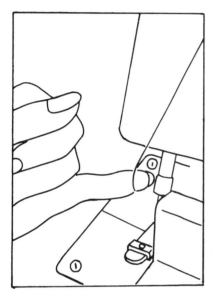

■ Pull the last stitch off the stitch fingers. Flip the fabric over and bring it around to the front of the needle.

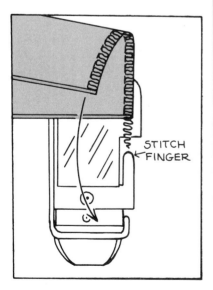

STITCH FINGER

■ Lower the presser foot and eliminate the slack by pulling on the needle thread, just above the tension dial. Serge over the previous stitching for about 1″ (2.5cm), then serge off the edge.

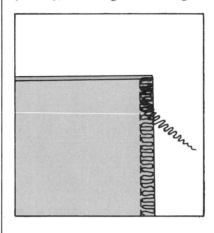

Tying Off

You may prefer to tie off the threads. There are two ways to do this. The first is quick, but a little bulky. The second method results in an almost invisible knot.

Method #1: Gently run your fingertips along the thread chain to smooth it out. Then, tie the threads as described for securing conventional machine stitching, page 91. To further secure the knot, add a drop of liquid seam sealant.

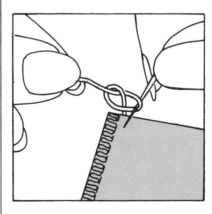

Method #2: Hold the project and the thread chain in one hand. With the other hand, use a pin (an extra-long quilting pin works very well) to loosen the needle thread. Pull the needle thread out of the chain. Now all the threads are free and can be tied in a small knot.

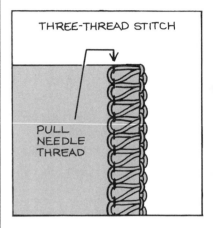

THREE-THREAD STITCH

PULL NEEDLE THREAD

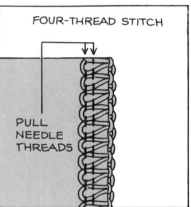

FOUR-THREAD STITCH

PULL NEEDLE THREADS

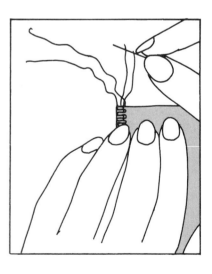

Burying the Threads

Thread the chain onto a large-eyed craft needle, then tunnel it back along the seam allowance, between the fabric and the stitches.

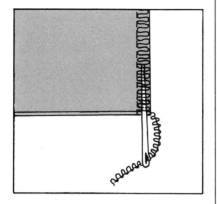

SEAMS

Your overlock can be used as a finishing machine for seams that will eventually be sewn on a conventional sewing machine . . . or it can be used to simultaneously finish and stitch a seam.

When sewing on a conventional machine, the top layer of fabric always feeds slightly faster than the bottom layer. As a result, the rule is to stitch with the grain whenever possible and practical.

With your overlock machine, this is a rule that you can happily break. Because the presser foot has a firmer pressure and the loopers "knit" the threads across the fabric, as well as along its length, shifting is virtually eliminated. As a result, you can stitch your seams in any direction you please.

Continuous Overcasting

If you plan to stitch your seams on a conventional machine, you can use your overlock, and the continuous overcasting technique, to speed up the mundane task of finishing the raw edges.

Depending on what type of overlock you own, use either a two-thread or three-thread stitch to overcast the edges. As you serge, the knife should skim the edge of the fabric so nothing is trimmed off the seam allowance except a few loose threads.

For continuous overcasting, you are going to line up all the garment sections so that the

stitching is not broken as you move from the edge of one section to the edge of another. Once the overcasting is finished, the thread chains are clipped and the garment sections are separated.

For example, suppose you are making a simple top and a matching pair of shorts. Here's how you would line up the pattern pieces and feed them into the overlock:

■ Begin by overcasting all the hem edges, cutting the threads in between, as shown in the top diagram below.

■ On the TOP FRONT (as shown in the stitching diagram, below), begin at the hemline and overcast one side seam (A), the two shoulder seams (B & C), and then the other side seam (D).

■ Without snipping the thread, and without raising the presser foot, move on to the TOP BACK. Overcast in the same sequence as for the TOP FRONT (E, F, G & H).

■ Without snipping the threads, overcast the outside legs of the

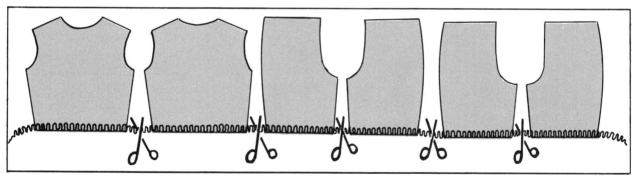

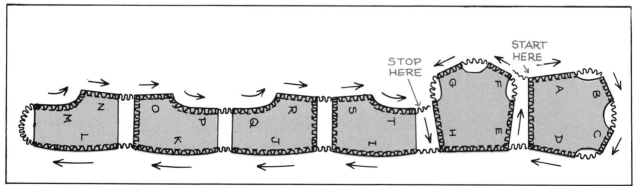

SHORTS FRONT and SHORTS BACK (I–L). Your work will begin to resemble an oddly shaped kite tail!

■ When you are finished with the outside legs, turn everything around and overcast the inside legs (M–S).

■ To separate the garment sections, simply snip the connecting thread chains.

Speed Seaming

This technique for joining the seams of a garment is similar to the sequence for continuous overcasting.

Suppose you are making a simple top and want to join and finish the seams using only the overlock machine.

■ Overcast the bottom hem edges, then cut the threads in between.

■ Pin the garment together at the side seams and shoulder seams.

■ Starting at the hemline, serge up one side seam (A). Chain off but do not cut the threads.

■ Serge the first shoulder seam (B), from armhole to neck edge, and chain off. Again, do not cut the threads.

■ Serge the second shoulder seam (C), from neck edge to armhole, and chain off.

■ Serge the remaining side seam (D), from armhole to hemline.

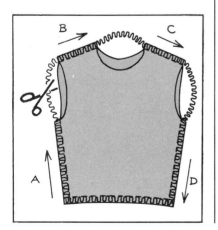

> **TIP** *On very stretchy knits or loosely woven fabrics, staystitch over elastic thread. In its relaxed position, elastic thread is strong enough to hold a shape. However, it will also stretch and give when you put the garment on and take it off.*

■ Snip the threads between the seams. Press the seams and you're ready to go on to the finishing details, such as facings, bands and hems.

Staystitching

Fabrics that require special handling on a conventional machine

> **TIP** *Some garment sections may not require any handling between the time you staystitch and the time you serge the seams. If this is the case, staystitch and join the seams at the same time. Pin the garment together along the seamline, position the twill tape, and serge the seam. (Reminder: Remove pins as they approach the knife.)*

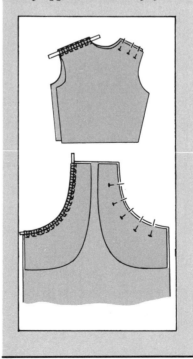

are a breeze to sew on the overlock. Stretchy sweater knits, stretch terry cloth and velour, slippery crepe de chine, jersey and nylon tricot are just a few of the difficult fabrics that your overlock will handle just like a piece of crisply woven cotton.

One of the reasons that many sewers have avoided these "special" fabrics is their tendency to stretch out of shape, during both handling and sewing. Staystitching is the time-honored way to prevent fabric distortion. On an overlock, it's really easy!

To staystitch, place a strand of 1/4" (6mm) twill tape, knitting ribbon or baby yarn so that it goes under the presser foot and over the finger guard, and serge slightly to the right of the seamline. If your machine has a presser foot with a hole for inserting cording, thread the tape, ribbon or yarn through the hole

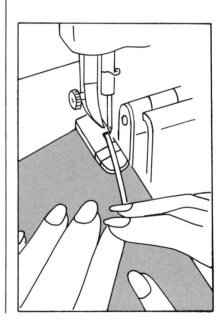

THE UNIVERSAL BASICS 113

first, then pull it under the back of the foot and serge.

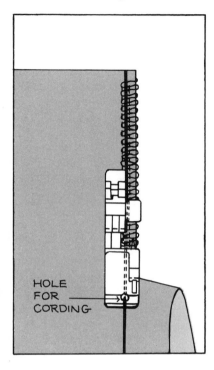

When you are ready to serge your garment together, remember that the knife on your overlock has trimmed away the excess seam allowance. Sections that are staystitched will now have ¼" (6mm) seam allowances.

SPECIAL TECHNIQUES

Serging Outside Corners

Because of the way an overlock creates the stitches, serging outside corners calls for some (very easy) special treatment. If you don't use the following procedure, one of two things will happen: either a small, untidy clover leaf of thread will form at the corner or you won't be able to pivot the fabric to get a sharp point.

■ Starting at one edge of the outside corner, make a 2" (5cm) long slash, parallel to and ⅜" (1cm) in from the edge of the

fabric. *Note:* If your project has ¼" (6mm) hem allowances, you won't be trimming as you overcast so you can skip this step.

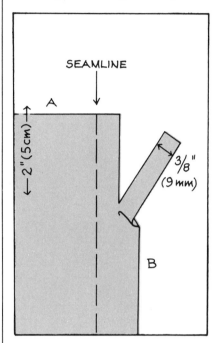

■ Beginning on side A, serge to the corner, going just one stitch past the edge of the fabric.

■ Lift the presser foot and gently pull on the needle thread to create a little bit of slack.

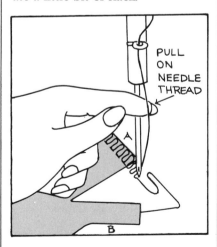

■ Carefully pull the last stitch off the stitch finger(s) and pivot the fabric, positioning it so that the new stitches will butt up against the previous stitches.

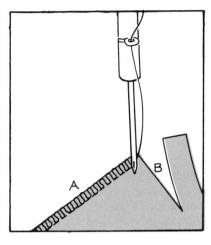

■ Pull the needle thread back up above the tension dial to remove the slack; serge. The result is a neat, clean corner.

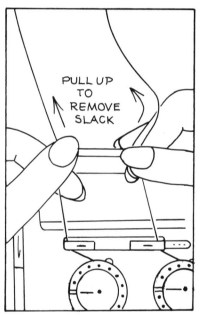

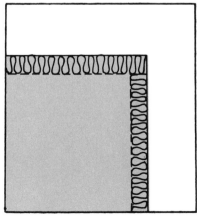

Serging Inside Corners

On rare occasions, you may want to serge an edge that includes an inside corner. This technique takes practice, so try it out first on some scraps of fabric until you're comfortable with the results.

■ Using a disappearing marking pen, mark the corner at the intersection of the ⅝″ (1.5cm) seamlines. If your fabric is soft, staystitch the inside corner on your conventional sewing machine.

■ Clip the corner, ending the clip ⅛″ (3mm) from the corner mark.

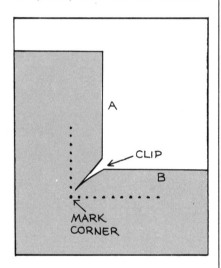

■ Starting at the clip, and working on side B of the corner, trim the seam allowance to ⅛″ (3mm) for approximately 1″ (2.5cm).

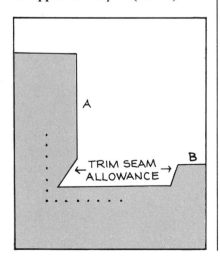

■ Beginning at side A, serge until side B is just in front of the knife. Spread the fabric open so that the cut edge of side B is even with the edge of the knife. (*Note:* A small pleat will appear in the fabric when you do this.) Continue serging side B.

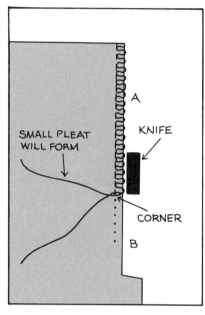

Serging in a Circle

Because overlock stitches must always begin and end at the edge of the fabric, and because an overlock cannot backstitch, sewing in a circle requires some special—but easy—techniques. Suppose you want to attach a circular band to a neckline . . . or a circular cuff to the edge of a sleeve . . . or finish the edges of an oval placemat or a round tablecloth. Here are two techniques:

Serge On/Serge Off. Since this is the fastest—but not the neatest—method, it is usually used when the seam will be hidden inside the garment. All the intersecting seams are serged before the circular seam is stitched.

■ With right sides together, pin the two garment sections together.

■ At some point along the seamline (usually the center back), make a 2″ (5cm) mark along the ⅝″ (1.5cm) seam allowance with a disappearing marking pen.

■ Serge, starting over just before the mark and angling the fabric until you are stitching along the mark.

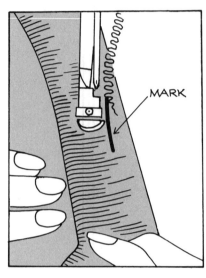

■ Serge around the circular area until the stitches meet at the mark. Serge off the fabric.

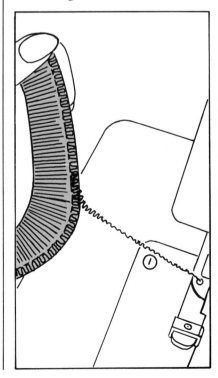

TIP *To prevent any "bumps" or distortion that might occur when serging over bulky, intersecting seams, press the seam allowances so that they will face in opposite directions when you serge.*

Clip Method. Use this method when you are finishing a continuous edge, such as the neckline or hemline of a garment, or hemming an item such as an oval placemat or a round tablecloth.

■ If you have a seam or hem allowance that is deeper than ¼" (6mm), make two parallel clips in the seam allowance 2" (5cm) apart. Trim the seam allowance away between the clips. If the project has a ¼" (6mm) seam allowance, skip this step.

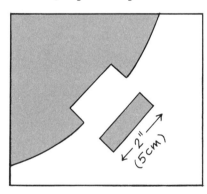

■ Raise the presser foot and place the fabric so that the trimmed edge is next to the knife and the needle is at the top of the clipped

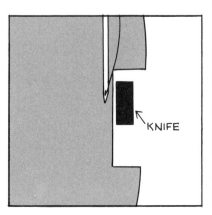

area. Carefully lower the presser foot onto the fabric.

■ Serge around the edge until the stitches meet and overlap for two or three stitches.

■ Pull the thread through the needles by hand to create about 3" (7.5cm) of slack. Lift the presser foot and pull the fabric toward the back so the stitches come off the stitch fingers. Separate the thread chain and tie off the threads (see page 110).

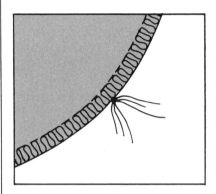

REMOVING STITCHES

"As she sews, so shall she rip!" Let's face it: Everyone, even the most experienced sewer, makes mistakes now and then.

Believe it or not, ripping out serger stitching is often easier than ripping out conventional stitching. However, when you go to restitch, remember that the knife has already trimmed the seam allowance.

For the Two-, Three- or Four-Thread Overlock Stitches:
Simply run a seam ripper along

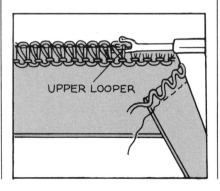

the edge of the fabric, under the upper looper threads, cutting them as you go.

For a Four-Thread Safety Stitch:
To remove the "chain" part of the stitch, work from the underneath side of the serged stitches and start ripping at the end of the chain. If you can locate the looper thread, pull it and the chain will come undone like ready-to-wear stitches often do. To remove the overedge stitches, turn the fabric to the wrong side and cut along the "V" created by the needle threads.

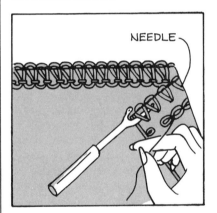

SEWING WITH YOUR IRON

Careful pressing is as important as accurate stitching. In fact, if you want professional results, you can't have one without the other! Note that the term "press" rather than "iron" is used in sewing. The difference? "To press" means to move the iron across the fabric by lifting it up and putting it back down in an overlapping pattern. "To iron" means to slide the iron across the fabric with a back-and-forth motion. Ironing may distort the shape of the garment; pressing won't.

The cardinal rule in sewing is "press as you go." This means that you should never, never

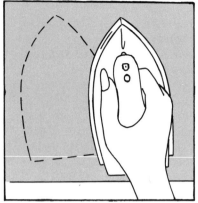

PRESSING

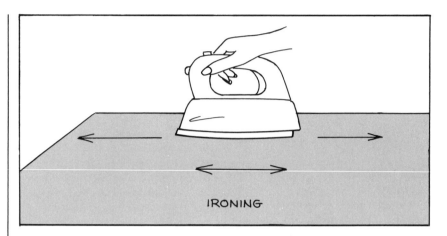

IRONING

cross one seam with another without first pressing the original seam.

This doesn't mean that you must be constantly hopping back and forth from ironing board to sewing machine. Two easy solutions:

■ Organize your sewing so that you are working on several different sections of the garment at the same time. Sew as far as you can on each section, then take them all to the ironing board and press everything that needs it.

■ Keep your iron and a tabletop ironing board or a sturdy sleeve board within arm's reach of your sewing machine. That way you can do small detail pressing without getting up.

Although some sewing procedures require special pressing techniques (see Chapter 6), there are three universal steps for achieving good results.

Step 1—Press flat along the stitching line to blend the stitches.

Step 2—Press the seam allowances open or to one side, as indicated in the pattern instructions.

Step 3—Press the seam or detail area from the right side. If necessary, protect the fabric with a press cloth.

As a rule, it's best to use light pressure, without resting the full weight of the iron on the fabric. Some delicate fabrics or fabrics with a texture that could be flattened, such as velvet or fake furs, can be finger-pressed. To do this, hold the iron above the fabric and apply a generous amount of steam. Then use your fingers, not the iron, to press seams, darts and edges.

PRESS-AS-YOU-SEW GUIDE

The chart on the opposite page is a useful guide to pressing today's common fibers and textures.

GLOSSARY OF PRESSING EQUIPMENT

In addition to your iron and ironing board, there's a wide range of pressing equipment available. Pressing aids are designed:

■ to provide a shaped pressing surface that simulates the curves of the body.

■ to allow you to press small detail areas without putting creases into the rest of the garment.

Don't think you have to run out and buy all the equipment listed. Start with a seam roll (or our no-cost substitute) and some press cloths. Then add to your collection as your sewing skills develop.

Seam Roll. Useful for pressing seams open on long, cylindrical garment sections, such as sleeves and pants legs. If you press the seams open using the tip of your iron, the curved surface prevents the seal allowances from creating imprints on the outside of the garment.

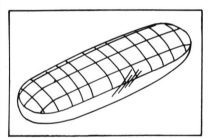

Press Cloths prevent scorch marks and iron shine. Use any of the following: specially treated press cloths, muslin in several different weights, a piece of your fashion fabric, or a man's handkerchief.

TIP *As a quick substitute for a seam roll, place a magazine on top of a piece of muslin, roll it up tightly and secure with a few rubber bands.*

PRESS-AS-YOU-SEW GUIDE

FIBER	PRESSURE	HEAT	MOISTURE	SPECIAL INSTRUCTIONS
Acetate	Light	Very low	Dry iron	Use press cloth on right side.
Acrylic	Light	Moderate	Dry iron	Use press cloth on right side.
Cotton	Light to moderate	Moderate to high		Press with steam iron. For more moisture, dampen fabric and press with dry iron. To avoid shine on dark colors, press from wrong side or use press cloth on right side.
Linen	Light to heavy	High		
Nylon	Light			Little or no ironing required.
Polyester	Moderate			May need press cloth on right side; test first.
Rayon		Low to moderate	Dry or steam iron	Use press cloth to prevent shine and water spots.
Silk	Light			Press light to medium weights with dry iron. For heavyweights, use steam iron and dry press cloth to avoid water spots.
Wool	Light to moderate	Moderate		Press with steam iron. For more moisture, press with dry iron and slightly dampened press cloth. Use press cloth on right side to prevent shine. Press crepe with dry iron.
Blends	Press according to requirements of the more delicate fiber.			
Texture				
Crepe	Light	Low to moderate	Dry iron	Use press cloth on right side.
Deep Pile	Finger-press	Moderate	Steam iron	See Pressure, above, for finger pressing.
Glossy	Light	Low	Dry iron	Same as Crepe.
Nap, Pile	Light or finger-press	Low to moderate	Dry or steam iron	Press fabric over needleboard, using light pressure; or finger-press.

Paper Strips. Slip them underneath the seam allowances as the seams are pressed open and you won't have any seam allowance imprints on the outside of your garment. Cut strips from brown bags, use #10 envelopes or rolls of adding machine tape.

Tailor's Ham. Useful for pressing curved areas such as darts, princess seams and sleeve caps.

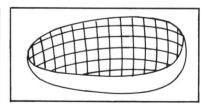

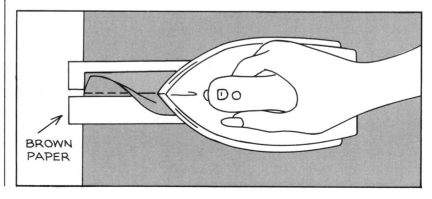

BROWN PAPER

Point Presser or *Tailor's Board.* A multi-edged surface that makes it possible to press seams open on small, detail areas such as collars, cuffs and facings.

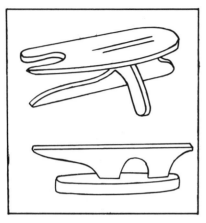

Sleeve Board. Great for pressing narrow garment sections that won't fit over the regular ironing board.

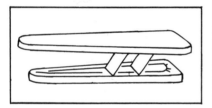

Needle Board. A good investment if you plan to sew with lots of velvets, velveteens or corduroys.

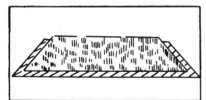

Place the fabric face down on the board and press. The short, dense needles keep the pile from being flattened.

TIP *A fluffy terry cloth towel or a scrap of self-fabric provides a cushioned surface that can substitute for a needle board.*

FUSIBLES, IRON-ONS AND FUSIBLE WEB

There are certain areas of sewing where you can put your sewing machine aside and "sew" with a wide range of heat-sensitive, iron-on sewing aids. Time-saving and easy to use, these fusibles, iron-ons and fusible webs are a fundamental part of today's sewing—provided you know how to use them. You'll find applications, hems, interfacing and tailoring, for example, throughout Chapter 6. But first, the basics.

A *fusible* is applied using a combination of heat, STEAM and pressure. Fusible products include interfacings and fusible web.

An *iron-on* is applied using heat and pressure only—NO STEAM. Mending tape, mending patches and some hem tapes are today's most common iron-ons. However, as technology improves, more iron-on products are available. For quick glamour, there are embroidered appliqués and sequinned trim that can be applied with the touch of your iron.

Both fusibles and iron-on

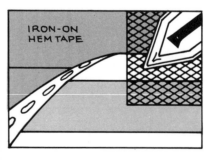

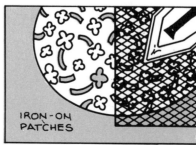

products come with instructions. Be sure to follow them carefully. To be on the safe side, ALWAYS use a press cloth to protect your fabric.

Fusible web is an adhesive web that "glues" two layers of fabric together. Don't confuse fusible web with fusible interfacing. Fusible web will not shape, support or reinforce your fabric the way fusible interfacing will. In fact, if you examine fusible web carefully, you'll see that it's not a fabric at all. It's a network of fibers. When the prescribed combination of heat, steam and pressure is applied, these fibers melt and "disappear", causing the two layers of fabric to adhere to each other.

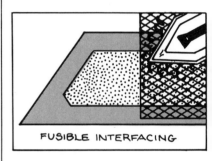

FUSIBLE INTERFACING

■ Use it as a substitute for hand tacking to keep facings, etc. from rolling to the outside of the garment.

■ Fuse-baste with fusible web. Position the web between the two layers of fabric, cover with a damp press cloth and press lightly for two to three seconds. This basting method is great for preventing ribbons, trims, etc. from rippling and shifting as they are

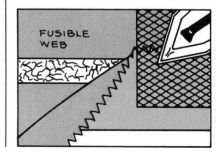

FUSIBLE WEB

HAND SEWING

Although most of your sewing will be done at the machine, there are times when only a hand stitch will do. The following stitches are the ones you'll use most frequently.

Basting: Useful for transferring markings to the right side of the garment and for temporarily holding the garment together. For more information, see Hand Basting, page 94.

Blindstitch: This stitch is useful for hemming knits and bulky fabrics. It will help prevent a ridge from forming at the hemline on the outside of the garment.

■ Fold back the garment slightly below the hem edge and hold it with your thumb.

■ Fasten the thread in the hem edge and, working from right to left, take a tiny stitch about ¼″ (6mm) to the left in the garment.

■ Take the next stitch ¼″ (6mm) away in the hem edge.

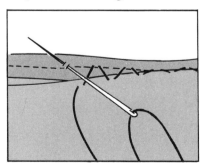

■ Continue, alternating from garment to hem and keeping the stitches evenly spaced.

Catchstitch: This stitch has some built-in stretch which makes it an especially good choice for hemming knits and for holding edges, such as facings, in place.

■ Fasten the thread to the wrong side of the hem or facing.

■ Work from left to right, with the needle pointing to the left. Take a tiny stitch in the garment ¼″ (6mm) to the right, close to the hem or facing edge.

■ Take the next stitch ¼″ (6mm) to the right in the hem or facing so that the stitches form an "X."

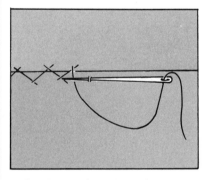

■ Continue, alternating from garment to hem or facing, keeping the stitches fairly loose.

Hemming Stitch: Use this stitch if the hem allowance is finished with seam binding.

■ Begin at a seam, fastening the thread in the seam allowance.

■ Take a tiny stitch through the garment, picking up a single thread.

■ Insert the needle between the seam binding and the garment and bring it out through the seam binding, about ¼″ (6mm) to the left of the first stitch.

stitched. It's also a useful technique when sewing lapped seams on fabrics that can't be pinned, such as synthetic suede.

■ Hems on casual clothes and children's garments can be fused in place instead of sewing. For more information, see HEMS, page 165.

■ Design your own appliqués and fuse them in place with fusible web. Draw the shape directly on the right side of the fabric. Place the fabric, right side up, over the fusible web, then cut out both layers at the same time. This is a great way to cover tears and worn spots in children's garments!

■ Take another stitch in the garment, ¼″ (6mm) to the left of the second stitch.

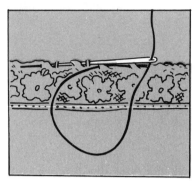

■ Continue, alternating from seam binding to garment, and taking several stitches on the needle before drawing the thread through the fabric.

Pickstitch: This stitch, also called a half-backstitch, is a good one to know if you are inserting a zipper in a fragile or hard-to-handle fabric, such as those used in bridal or evening wear. Use it in place of the final topstitching. To assure a straight line of pickstitches, add a row of hand basting stitches as a guideline.

■ Starting from the bottom of the zipper, fasten the thread on the underside of the zipper and bring the needle up through the zipper tape and the garment layers.

■ Insert the needle back down through all the layers, a thread or

two behind the point where it first emerged, as shown at bottom left.

■ Bring the needle up again about ¼″ (6mm) ahead of the first stitch. Continue along the length of the zipper.

Slipstitch: This is a good choice for securing turned-under edges because the stitches are invisible on both the inside and the outside of the garment.

■ Fasten the thread in the fold of the fabric.

■ Working from right to left, pick up a single fabric thread just below the folded edge.

■ Insert the needle into the fold directly above the first stitch and bring it out ¼″ (6mm) away.

■ Pick up another single thread in the garment directly below the point where the needle emerged.

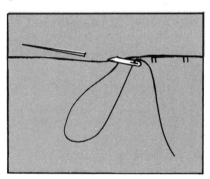

■ Continue, alternating between garment and fold.

Tacking: This stitch helps keep facings in place at the seams. Holding the edge of the facing and the seam allowance together, take three or four short stitches in one place through both layers.

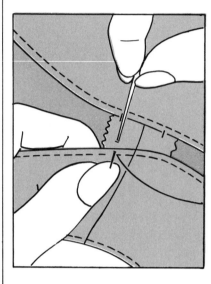

Do not sew through the garment fabric. Repeat on the other seam allowance.

> **TIP** *This same stitch is useful for permanently attaching snaps or books and eyes. For more information, see the section in Chapter 6 on Closures.*
>
> **TIP:** *Stitch-in-the-ditch (see page 93) is the quick machine alternative to hand tacking a facing in place.*

HAND SEWING TIPS

For tangle-free sewing:

■ Cut the thread in lengths no longer than 18″ (45.5cm).

■ Draw the thread through beeswax. This will also make the thread stronger.

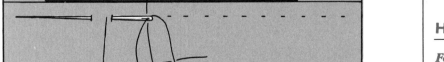

For easy needle threading:

■ Cut the thread diagonally by holding your scissors at a slant.

■ Hold the needle up against a white background so you can see the eye clearly.

■ Use a needle threader. Push the wire through the eye of the needle, then insert the thread through the wire (a). Pull the wire back out of the needle, drawing the thread through the eye (b).

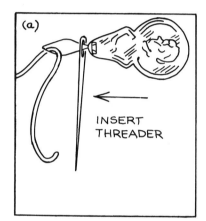

■ Use a calyx-eyed needle. These are designed with a tiny opening at the top for easy threading.

To knot the thread:

■ Insert the thread through the eye of the needle, then cut it off to the desired length.

■ Working with the end you just cut off the spool, hold the thread between your thumb and index

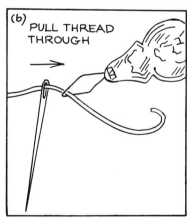

finger, then wrap the thread around your index finger (a).

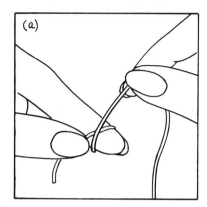

■ While holding the thread taut, slide your index finger back along your thumb until the thread ends twist into a loop (b).

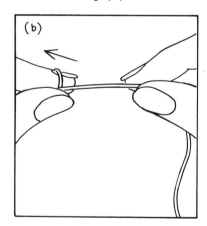

■ Continue sliding your index finger back until the loop slides off your finger (c).

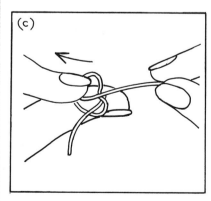

■ Bring your middle finger down to hold the open loop, then pull on the thread to form a knot (d).

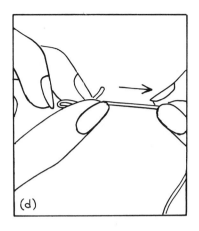

To secure the stitching:

■ Form a thread loop by taking a very small backstitch at the point where the needle last emerged.

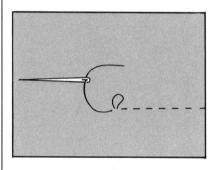

■ Take a second small backstitch on top of the first. As you complete the stitch, bring the needle and thread through the loop.

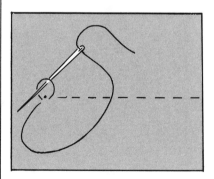

■ Pull on the thread, drawing up the loop and making both stitches taut.

■ If the stitching is subject to a great deal of strain, repeat to form a second "knot."

■ Cut the thread.

CHAPTER 6

SIMPLY THE BEST SEWING TECHNIQUES

You may wonder why this section is devoted to many of the same techniques included on your pattern's Instruction Sheet. After all, the Instruction Sheet contains carefully sketched and expertly written step-by-step directions for putting the project together. However, there are times when you may want more information than the pattern is able to supply.

■ Pattern companies usually select the techniques that are suitable for the broadest range of fabrics. But suppose your choice of fabric creates a special sewing situation. For example, it might be very sheer, or have a nap, or be quite bulky. In that case, you might want to vary the sewing techniques to suit your fabric.

■ If a technique is confusing to you, reading "how to do it" in slightly different words, or looking at a sketch with a slightly different perspective, may clarify it for you.

■ As your sewing skills progress, you'll want to look for patterns with design details that expand your sewing knowledge. Use this section as a guide to decide what techniques you want to focus on with each new pattern purchase.

■ Although many patterns are identified as containing special overlock instructions, almost every pattern can benefit from a blending of overlock and conventional sewing techniques. Here's where you find out what your options are.

■ For quick reference, this 🅢 will alert you every time a technique utilizes the overlock machine. In some instances, it makes no difference whether you use the conventional or overlock machine but the symbol appears because you may not have thought of using the overlock machine for the technique described.

HOW TO USE THE OVERLOCK CHARTS

Many of the overlock techniques in this section include a chart with the recommended settings for two-, three- or four-thread overlock stitch settings, as appropriate. Because every overlock machine, like every conventional machine, has its own "personality," there's also a space for you to record the appropriate settings for your machine. A sample of the overlock stitch chart appears below. On it, you will find the following four pieces of information:

1. TYPE OF OVERLOCK STITCH

This identifies the overlock settings for a two-, three- or four-

TYPE OF OVERLOCK STITCH:	3	4	MINE
Stitch Length:	4mm–5mm	4mm–5mm	
Stitch Width:	Widest	Widest	
Tensions—Needle:	Tight	Tight	
Rt. Needle:	N/A	Normal	
U. Looper:	Normal	Normal	
L. Looper:	Normal	Normal	

thread stitch. If you don't know what type(s) your overlock machine can make, check your owner's manual. The spaces under the third column, "Mine," have been left blank so that, once you use a technique, you can record the settings that are appropriate for your machine.

2. STITCH LENGTH

When serging seams on a woven fabric, a shorter stitch length provides greater durability. You might also want to shorten your stitch for some decorative effects or when making a narrow rolled hem. Where durability is not an issue, such as when overcasting the raw edges of a conventional seam, lengthening the stitch saves thread.

The stitch-length adjustment is usually located somewhere on the bottom left of the overlock machine. It's turned either by hand or by using a screwdriver and a lock screw. The stitch length is calibrated according to the metric system and ranges from slightly shorter than 1mm to about 5mm.

3. STITCH WIDTH

When serging on a woven fabric, you might want to widen your stitch so that your seam allowances will be deeper, resulting in seams that are more durable. When serging on knits, where raveling isn't a problem, a narrower width will give you a daintier seam. On sheer fabrics that do not ravel excessively, a narrow width creates a neater look, both inside and out.

Stitch width is generally determined by the throat plate and presser foot or by whether you use the right or the left needle. However, instead of changing throat plates, some machines use a dial-type width adjustment for both three-thread and four-thread serging.

On a three-thread overlock machine:

- use a throat plate with a narrow stitch finger for a narrow width (approximately 1mm–2mm).
- use a throat plate with a wider stitch finger for the widest setting (usually 4mm–5mm, although some new machines go as wide as 7.5mm).

On a four-thread overlock machine:

- use the right needle to create a three-thread stitch with the narrowest width (approximately 1mm–2mm). To fine-tune the width, use a throat plate with a narrow stitch finger.
- use the left needle for the widest stitch (approximately 4mm–5mm). To fine-tune the width, use a throat plate with a wide stitch finger.

Note: Some overlock machines have adjustable stitch fingers that move in and out so you don't have to change the throat plate. Check your owner's manual for specifics.

4. TENSIONS

NEEDLE AND RIGHT NEEDLE:

- The three-thread overlock stitch uses only one needle, so follow the guidelines for "Needle" tension.

> **TIP** *Once you have established what the "normal" setting is for your machine, write it on a piece of masking tape and stick it on your machine for future reference.*

- The four-thread overlock has a left and a right needle. Follow the "Needle" tension guidelines for the left needle and the "Right Needle" guidelines for the right needle.
- When "N/A" appears next to the words "Right Needle" it means this needle setting is not appropriate for that type of stitch.

UPPER LOOPER: This identifies how to set the tension on the upper looper. Thread suggestions may also be included.

LOWER LOOPER: This identifies how to set the tension on the lower looper.

Tension Settings
Thread tension dials are usually numbered or calibrated to indicate the tension settings.

NORMAL: When the tension is "normal," the looper threads are smooth on both sides of the fabric and lock together evenly along the fabric edge. When a seam with normal tension is pressed to one side, you won't see any puckering or threads pulled to the surface on the right side of the fabric.

VERY LOOSE: Set the appropriate tension dial approximately $\frac{1}{3}$ of the way between "0," or no tension, and your "normal" setting.

LOOSE: Set the appropriate tension dial approximately $\frac{1}{2}$ way between "0," or no tension, and your "normal" setting.

TIGHT: Set the appropriate tension dial approximately $\frac{1}{3}$ to $\frac{1}{2}$ way between your "normal" setting and the tightest possible tension setting for your overlock.

VERY TIGHT: Set the appropriate tension dial almost as tight as it can be adjusted.

BANDS AND RIBBING

Bands are a neat, decorative way to finish necklines, armholes and front closings.

LAPPED V-NECK BAND

This type of band is particularly popular on knit garments that pull on over the head. It can be made from matching or contrasting fabric.

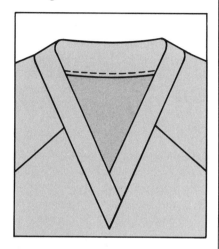

■ With wrong sides together, fold the band in half lengthwise; pin or baste the raw edges together.

■ On the garment front, reinforce the "V" at the tip of the neckline with a row of small machine stitches placed just inside the ⅝" (1.5cm) seamline.

■ With right sides together, and beginning on side A of the garment, pin the band to the neck edge. For a smooth, accurate fit, carefully match the band markings to the neckline markings. Leave the end of the band free on side B.

■ Begin stitching at the first marking on side A of the band, as shown. (This marking should be matched exactly to the tip of the "V.") Stop stitching when you reach the next-to-the-last marking on side B of the band. Tie the thread ends.

■ Clip the garment seam allowance only at the tip of the "V" just to, but not through, the reinforcement stitching. (Be careful—don't clip the band!) This will make it easier to fold the seam allowances to the inside and finish the band.

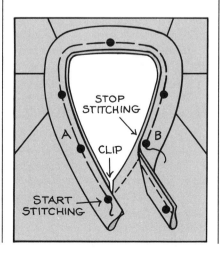

■ Turn the band up and tuck the ends inside the garment.

■ On the inside of the garment, lap the free end of the band (B) over the stitched end (A), carefully matching all the markings at the tip of the "V." Hand-baste the ends of the bands together at the "V."

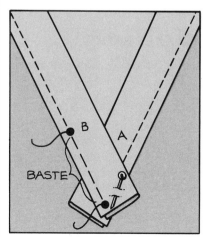

■ Turn the seam allowances up and finish stitching the seam along side B of the neckline. End the stitching at the point of the "V" and tie off the threads.

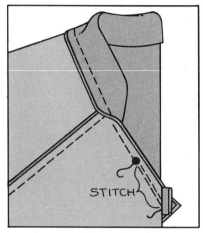

■ To secure the loose end of the band, turn the seam allowances up along side A of the neckline "V" and stitch between the markings, right on top of the previous stitching.

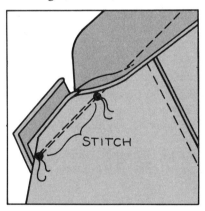

PLACKET BAND

This classic band is often used at the necklines of tailored dresses, shirts, tops and blouses. Traditionally tailored shirts or shirt jackets may feature a variation of this band as a finishing technique on the sleeve opening.

Before you begin, make sure you have transferred ALL the markings, including stitching lines and foldlines, to the garment front and the band sections.

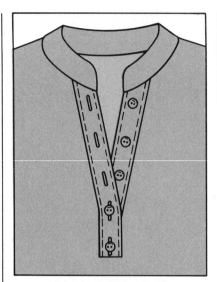

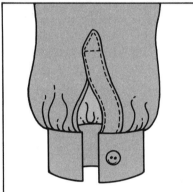

Note: The following directions will result in a classic women's right-over-left closing. However, your pattern may feature a menswear left-over-right closing.

■ On the garment front, machine-stitch along the marked stitching lines. This will reinforce the corners, as well as provide you with a stitching guide when you attach the band sections.

■ Slash the garment apart exactly in the middle of the two stitching lines. Make a small flap at the bot-

> **TIP** *If your fabric has a tendency to fray, treat the edges of the flap with a bit of liquid seam sealant, such as Fray Check.™*

tom by taking diagonal clips just to the corners of the stitching line. Be careful—don't clip through the stitches!

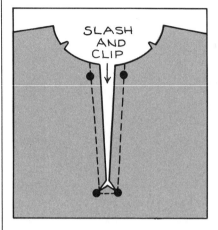

■ Interface the band sections according to your pattern instructions.

> **TIP** *If you're working with a slippery or stretchy fabric, you may want to interface the entire band. To keep it from becoming too stiff, use a light or sheer weight fusible interfacing.*

■ Press the seam allowance under on one long edge of one band section and trim to ¼" (6mm).

■ With right sides together, pin the other long edge of the band to the garment front, matching markings.

■ Machine-stitch along the stitching line, ending the stitching exactly at the bottom marking.

■ Trim and grade the seam allowances, then press them toward the band.

■ Fold the band to the outside of the garment and pin the pressed edge in place along the stitching line (a).

■ Edgestitch close to both long edges of the band, ending the stitching at the lower markings (b).

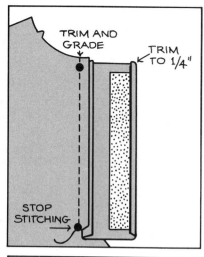

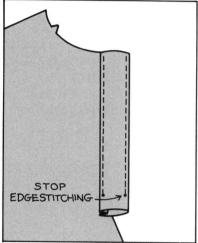

■ Repeat, attaching the remaining band to the other side of the slashed opening.

■ Slip the ends of the bands

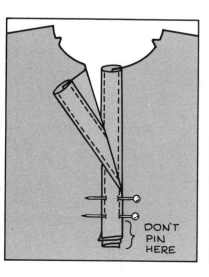

through to the inside of the garment. On the inside, lap the left band over the right. (For a menswear closing, lap the right over the left.) Pin, as shown, above the lower markings.

■ Working with the wrong side of the garment face down, fold the lower portion of the garment up to expose the flap at the bottom of the opening. Baste the flap and the bands together along the stitching line, then machine-stitch as basted, keeping the garment free. Finish according to the pattern instructions.

RIBBED BANDS

This type of band can be found at the neckline or the wrists . . . at the lower edge of a sweater-style top . . . or at the ankles of a pair of sweatpants.

Use either rib-knit trim or by-the-yard tubular sweater knit fabric.

Measuring and Cutting

Sometimes the hardest part about sewing ribbing is cutting it out. It slides and curls as you try to pin that long, narrow pattern piece to the fabric. This measuring and cutting technique does not require a pattern piece. It works equally well whether you're sewing ribbing on a conventional or an overlock machine.

WIDTH:

■ Decide on a finished width. If you have a pattern piece for ribbing, use it as a guide. Double the width, then add 1¼″ (3.2cm) for seam allowances.

■ Fold the ribbing lengthwise into two to four thicknesses, mark the width, and cut the band out. Be sure to position the band crosswise so that the ribs run up and down—this way the greatest amount of stretch goes around the body.

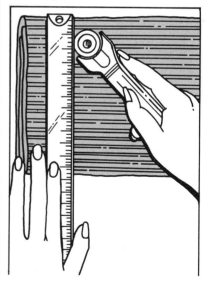

LENGTH:

Now that your band is the desired width, the next step is to determine how long it should be.

■ Using your pattern pieces as a guide, measure the garment opening, eliminating any seam allowances.

■ For a crew neck, the length of the band should equal ⅔ of the neckline opening.

■ For a V neck, U neck, waistband or cuff, the length of the band should equal ¾ of the garment opening.

■ Before you actually cut the ribbing into what you've determined to be the correct length, check your calculations by pin-fitting. To do this, mark off the length, pin the ribbing together, slide it over the appropriate part of the body, and analyze the fit. Ankle bands must slide over the widest part of the foot, wrist bands over the hand, neck bands over the head, and waist bands must slide down over the shoulders or up over the hips.

■ Now add 1¼″ (3.2cm) to the pin-fit length measurement to allow for a ⅝″ (1.5cm) seam.

■ Cut the band to the correct length.

The Flat Construction Method

Since it's easiest to apply rib-knit trim while the garment is still flat, leave one side seam, shoulder seam, leg seam or the sleeve seam unstitched.

■ With wrong sides together, fold the band in half lengthwise and baste the edges together.

■ Use pin markers to divide the garment edge and the band into four equal parts.

■ Pin the band to the right side of the garment, matching markings, as shown above.

■ With the band side up, machine-stitch, stretching the ribbing to fit between the markings. Stitch again, ¼″ (6mm) from first stitching, using a straight stitch or a zigzag stitch; trim close to the

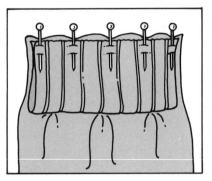

stitching. Or serge on your overlock machine.

■ Press the seam allowance toward the garment.

■ Stitch the garment seam allowance, beginning at the folded edge of the band. Stitch again, ¼

(6mm) from first stitching. Trim the seam allowance close to the stitching. Or, using your overlock machine, chain for 2″ (5cm), then lift the presser foot, slide the folded edge of the band under it and serge the seam.

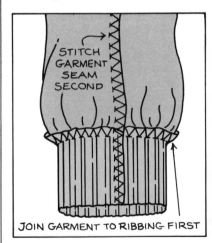

STITCH GARMENT SEAM SECOND

JOIN GARMENT TO RIBBING FIRST

■ Press.

S The Round Method

Many sewers shy away from sewing with sweater knits, stretch terry cloth or stretch velour because they think that the ribbing will be difficult to work with. You'll be delighted at how easy it is to attach it with your overlock.

■ Cut the ribbing to size.

■ With right sides together, serge the side seam to form a circle.

■ Fold the band in half, wrong sides together, so the raw edges meet, and pin. If the ribbing curls, baste the edges together with a long, wide zigzag stitch on your conventional machine.

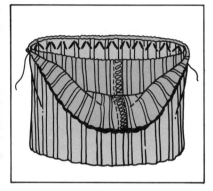

■ Mark the band into quarters with pins or a marking pen. Do the same for the garment opening.

■ With right sides together, pin the band to the garment opening, matching markings. Position the seam in the band so it matches a garment seam. With the band side up, serge, stretching the ribbing to fit the opening (see drawing below). Press the seam allowance toward the garment.

■ For that ready-to-wear look, use your conventional machine and a twin needle to topstitch on both sides of the seamline.

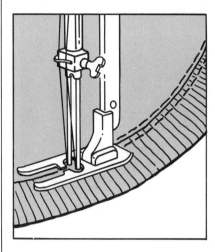

BELTS AND BELT LOOPS

Belts add the finishing touch to many an ensemble. In fact, your local fabric store is probably a wonderful source for a wide array of gorgeous buckles.

COVERED BELTS

If you're going to make your own covered belt, check your fabric store for the stiffening material that is specifically designed to use inside belts. It's available in several widths and has the right blend of rigidity and flexibility necessary for a belt that is comfortable but won't curl. Don't be tempted to substitute several layers of interfacing. You'll end up with a belt that collapses into folds after several wearings.

The stiffening material is sold by the yard or in kits with an accompanying buckle to cover. If it's your first belt, buy the kit and follow its directions to cover the belting.

SOFT BELTS

Done on either the conventional or overlock machine, this simple stitched-and-turned method can be used to make a fabric sash or a soft, crushed belt that's attached to a slip-through buckle.

■ Cut a lengthwise strip of fabric that's equal to the desired length plus 1¼" (3.2cm) and twice the desired width plus 1¼" (3.2cm).

The Conventional Method:

■ With right sides together, fold the belt in half lengthwise.

■ Stitch along the ⅝" (1.5cm) seamline, leaving an opening at

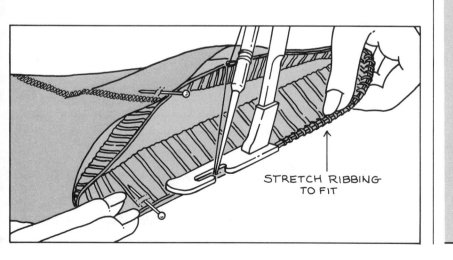

STRETCH RIBBING TO FIT

> **TIP** *Many sewers, even those with a great deal of experience, find it difficult to achieve the same crisp look that they admire on ready-to-wear covered belts. The solution is to get a professional to do it for you. Ask at your favorite fabric store or look in your local Yellow Pages. If you can't find a home town source, there are mail-order companies that will do it for you. Look in the advertising section of your favorite sewing publications.*

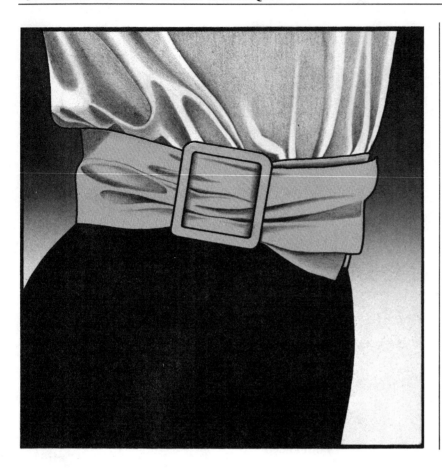

S The Overlock Method:

■ With wrong sides together, fold the belt in half lengthwise.

■ Serge around the outside edges. For fine fabrics, use all-purpose thread and a rolled hem. For heavy fabrics, try pearl cotton or 1/16″ (2mm) silk or rayon ribbon in the upper looper.

STRETCH BELTS

Stretch belting and elasticized trims are available by the yard in a wide range of widths and styles, from solid colors to simple patternings to elaborately embellished surfaces. For your most gala evenings, there's even sequinned or beaded stretch trim.

Purchase enough stretch belting or trim to fit comfortably around your waist, plus 2″ (5cm). Buy a clasp buckle or interlocking buckle that fits the width of your trim.

■ To keep the ends of the belting from raveling, seal them with Fray

the center back for turning. To secure the stitching, backstitch at the corners and at either end of the opening.

■ Trim the seams and corners. If possible, press the seam allowances open. Otherwise, press the top seam allowance toward the body of the sash. This will ensure that your finished sash will have crisp edges.

■ Turn the belt right side out, press, and slipstitch the opening closed.

TIP *Use a ruler to turn the belt right side out. Push one end toward, and out through, the opening. Repeat for the other end.*

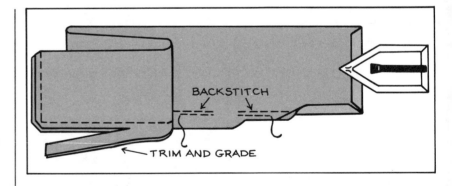

BACKSTITCH

TRIM AND GRADE

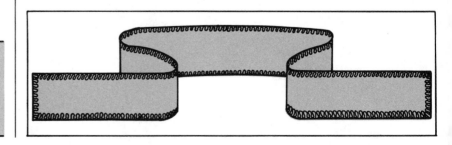

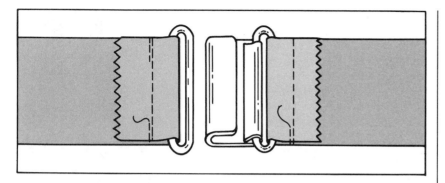

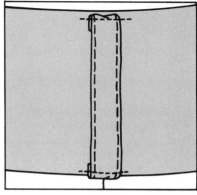

Check™, finish them on the overlock machine OR trim them with pinking shears.

■ Slip the ends of the belting through each half of the buckle and fold back 1″ (2.5cm).

■ Pin and stitch the edges in place, backstitching to secure. If your stretch belting is sequinned or beaded, stitch by hand.

BELT LOOPS

No matter what type of belt you choose to make or buy, belt loops will help it stay put when you wear your garment. On a garment without a waistline seam, they'll serve as anchors to keep the hemline from shifting and dipping as you stand up and sit down.

Placement

A pattern that calls for fabric loops will include a pattern piece and markings for placement. If you're adding loops, center them over the waistline. Plan on at least three loops—one at center back and one at each side seam. If your belt has a heavy buckle, you might want to add them to the front. Depending on the style of buckle, position one slightly off-center, so that it's hidden from view when the buckle is fastened or add two, each one midway between the side seam and the center front.

Fabric Loops

If you want fabric loops, and the instructions aren't included in your pattern, do the following:

■ Cut a strip of fabric along the selvage, three times the width of the finished loop. To determine how long this strip should be, add ¾″ (2cm) to the width of the belt, then multiply by the number of loops.

■ Fold the strip lengthwise in thirds with the selvage on top. Edgestitch along both folded edges.

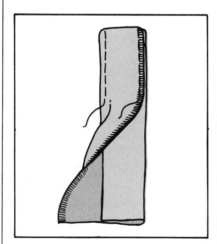

■ Cut apart into the desired number of loops.

■ To attach the loops to the garment, press the short ends under ¼″ (6mm). Position one loop at each marking. Topstitch it to the garment by machine or slipstitch in place by hand.

Machine Thread Loops

On many ready-to-wear garments, fine thread chains are used as belt loops or button loops at the cuffs or neckline. They're not bulky and they're almost invisible.

THE CONVENTIONAL METHOD:

■ Take two or three lengths of fine cording, such as buttonhole twist, crochet cotton or tatting thread, and twist them tightly together.

■ Stitch over them twice using a close, narrow zigzag stitch.

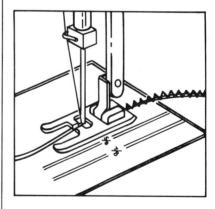

■ Cut the thread chain into loops. To make them easy to handle, each loop should be three times its finished length.

⑤ THE OVERLOCK METHOD:

■ Thread the machine with all-purpose sewing thread that

TIP *If your overlock can do a narrow rolled hem, you can also use that stitch setting to create a thread chain suitable for loops. Set the machine for a narrow rolled edge and serge, without feeding fabric through the machine.*

matches the garment fabric. Set the tensions for general serging and shorten the stitch length so that the stitches lock into a tight chain.

■ Serge a chain that is three times the finished length of each loop. As you serge, pull tightly on the thread tails so that the chain comes off the stitch fingers smoothly.

■ Cut the chain apart into the desired number of lengths.

Once you have made the chains, either by the conventional or overlock methods, you will need to attach them to the garment. Do one of the following:

■ Make the belt loops first, then catch them in the seamline as the garment is sewn together.

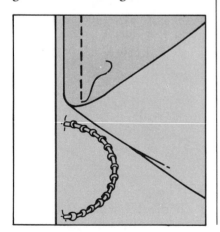

TIP *Use thread loops to help keep children from losing their winter gear! Sew buttons on the inside of a child's coat, at the sleeves and back of the neck. Sew loops onto mittens, hats, and scarves, then button them in place.*

OR:

■ Sew the garment together first. Then, thread the loop through the large eye of a needle. Insert the needle between the stitches in a seamline or between the threads of the fabric (if there is no seamline) and gently pull the tail of the thread chain to the wrong side of the garment. Knot to secure. Repeat for the other end of the loop.

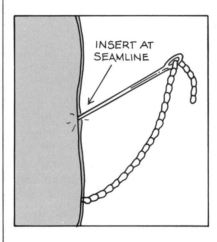

INSERT AT SEAMLINE

BINDINGS

Bindings are a clever way to decorate and finish a raw edge at the same time.

Some patterns already include bindings as a design detail. Don't, however, feel you're limited to putting binding on only these patterns.

■ Used at necklines, armholes, even hemline edges, bindings are an alternative to facings.

■ Made in a contrasting color, bindings are a great way to liven

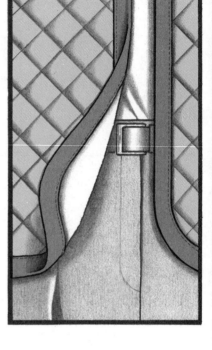

up a simple garment, particularly for children's clothes.

■ On sheers, narrow, self-fabric (i.e., cut from your fashion fabric) bindings eliminate unsightly facing show-through. The drawing on page 161 illustrates the use of this technique.

■ Bindings are an easy way to finish the edges of a reversible garment, such as a jacket or vest.

■ Bindings are a popular way to add emphasis to home decorating items such as placemats, napkins, tablecloths, even curtain edges.

TIP *If you're adding binding to a pattern that doesn't call for it, trim off the seam allowances on the garment edge(s) that will be encased in the binding.*

If your pattern already utilizes binding, check the back of the pattern envelope to determine the recommended width. Most patterns are designed for a ¼″ (6mm) or ½″ (1.3cm) finished width binding. You can make your own bias binding or use purchased double-fold bias tape or foldover braid.

MAKING YOUR OWN BINDING

To provide give and flexibility, binding is always cut on the bias.

The continuous bias method is an easy way to mark and join make-your-own bias strips.

■ Cut a rectangle of fashion fabric. The longer side of the rectangle can follow either the lengthwise or the crosswise grain of your fabric. Trim each side of the rectangle so that it EXACTLY follows a thread of the fabric.

■ Fold one corner of the rectangle so that the crosswise and the lengthwise edges meet; press, then open out the rectangle. (This crease is the true bias.)

■ Cut a cardboard template the width required for your bias

> **TIP** *Using 45" (115cm) wide fabric, a 5"×45" (12.5cm ×115cm) rectangle will yield approximately 2½ yds. (2.3m) of ½" (1.3cm) finished width binding or 5 yds. (4.6m) of ¼" (6mm) finished width binding.*

strips. Each strip should be four times the width of the finished binding. For example, for ¼" (6mm) finished binding width, mark 1" (2.5cm) wide strips; for ½" (1.3cm) binding, mark 2" (5cm) wide strips. Using the crease as your starting point, and the cardboard template as your guide, pencil-mark parallel lines across the width of the fabric until you reach a corner.

■ Cut off the triangles of unmarked fabric at either end of the rectangle.

■ With right sides together, fold the fabric into a tube. Match the

pencil lines so that one width of binding extends beyond the edge on each side. Sew a ¼" (6mm) seam and press open.

■ Starting at one end, cut along the pencil line, working your way around the tube until you've separated it into one long, continuous strip.

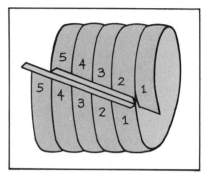

PIECING INDIVIDUAL STRIPS

You may not have enough fabric left over after cutting out your project to make a rectangle large enough to construct one long continuous strip . . . or you may need to piece strips of purchased binding. In either case, here's the professional-looking way to join them:

■ Using bias-cut strips the required width and with right sides together, pin the ends of the strips so they form a right (90°) angle. Stitch a ¼" (6mm) seam.

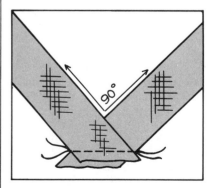

■ Press the seam open and trim away the points that extend beyond the edge of the binding.

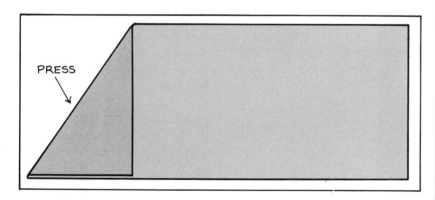

PRESS

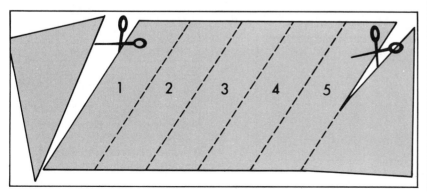

1 2 3 4 5

TWO-STEP APPLICATION METHOD FOR MAKING-YOUR-OWN BINDING OR DOUBLEFOLD BIAS TAPE

Because it's the fastest method, many patterns tell you to apply the binding entirely by machine. However, many sewers find it difficult to achieve professional results using this method. The following combination of machine and hand sewing may take you a few minutes longer, but that extra time will pay off in great results!

■ When applying 1" (2.5cm) wide bias strips, use ¼" (6mm) wide seams.

■ When applying 2" (5cm) wide bias strips, use ½ (1.3cm) wide seams.

■ When applying double-fold bias tape, open it out and follow the foldlines for your seam widths.

On binding that you've made yourself, fold and press under on one long edge before you begin.

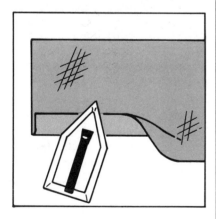

The fold should be equal to ¼ of the width of the binding. This will give you the folded edge you need for Step 2.

Step 1: With right sides together, machine-stitch the binding to the garment edge. Press the seam toward the binding.

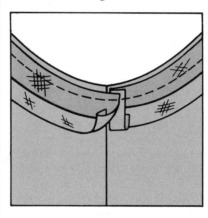

Step 2: Turn the folded edge of the binding to the inside so that it encases the raw edge and just covers the stitching line. Slipstitch in place.

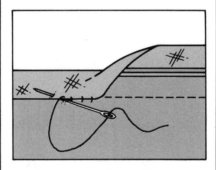

At an Outside Corner:

■ Before you begin, use a fabric marking pen or dressmaker's pen-

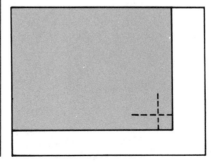

cil to mark where the seam allowances intersect at the corner.

■ Follow **Step 1**, ending your stitching where the seamlines intersect at the corner. Backstitch one or two stitches and cut the thread.

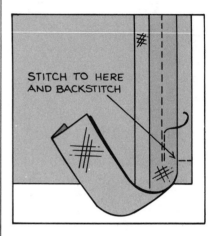

■ Fold the binding back on itself to create a diagonal crease at the corner. Now fold the binding back again so that this new fold is even with the edge of the binding on side A and the seamlines of binding and garment match on side B.

■ Insert the needle exactly at the corner marking and continue stitching.

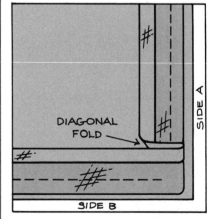

■ Finish according to **Step 2**, making a diagonal fold at the corner and slipstitching the binding

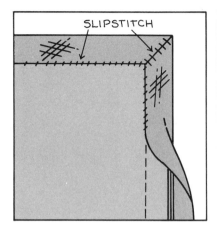

in place. If desired, slipstitch the corner folds also.

At an Inside Corner:

■ Reinforce the corner with small stitches along the seamline. Clip the corner just to the stitches.

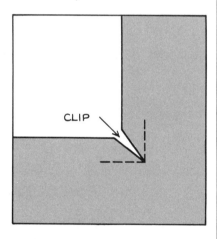

■ Following **Step 1**, stitch binding to one fabric edge. Stop stitching when you reach the corner.

■ Keeping the needle in the fabric, raise the presser foot and spread the fabric open at the clip so that it lines up with the edge of the binding. Lower the presser foot and continue stitching.

■ Press the seam allowances toward the binding. As you do this, a diagonal fold will form at the corner.

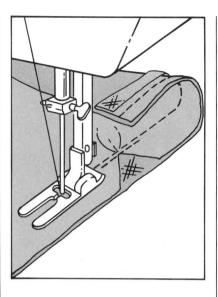

■ Finish according to **Step 2**, forming another diagonal fold at the corner. If desired, slipstitch the corner folds.

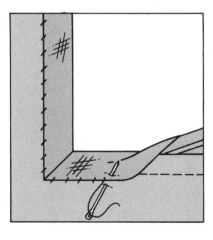

EDGESTITCHED APPLICATION

Use this method with purchased double-fold bias tape or foldover braid.

■ Slip the binding over the raw garment edge. Note that these tapes and braids are folded so that one side is slightly wider than the other. Always sandwich your fabric between the folds with the wider side of the tape on the bottom. Then, working on the right side of the fabric, edgestitch the tape in place.

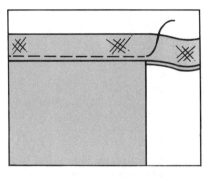

TIP *To keep the binding from shifting as you sew, apply glue stick to the inside of the binding, then press it into position. Let the glue dry, then edgestitch.*

TIP *To begin and end the binding, press under along one short end. As you apply the binding, lap the pressed end over the unpressed end. Do this at an inconspicuous place on the garment, such as the center back or underarm.*

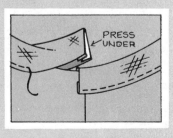

At an Outside Corner:

■ Edgestitch the binding all the way to the raw edge of the fabric. Remove the fabric from the machine and cut the threads.

■ Turn the binding around the corner and down the next side. Pin.

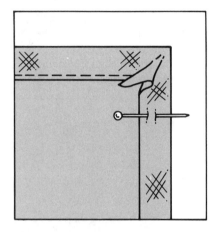

■ Make a diagonal fold on both sides of the corner; press.

■ Beginning just below the diagonal fold, backstitch to fold, then edgestitch along the binding. If desired, slipstitch the corner folds.

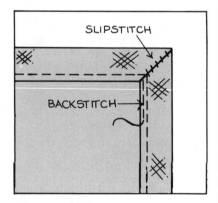

At an Inside Corner:

■ Reinforce the corner with small machine stitches. Clip the corner just to the stitches.

■ Edgestitch the binding to the garment, stopping when you reach the corner.

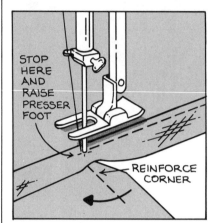

■ Keeping the needle in the fabric, raise the presser foot and spread the fabric to straighten the garment edge. Slip the binding over the fabric, lower the presser foot, and continue edgestitching.

■ Press the binding at the corner so that a diagonal fold forms on both sides of the garment. If desired, slipstitch the corner folds to keep them in place.

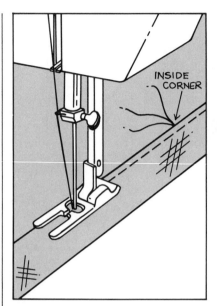

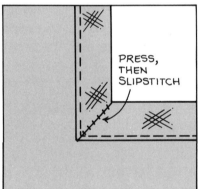

TIP *Be careful not to stretch the binding as you sew, particularly when you are working on a curved edge. You may find it helpful to use steam to preshape the binding before you apply it. Pin the binding to your ironing board in a curve that matches the shape of the garment edge. Using a generous amount of steam, shrink out the excess fullness, let the binding dry, then attach it to the garment.*

CASINGS AND ELASTIC

When elastic or a drawstring is used to control fullness in a garment, it is often inserted into a tunnel of fabric, called a casing. However, with some techniques, the casing is created at the same time the elastic is applied. This is called the direct application method. Elastic can also be applied directly to a garment edge with no casing at all. These exposed applications are commonly used on lingerie.

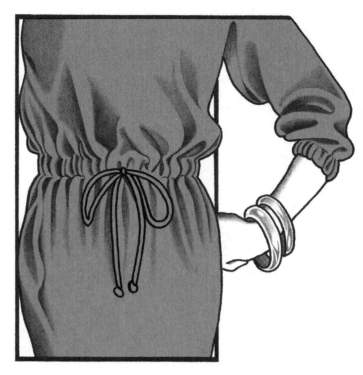

TUNNEL CASINGS

There are three common types of tunnel casings:

■ A *Folded Casing* can be found at waistline, sleeve and pants leg edges. The pattern is designed with an extended garment edge that is pressed under ¼" (6mm), pressed under again along the foldline, and then edgestitched along both folds.

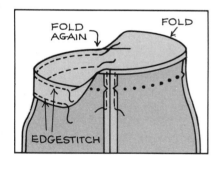

S TIP *To reduce bulk on a folded casing, finish the raw edge on your overlock machine instead of turning it under ¼" (6mm). Knits and firmly woven fabrics that do not ravel don't have to be pressed under ¼" (6mm) or finished on an overlock.*

■ An *Applied Casing* is a bias strip that is seamed to the edge of the garment. Then it is folded to the inside and stitched close to both edges of the casing. When you're done, it looks like a folded casing from the outside of the garment. This technique is used in place of a folded casing if the garment edge is shaped or curved.

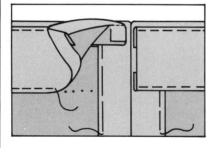

■ A *Bias Casing* is created by applying single-fold bias tape or a strip of bias fabric a specified distance from a garment edge. Bias casings are often used on the inside of a one-piece dress, a tunic or a jacket to create waistline definition. If the bias casing is placed a short distance in from the gar-

ment edge, a heading, or ruffle, forms once the elastic is inserted.

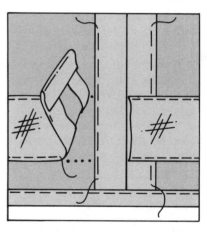

TIP *Before applying the bias tape, use steam to preshape it into a curve that matches the garment edge.*

TIP *If your fabric is too bulky, too scratchy or too loosely woven for a folded casing, make an applied facing instead. Use the casing foldline as your seamline.*

TIP *Use a sheer tricot seam binding, such as Seams Great® or Seam Saver™, as a lightweight substitute for bias tape. No need to turn the raw edges under as they will not fray.*

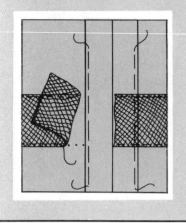

General Information

■ For accurate placement, be sure to mark the necessary fold-lines or stitching lines.

■ To keep the elastic from getting stuck in the seam allowances as it's inserted, use fusible web or machine basting to anchor them to the garment within the casing area. Do this before you create the casing.

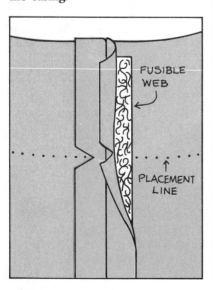

FUSIBLE WEB

↑ PLACEMENT LINE

TIP *If you're making a one-piece garment, you may want to change the design slightly to add waistline definition. To do this, make a bias casing, centering it over the waistline marking on your pattern, then insert elastic through the casing.*

■ Purchase elastic that is ⅛"–¼" (3mm–6mm) narrower than the casing or you'll have trouble inserting it.

■ For drawstring openings that occur at a seamline, reinforce the opening with small pieces of lightweight fusible interfacing or by including small squares of seam binding in the backstitching.

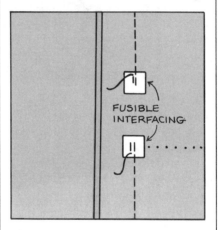

FUSIBLE INTERFACING

Inserting Elastic

■ Cut the elastic 1" (2.5cm) larger than the body measurement, or according to the pattern guide.

■ Fasten a safety pin or bodkin to one end of the elastic and thread it through the casing opening. To avoid accidentally pulling the elastic all the way through the casing, use a safety pin to fasten the other end of the elastic to the garment just below the casing. Do this before inserting the elastic into the casing opening.

■ Overlap the elastic ends ½" (1.3 cm), and stitch together in a square or with parallel rows of stitches. (*Note:* If you have any doubt about the fit, try the gar-

ment on and pin-fit the elastic before permanently securing it.) Then stitch the casing opening closed.

■ To keep the elastic from rolling and twisting during wear, stitch in the ditch, or groove, formed by each seam.

DIRECT APPLICATION METHODS

With these methods, you stitch right through the elastic so there's no chance of the elastic twisting or curling.

TIP *Many of these elastic application methods suggest dividing and marking the elastic and the garment edge into quarters. However, if you're a beginning sewer, or if you're working on a long edge, you'll have an easier time if you divide and mark into eighths.*

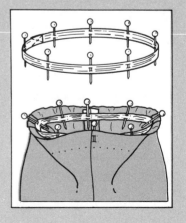

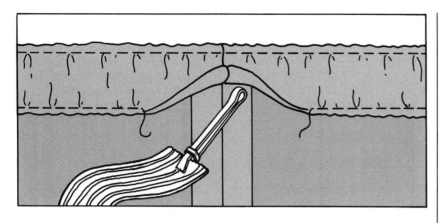

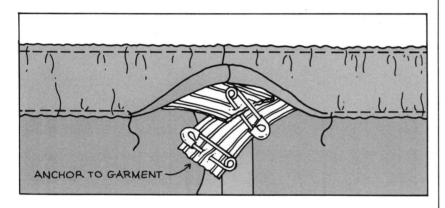

ANCHOR TO GARMENT ➝

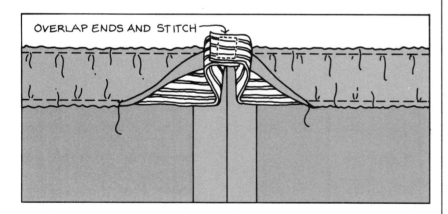

OVERLAP ENDS AND STITCH

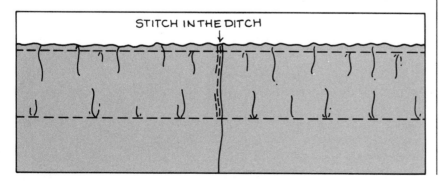

STITCH IN THE DITCH

Hidden Elastic Application

Use this quick technique to create a casing at the edge of a garment and apply the elastic at the same time. It's a no-twist method suitable for knits or wovens that won't ravel, for aerobic wear, swimwear and lingerie.

■ Cut the elastic the required length, generally 3″ (7.5cm) smaller than the body measurement. Overlap the ends ½″ (1.3cm) and stitch.

■ Trim the seam allowance on the garment edge to equal the width of the elastic.

■ Divide the elastic and the garment edge into quarters or eighths and mark.

■ Pin the elastic to the wrong side of the garment, matching the markings and keeping the edge of the elastic even with the edge of the garment. Zigzag, overcast or straight-stitch the elastic to the edge of the garment. Be sure to stretch the elastic to fit as you sew.

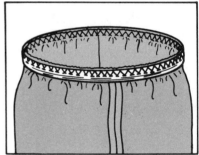

■ Fold the elastic to the inside of the garment. Stitch close to the raw edge of the fabric, through all

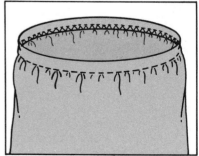

TIP *When applying elastic with the overlock, you'll find it easier to serge it on straight if there's a wide margin of fabric for the overlock's knife to trim away. Before you cut out your pattern, check the distance between the foldline and the cut edge of the garment. It should be at least ½" (1.3cm) wider than the width of the elastic. For ¼" (6mm) wide elastic, you should have at least a ¾" (2cm) wide seam allowance; for ⅜" (1cm) wide elastic, at least a ⅞" (2.2cm) wide seam allowance. If necessary, adjust the seam allowances, then cut out the garment.*

the layers, with a straight stitch or a zigzag stitch. Again, stretch the elastic to fit as you sew. For increased stretch and recovery, use a straight stitch with elastic thread in the bobbin (see TIP, page 141) or a zigzag stitch with nylon thread in the top and the bobbin.

S *Hidden Elastic Application*

Here's where your overlock really shines!

■ Adjust your overlock machine to the appropriate settings; see chart below.

■ Leave one seam open. Divide and mark the elastic into quarters or eighths.

■ Divide and mark the garment edge into quarters or eighths.

■ Pin the elastic to the wrong side of the garment, placing the inside edge along the foldline and matching the markings.

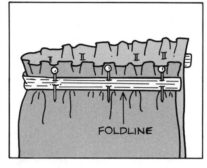

FOLDLINE

■ With the elastic side up, position the outer edge of the elastic

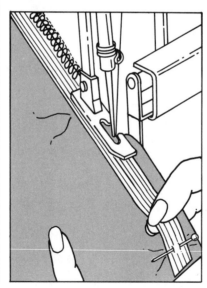

next to the knife. Serge a couple of stitches to anchor the elastic. Be careful—don't cut the elastic! Continue serging, holding the elastic up slightly off the fabric against the toe of the presser foot. As you do, stretch the elastic to fit between the pins. *Remember to remove the pins before the presser foot reaches them.*

■ Adjust your overlock to a balanced stitch setting and serge the remaining seam all the way up through the elastic.

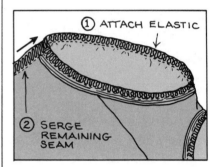

① ATTACH ELASTIC

② SERGE REMAINING SEAM

■ Fold the elastic to the inside of the garment. *Using your conventional machine*, stitch close to the edge of the fabric, through all the layers. To keep this row of stitches from popping when you wear the garment, use elastic thread in the bobbin (see TIP) or use a zigzag stitch and nylon thread in the top and bobbin.

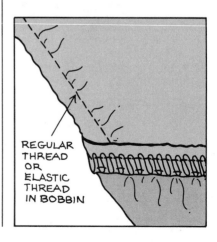

REGULAR THREAD OR ELASTIC THREAD IN BOBBIN

TYPE OF OVERLOCK STITCH:	3	4	MINE
Stitch Length:	4mm–5mm	4mm–5mm	
Stitch Width:	Widest	Widest	
Tensions—Needle:	Tight	Tight	
Right Needle:	N/A	Tight	
U. Looper*	Normal	Normal	
L. Looper:	Normal	Normal	
* (can use woolly nylon thread)			

TIP *Here's a technique borrowed directly from ready-to-wear swimwear and aerobic wear. For your final row of stitches, put elastic thread in the bobbin and stitch with the right side of the garment facing you. For best results, use nylon thread in the needle.*

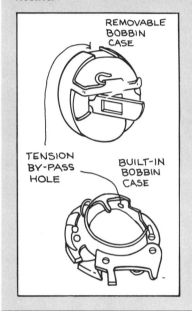

■ *How you wind the bobbin thread depends on how your conventional machine is designed. If it has a self-winding bobbin, wind the elastic thread on by hand, stretching it slightly. If you must remove the bobbin from the bobbin case to wind it, guide the elastic thread onto the bobbin while it's turning on the bobbin winder, being careful NOT to stretch it.*

■ *If your bobbin case has a tension bypass hole, insert the elastic thread through it, replace the bobbin case and bring the thread up through the hole in the throat plate. This gives you a lighter bobbin tension.*

■ *Set your machine for a straight stitch, 3mm long or 8 stitches per inch.*

■ *Working on the right side of the garment, topstitch close to the inner edge of the elastic, through all the layers.*

If you want the seam to be flat against the body, with the ladder stitches on the outside, pin the elastic to the RIGHT side of the fabric. If you want the seam on the outside, with the ladder stitches against the body, pin the elastic to the WRONG side of the fabric.

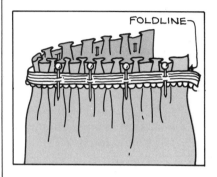

■ With the elastic side up, position the straight edge of the elastic next to the knife. Serge a couple of stitches to anchor the elastic. Be careful—don't cut the elastic. Continue serging, holding the elastic up slightly off the fabric, against the toe of the foot. As you do this, stretch the elastic to fit between the pins. Remember to remove the pins as you come to them.

S *Flatlock or Exposed Application*

This professional one-step application makes for fast sewing and comfortable wearing. Because the elastic is exposed, this technique is most frequently used for lingerie. For the most attractive results, use lingerie elastic, a soft, stretchy elastic with one picot or decorative edge.

■ Adjust your overlock machine to the appropriate setting, see chart below.

■ Leave one garment seam open. Divide and mark the elastic into quarters or eighths.

■ Divide and mark the garment edge into quarters or eighths.

■ Position the elastic so that the straight edge is along the foldline.

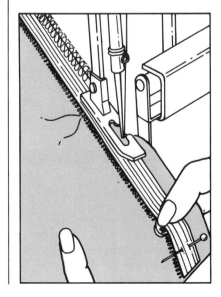

TYPE OF OVERLOCK STITCH:	2	3	MINE
Stitch Length:	3mm–4mm	3mm–4mm	
Stitch Width:	Widest	Widest	
Tensions—Needle:	Very Loose	Very Loose	
Rt. Needle:	N/A	N/A	
U. Looper:	N/A	Loose	
L. Looper:	Normal	Very Tight	

S TIP *Get some practice on your overlock machine— and make yourself a present 1-2-3. Using an old half-slip as a guide, cut a piece of tricot the desired width and length. Allow 1¼" (3.2cm) for side seams and ½" (1.3cm) for the waistline seam.*

1. Flatlock a piece of flat lace to one end of the slip. (See TRIMS, p. 197.)

2. Attach elastic to the other end using the flatlock method.

3. Adjust your overlock for a balanced stitch setting and serge the side seam.

For a bit of custom comfort, cover the seam in the elastic with a piece of ribbon. Use a dot of glue stick to hold it in place, then stitch it on your conventional machine. That's it!

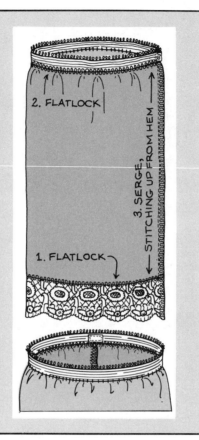

2. FLATLOCK

3. SERGE, STITCHING UP FROM HEM

1. FLATLOCK

■ Pull on the elastic until the picot edge is up and the seam is flat.

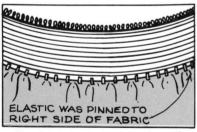

ELASTIC WAS PINNED TO RIGHT SIDE OF FABRIC

ELASTIC WAS PINNED TO WRONG SIDE OF FABRIC

■ Adjust your overlock for a balanced stitch setting and serge the remaining seam, all the way up through the elastic.

CLOSURES

When you make a garment, you, not the pattern company, are the ultimate designer. This means that you can make the closures as subtle or as obvious as you wish. Buttons can match or contrast . . . or be replaced by snaps, toggles, frogs, ties or self-gripping hook and loop fasteners, such as Velcro®.

Other than the quickie overlock technique for making ties that appears at the end of this section, closures are sewn on by hand or on the conventional sewing machine. Here's where your overlock machine gets a rest!

Note: Zippers are another popular closure. For more information about them, see page 208.

BUTTONS AND BUTTONHOLES

Once upon a time, anyone who learned to sew had to struggle with learning how to make bound buttonholes. Not so in today's machine age! Look around you at some of the most expensive ready-to-wear garments. Even those buttonholes are made by machine.

In Chapter 5, we talked about the importance of making friends with your sewing machine. Here's one place it really pays off. Take a rainy weekend afternoon to practice making buttonholes in a variety of fabrics. Read your sewing machine manual and learn what, if any, tension or pressure adjustments are required.

If you're not satisfied with the buttonholes your machine makes, do one of the following.

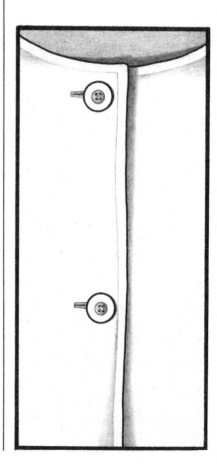

- Take it to the dealer and get it cleaned and overhauled. Bring your sample buttonholes with you so the dealer can see where you are having problems.
- Find someone else to make them for you. Ask at your local fabric store and check out the Yellow Pages.
- Consider substituting with a closure that doesn't require buttonholes. Sometimes the substitute is a better choice. For example, small children who are learning to dress themselves will find Velcro® closures easier to maneuver than buttons and buttonholes.

Some Button and Buttonhole Basics:

- Stick to the size button recommended on the pattern envelope. If you can't find a button you like in the right size, don't go more than 1/8" (3mm) larger or smaller. Otherwise, the buttons will either look out of proportion on the garment or the buttonholes may have to be respaced.
- ALWAYS make a test buttonhole first on a scrap of fabric. Use the same number of layers (fashion fabric, interfacing, facing, etc.) as the garment will have.
- To make sure your buttonholes are accurately placed, begin

stitching horizontal buttonholes at the marking closest to the garment edge; begin stitching vertical buttonholes at the marking closest to the upper edge of the garment.

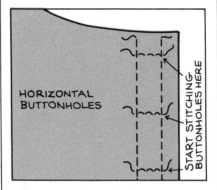

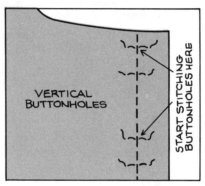

Transferring the Markings

Buttonhole placement should be marked on the right side of your fabric. You can do this during the cutting and marking stage, when you transfer all the other markings, or you can wait until just before you're ready to stitch.

Even if you marked the placement lines when you cut out the garment, it's a good idea to check them when you're ready to make the buttonholes. Here's how:

- Place the pattern tissue on top of the garment, aligning the pattern seamline with the garment opening edge.
- Stick pins straight through the tissue and the fabric at both ends of each marking; then, carefully

remove the pattern without disturbing the pins.

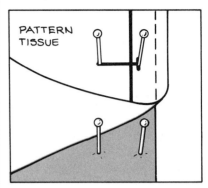

- If appropriate for your fabric, mark between the pins with a water-soluble or evaporating marking pen. If these are not suitable, place a strip of 1/2" (1.3cm) wide transparent tape or masking tape alongside, but a scant 1/8" (3mm) away from, the pins. Mark the position of each pin on the tape. When you make the buttonhole, stitch next to the tape, being careful not to stitch through it. Caution: Tape mars some fabrics. Test first on a scrap of the fabric, experimenting with cellophane tape and masking tape.

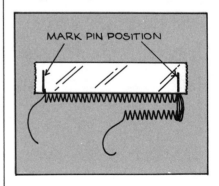

Determining Buttonhole Size

The buttonhole markings on the pattern tissue indicate the placement, not the size, of the buttonhole. Buttons are sized according to their diameter. However, it's a button's circumference (the diameter plus the height) that determines how large the buttonhole needs to be. For example, a flat ⅝″ (1.5cm) button will probably require a smaller buttonhole than a domed button of the same size.

■ To determine the circumference, wrap a piece of narrow ribbon, seam binding or twill tape around the widest part of the button and pin the ends together.

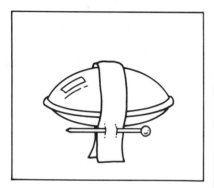

■ The length of your test buttonhole should be equal to half the circumference + ⅛″ (3mm). If your button is very thick, you may need to increase the size a little bit more. Test the size out before making any buttonholes on your garment.

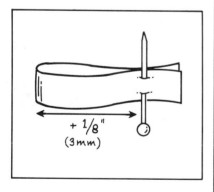

+ ⅛″
(3mm)

Cutting the Buttonhole Open

Once all the buttonholes are stitched, cut them open using a razor blade, X-Acto knife and a cutting board, or a pair of small, sharp scissors. Start at the center and cut toward each end. To prevent cutting too far, put straight

pins at each end of the buttonhole opening.

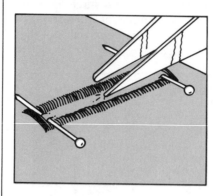

> **TIP** *If, despite all your good intentions, you cut into the stitches, repair the damage with a dot of Fray-Check.™*

> **TIP** *If your fabric frays, trim off all the loose threads, then treat the edges of the buttonhole with a thin beading of Fray-Check™. If it comes out of the bottle too fast, apply it with a very fine paintbrush.*

Sewing on the Button

Buttons come in two styles: sew-through and shank. The shank is designed to compensate for the thickness of the garment layers. On sew-through buttons, you'll need to use thread to create a

shank. You're going to do this at the same time you sew the button on.

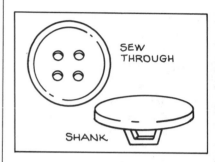

SEW THROUGH

SHANK

To Locate the Button Position:

■ After making the buttonholes and cutting them open, lap the garment edges, matching centers, so it looks like it's buttoned.

■ For a horizontal buttonhole, stick a pin through at the center front or back marking, ⅛″ (3mm) in from the end of the buttonhole.

For a vertical buttonhole, insert the pin ⅛ (3mm) below the top of the buttonhole.

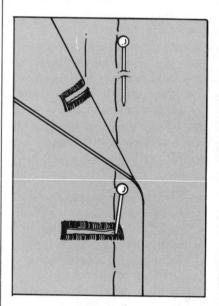

To Attach the Button:

■ Thread the needle with a double thread. Take a few small backstitches to lock the thread at the point of the pin marking.

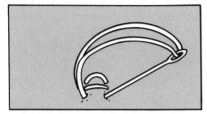

■ Bring the needle through the button and back into the fabric. Sew back and forth several times. To create a thread shank on a sew-through button, place a toothpick or wooden match on top of the button and sew over it. Sew back and forth several times. Then remove the toothpick and wind the thread round and round the extra thread under the button.

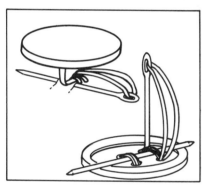

■ Instead of making an ugly knot on the underside of your garment, do this:

1. Draw the needle to the underside of the garment and fasten with several small, tight backstitches.

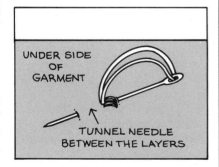

UNDER SIDE
OF
GARMENT

TUNNEL NEEDLE
BETWEEN THE LAYERS

2. Insert the needle into the fabric and tunnel it between the gar-

ment layers for about 1″ (2.5cm).
3. Bring the needle out and clip the thread close to the fabric. If your garment is only one layer thick, or your fabric is sheer, clip the thread close to the backstitches instead of tunneling it.

FROGS AND TOGGLES

Your pattern may recommend these two-part closures . . . or you can choose them as a substitute for buttons and buttonholes. In general, toggles add a sporty touch, while frogs are more decorative.

■ Lap the garment edges so that the center fronts match or the edges meet.
■ Position the toggle or ball part of the closure on the left side of the garment and the loop part on the right, so that they close directly over the center front, as shown below. (For men's clothes, the toggle part goes on the right and the loop part goes on the left.) Hold them in place with pins, double-faced basting tape or glue stick.
■ Machine-stitch or hand-tack them in place, as appropriate.

TIP *To sew on buttons super-quick, double your thread, then thread the needle so you're sewing with four thickness of thread rather than two.*

TIP *To keep your thread strong and tangle-free, run it through beeswax before you begin.*

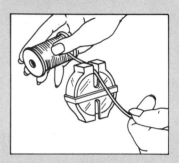

TIP *If your sewing machine makes a zigzag stitch, you can probably use it to attach sew-through buttons by machine. Check your manual for information.*

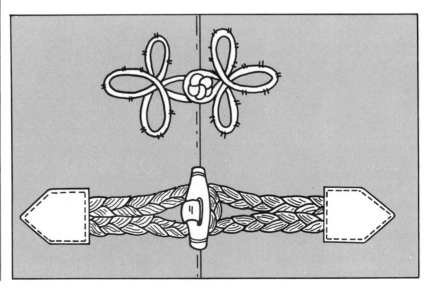

HOOKS AND EYES

Hooks and eyes may be used alone or in combination with another fastener. For example, you may want to add one at the top of a zipper. They range in size from 0 to 4, for light to heavy weight fabrics. Most hooks come with both loop eyes and straight eyes. Which eye you use depends on where the hook and eye is placed on your garment.

> **TIP** *When attaching hooks and eyes, your stitches should NEVER show on the outside of the garment.*

FOR EDGES THAT MEET, use a hook and a loop eye:

■ On the inside, sew the hook ⅛″ (3mm) from the right-hand edge of the garment by making a few tacking stitches through the holes. Then sew across the end, under the curve of the hook.

■ Sew the eye opposite the hook, letting it extend slightly beyond the garment edge. Take a few stitches along the sides of the loop to hold it flat.

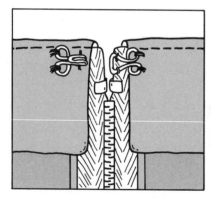

FOR EDGES THAT LAP, use a hook and a straight eye. For a waistband, use two sets of regular hooks and eyes or one set of the heavy-duty-hooks and eyes especially designed for waistbands.

■ Sew the hook(s) to the inside of the garment on the overlap, ⅛″

(3mm) from the edge. Hand-tack in place, sewing through the holes, then across the end, under the curve of the hook. Don't let the stitches for the hook(s) show on the outside of the garment.

■ Close the zipper or other closure, then mark the eye position(s) with pins.

■ Sew the eyes to the outside of the underlap.

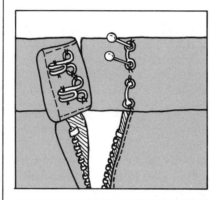

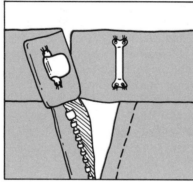

No-Sew Hooks and Eyes

This type of waistband hook and eye requires no sewing—just

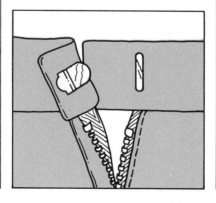

hammer them or clamp them on. Use them on sturdy or firmly woven fabrics only. No-sew hooks and eyes should be applied before the waistband is finished, following the manufacturer's instructions.

SNAPS

Snaps are used when a garment edge needs to be held flat but where there is no strain. Decorative snaps can be used as a substitute for buttons on loose-fitting, casual garments.

Snaps, like hooks and eyes, come in many sizes, for light to heavy weight fabrics, and in sew-on and no-sew versions.

Sew-on Types

■ Sew the ball half to the inside of the garment on the overlap. Positioning it approximately ⅛″ (3mm) from the edge, make several tacking stitches through each hole. To keep the stitches from showing on the outside, pick up only one or two threads of fabric with each stitch and tunnel the needle between the layers of fabric as you go from hole to hole.

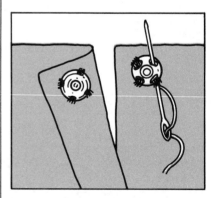

■ To mark the socket position, close the garment and stick a pin through the center of the ball to the underlap.

■ Sew the socket half in place the same way as you did the ball half.

TIP *Baste the snap sections in place with a dot of glue stick. Let them dry thoroughly before you sew.*

No-Sew Snaps

These sturdy, hammer-on snaps are a fast substitute for buttons and buttonholes on children's garments and sportswear. Follow the package instructions to hammer them in place or purchase a plier-like tool, which also comes with instructions.

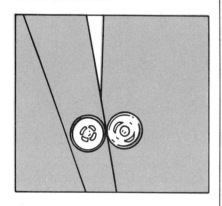

Snap Tape

Available in a range of colors, this tape comes with the snaps already attached. To apply, preshrink the tape first in cool water. Then, using a zipper foot, edgestitch the tape in place, turning the raw ends under. Sew the ball strip to the underlap and the socket strip to the overlap.

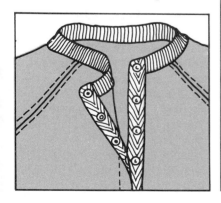

SELF-GRIPPING HOOK AND LOOP FASTENERS

These flexible, two-part fasteners have tiny, stiff hooks and soft loops that interlock when you press them together. They're an easy substitute for buttons or snaps and are available in precut dots and squares or in strips. The light adhesive backing will hold them in place for permanent stitching.

■ Position each part at least ¼" (6mm) from the garment edge. The loop part goes on the overlap, the hook part on the underlap.

■ To attach, machine-stitch the dots in a triangular pattern; edgestitch the squares and the strips. If you don't want the stitching to show on the outside of the garment, hand-sew in place all around the edges.

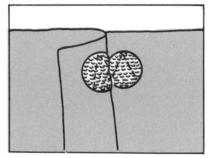

TIES

If your pattern calls for self-fabric ties, here's a quick way to do it. The method varies slightly, depending on whether you're using a conventional or an overlock machine. But, either way, the result is a neat, narrow tube of fabric that can be used for ties, belt loops, button loops or spaghetti straps.

THE CONVENTIONAL METHOD:

■ Cut a piece of string twice the length of the finished tie, plus 5" (12.5cm).

■ With right sides together, fold the tie in half lengthwise, placing the string inside the fold, as shown.

■ Sew back and forth across the top of the tie to secure the end of the string. Then stitch the tie together along its length, being

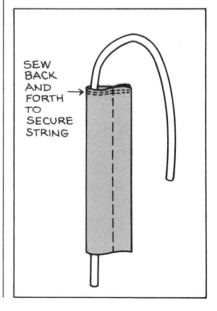

SEW BACK AND FORTH TO SECURE STRING

> **TIP** *Ribbon is a quick and easy substitute for fabric ties. Pick matching or contrasting ribbon. To prevent raveling, notch or cut the ends diagonally. If necessary, apply a little bit of Fray Check™.*

careful not to catch the string in the stitching. This will be easier to do if you use your machine's zipper foot.

■ To turn the tie, pull on the string.

■ To remove the string, trim off the end where it is attached.

S THE OVERLOCK METHOD:

■ Serge a chain the length of the tie, plus 2″ (5cm). DO NOT CUT THE CHAIN. Pull the chain around to the front of the foot.

■ With right sides together, fold the tie in half lengthwise, placing the thread chain inside the fold.

■ Serge the tie together, being careful not to catch the thread chain in the stitching.

■ To turn the tie, pull on the inside chain.

If you need to finish the ends, tie them in a knot or tuck them in and slipstitch the openings closed.

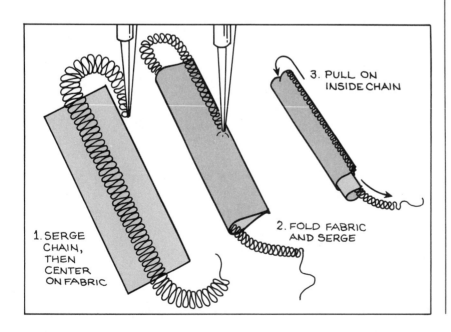

1. SERGE CHAIN, THEN CENTER ON FABRIC

2. FOLD FABRIC AND SERGE

3. PULL ON INSIDE CHAIN

COLLARS

In sewing terminology, a collar has two visible layers: the top layer, called the collar or upper collar, and the bottom layer, called the undercollar or facing. Almost every collar has a third, unseen, layer of interfacing. Some collars, called one-piece collars, are designed so that the undercollar is an extension of the upper collar. As a result, the outer edge is a fold rather than a seam.

Although there are many different fashion terms that describe collars, they all fall into three basic categories:

A *Flat Collar* lies flat against the neck edge of the garment. If you compared the neckline seam of the collar with the neckline seam of the garment, you would find that the curves are almost identical.

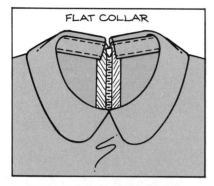

FLAT COLLAR

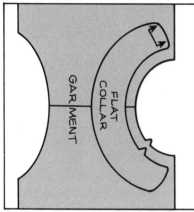

GARMENT · FLAT COLLAR

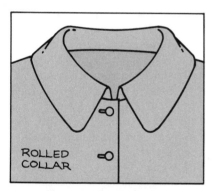

ROLLED COLLAR

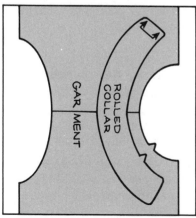

GARMENT · ROLLED COLLAR

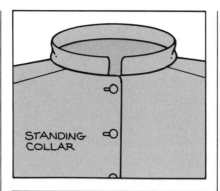

STANDING COLLAR

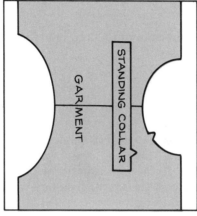

GARMENT · STANDING COLLAR

A *Rolled Collar* rises straight up from the neck edge for a short distance, then rolls down to rest on the garment. The part that rises is called the stand; the part that rolls down is called the fall. On a rolled collar, the collar neckline seam has a shallower curve than the garment neckline seam.

A *Standing Collar* is a band that rises straight up from the neckline seam. It can be a narrow, single-layer band or a double-layer band that folds back onto itself. On a standing collar, the collar neckline seam is very straight in comparison to the garment neckline seam.

COLLAR BASICS

Regardless of the style of collar, the techniques for professional results are basically the same.

Interfacing

Most collars have a layer of interfacing sandwiched between the collar and undercollar. Your pattern instructions will tell you what pattern piece(s) to use and where to apply the interfacing. In most cases, the interfacing is fused or machine-basted to the upper collar. This way it acts as a cushion against all the seam allowances.

To reduce bulk, it's a good idea to trim ½" (1.3cm) off the interfacing's seam allowances. For sew-in interfacings, trim the seam allowances after the interfacing is machine-basted in place. For fusibles, trim the seam allowances first, then fuse the interfacing. To reduce bulk at the corners, trim the interfacing diagonally, just inside the seamline.

Stitching It Together

Instead of starting at one edge of the collar and stitching all the way around to the other edge, you'll get a more symmetrical collar if you stitch it together in two steps.

Step 1: Begin at the center back and stitch to one edge of the collar.

Step 2: Begin again at the center back, overlapping several stitches, and stitch to the other edge of the collar.

> **TIP** *When using fusibles on light to medium weight fabrics, forget about pre-trimming the interfacing. The amount of bulk these interfacings add is almost imperceptible. Once the collar is stitched, careful trimming and grading, as well as good pressing, will take care of any bulk.*

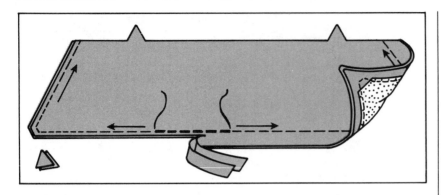

your scissors—it's all too easy to poke them right through the fabric.

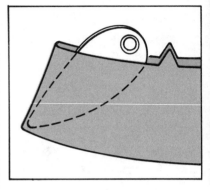

Press the collar. As you press, roll the seamline slightly underneath to the undercollar side.

Understitching

Understitching is that extra bit of security that keeps the undercollar from rolling to the outside.

■ Turn the collar inside out again and slip it under your presser foot so that the right side of the undercollar is facing you. Stitch on the undercollar, next to the seamline, catching all the seam allowances in your stitching.

Note: If your collar is curved, you'll be able to understitch along the entire length of the collar. If your collar is pointed, understitch (see page 151) along the back edge, between, and almost to, the points.

■ Turn the collar right side out and press again.

Preparing the Garment

The finished collar won't look smooth and neat unless you've done some preliminary work on your garment.

■ ALWAYS staystitch the garment's neckline edge to keep it from stretching out of shape as you sew.

TIP *If your collar has corners or sharp curves, remember to use a smaller stitch for about 1" (2.5cm) on either side. For sharper corners, take one stitch across the point.*

Trimming and Grading

Trim the seam allowances and the corners. On medium and heavy weight fabrics, grade the seam allowances so that the undercollar seam allowance is narrower than the upper collar seam allowance.

Remember to notch your curved collars.

Pressing

Before turning the collar right side out, press it flat on both the collar side and the undercollar side. This blends the stitches.

To insure a sharp edge once the collar is turned, do one of the following:

■ Press the seam allowance open over a point presser.

OR:

■ Place the collar flat on the ironing board with the undercollar side facing up. Press the undercollar seam allowance toward the collar.

Turn the collar right side out. If the collar has points, gently coax them out from the inside with the eraser end of a pencil or the tip of a point turner. Resist the temptation to use the tip of

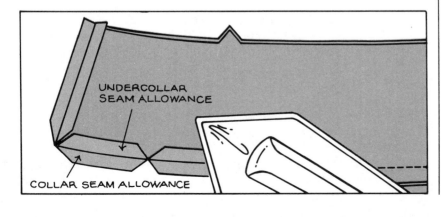

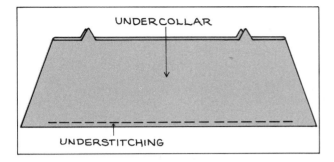

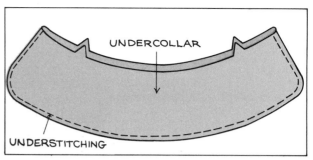

■ You'll also need to clip the neckline seam allowance at regular intervals, just to, but not through, the staystitching. This releases the fabric and helps it to lie flat as you pin and stitch the collar in place. The greater the difference between the neckline curves of the garment and the collar, the more clipping you'll have to do. For flat collars, very little clipping is necessary. For standing collars, you may need to clip every ½" (1.3cm) or more.

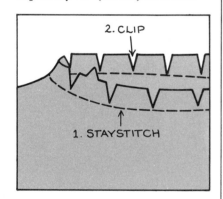

Attaching the Collar

There are many different methods of attaching the collar. Sometimes it is attached at the same time as the neckline facing so that the facing hides the neckline seam allowances. Sometimes there is no facing. Instead, the collar is attached so that the garment neckline seam allowance is sandwiched between the collar and the undercollar. Follow your pattern directions, making sure that

TIP *When making a collar from sheer fabric, seams should be as inconspicuous as possible. To do this, use one of the following seam techniques. Note that clipping, grading and understitching are not necessary.*

THE CONVENTIONAL METHOD:

■ *Stitch along the seamline over a filler cord of pearl cotton or crochet thread, using a fine zigzag stitch. Trim the seam allowance close to the stitching, then turn and press the collar.*

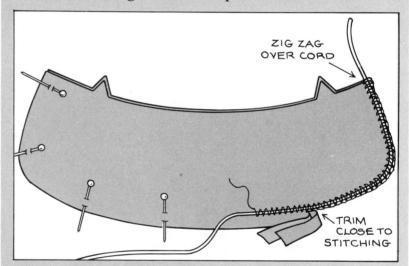

S THE OVERLOCK METHOD:

■ *Set the machine to make a narrow seam; see chart below.*

TYPE OF OVERLOCK STITCH	3	MINE
Stitch Length:	2–3	
Stitch Width:	Narrowest	
Tension—Needle:	Normal	
U. Looper:	Normal	
L. Looper:	Normal	

■ *Serge along the seamline, then turn and press the collar.*

Note: These two techniques work equally well for cuffs.

you trim, grade and clip the neckline seam, then press the seam allowances as indicated.

CUFFS

Buttoned and snug, or turned up and loose, cuffs are a popular detail on sleeves and pants.

As you read your pattern instructions, keep in mind that most cuffs, like most collars, are made up of three layers. The top layer is called the cuff; the underneath layer is called the facing. In between is the interfacing.

THE ATTACHED CUFF

Sewing an attached cuff is very similar to sewing a collar. In fact, the basics of assembling—interfacing, stitching, trimming and grading, and pressing—are exactly the same. Before you make a cuff,

reread the previous sections on collars, pages 149–150.

An attached cuff can be a continuous band cuff or it can have a cuff opening. If the cuff opens, there is a corresponding sleeve opening, or placket, that can be finished in a variety of ways.

The easiest "placket" is an *opening in the sleeve seam*. To do this, stitch the seam to the marking and backstitch, then press the entire seam open.

The *faced opening* is another style of placket. If your pattern calls for this type of opening, it will include a pattern piece for the facing and complete instructions.

Two other common openings are the *continuous lap* and the *hemmed opening*. A fifth opening, the *tailored placket*, is similar to the conventional neckline placket band. If you're making this type of placket, review the information on BANDS, pages 126–127.

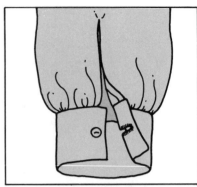

SEAM OPENING

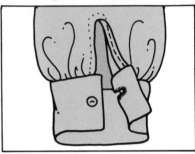

FACED PLACKET

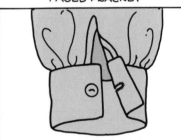

CONTINUOUS LAP

HEMMED OPENING

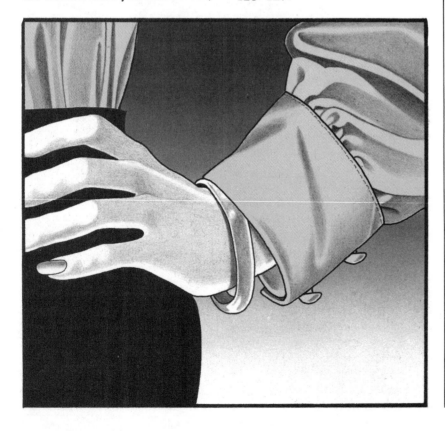

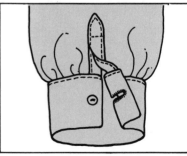

TAILORED PLACKET

Hemmed Opening

Some patterns have a small sleeve opening that's formed by turning up part of the seam allowance.

■ Reinforce along the seamline, as indicated on your pattern, extending the stitching ½" (1.3cm) beyong the markings.

■ Clip to the stitching at the markings.

■ Fold the flap up and press. Then turn the raw edge of the flap in to meet the stitching line and press again.

■ To secure the flap to the sleeve, use fusible web or slip-stitch it in place across the top of the fold.

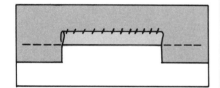

> **TIP** *If your fabric has a tendence to fray, treat the cut edges of the flap with a liquid seam sealant. Test first to make sure it isn't visible on your fabric when dry.*

Continuous Lap

Cuffs on a tailored shirt may have an opening that is bound with a strip of fabric. This is done before the underarm seam is stitched. Your pattern either includes a pattern piece for this strip or tells you how to measure and cut it.

THE CONVENTIONAL METHOD:

The following method may be slightly different from the one in your pattern instructions. Contin-

> **TIP** *If you're worried about your fabric fraying at the point, treat the cut edges of the opening with a liquid seam sealant, such as Fray Check™.*

uous laps can be tricky but with this method even your first attempt will be successful.

The first step is to create the opening at the lower edge of the sleeve.

■ Mark the slash stitching lines.

■ Stitch along these lines, using reinforcement-length stitches for 1" (2.5cm) on either side of the point and taking one stitch across the point.

■ Cut an opening between the stitching lines, being careful not to slash through the stitch at the point

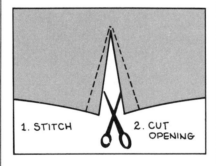

1. STITCH   2. CUT OPENING

To attach the lap:

■ Spread the edges of the opening apart so that they almost form a straight line.

■ With right sides together, pin the fabric strip to the slashed edge so that the stitching line of the opening is ¼" (6mm) from the edge of the strip (*top right*).

■ Working with the sleeve on top, machine-stitch, stitching just to the left of the previous stitching. As you come to the point of the opening, fold the extra sleeve fabric out of the way.

■ Press the seam allowances toward the strip (*bottom right*).

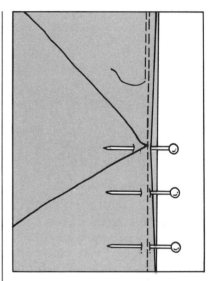

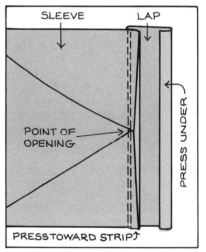

SLEEVE   LAP

POINT OF OPENING

PRESS UNDER

PRESS TOWARD STRIP

■ Press under ¼" (6mm) on the remaining long edge of the strip.

> **TIP** *To reduce bulk, eliminate one of the ¼" (6mm) seam allowances, cut the strip along the selvage edge of your fabric. Then there's no need to press this edge under.*

■ Pin this edge over the seam on the inside of the sleeve and slip-stitch in place.

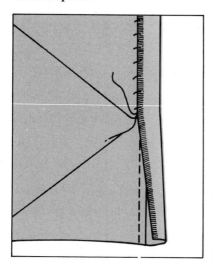

■ Press the front portion of the lap to the inside and baste it in place across the lower edge of the sleeve.

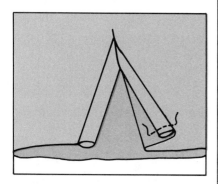

S THE OVERLOCK METHOD:

■ Measure the length of the placket opening on your pattern tissue. Then cut a 1″ (2.5cm) wide bias strip of fabric twice the length of the placket opening.

■ Reinforce and slash the placket opening as for the conventional machine technique.

■ With right sides together, pin the bias strip to the slashed edge so that the stitching line of the opening is ¼″ (6mm) from the edge of the strip.

■ Working with the sleeve on top, serge until the knife reaches

the point of the slash. Be sure to keep the fabric in front of the blade clear. Rearrange the sleeve folds and continue serging. *Note:* As you stitch, guide the bias strip under the needle with your right hand, while holding the placket edge straight with your left hand.

HOLD PLACKET EDGE STRAIGHT

GUIDE BIAS STRIP UNDERNEATH

■ Serge the remaining raw edge of the bias strip, trimming away about ⅛″ (3mm) as you serge.

■ Press the seam allowance toward the bias strip.

■ Fold the bias strip to the wrong side of the garment so the edge

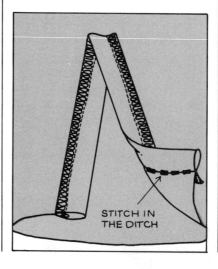

STITCH IN THE DITCH

of the strip extends ⅛″ (3mm) over the line of reinforcement stitching. Press, then stitch in the ditch, using your conventional machine.

■ Press the front portion of the lap to the inside and baste it in place across the lower edge of the sleeve.

Attaching the Cuff

Once the cuff is assembled and the sleeve opening is finished, you're ready to attach the cuff.

THE CONVENTIONAL METHOD:

Your pattern will probably tell you to attach the cuff in one of the following conventional ways. **Technique #1:** Stitch the cuff to the lower edge of the sleeve. Then, working on the inside, slip-stitch the facing in place over the seam allowances.

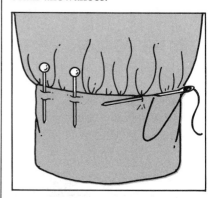

Technique #2: Stitch the cuff facing to the lower edge of the sleeve. Then, working on the outside, edgestitch the cuff in place over the seam allowances.

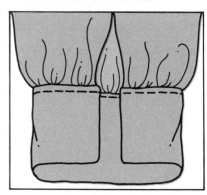

> **TIP** *When you are attaching the cuff to the sleeve, the pattern directions usually tell you to trim and grade the seam allowances. However, if you are using a sheer or loosely woven fabric, DO NOT trim and grade. If you do, you may find that the first time you bend your elbow and rest it on a table, the strain may cause the trimmed seam allowance to pull away along the stitching line.*

Although Technique #2 sounds much easier (and has a sportier look), you may find it more difficult to get neat results, particularly if this technique is new to you. Feel free to substitute Technique #1 for Technique #2. Then, to achieve the sportier look, you can go back and edge-stitch the cuff on the outside.

S THE OVERLOCK METHOD:

Note: This technique is successful ONLY if your "placket" is an opening in the sleeve seam. On sleeves with a faced opening, a hemmed opening, a continuous lap or a tailored placket, the cuff should be attached using the conventional machine.

■ With right sides together, pin the cuff to the lower edge of the sleeve, matching markings.

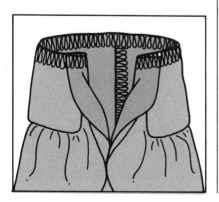

■ Roll the edge of the opening over the ends of the cuff and pin. Diagonally trim the corners before stitching. This eliminates bulk at the corner once the seam is serged.

■ Serge the cuff to the sleeve and secure the thread ends.

■ Turn the lap edges of the opening to the inside. Press the seam allowance toward the sleeve.

RIB-KNIT CUFFS

These cuffs are a good way to finish the legs or sleeves of a sporty garment. For more information on this and other types of continuous bands, see BANDS AND RIBBING, p.127–129.

FOLD-UP CUFF

This type of cuff is often found on pants, particularly trouser styles, and short sleeves. Patterns styled this way include the extra length that's needed to form the cuffs.

The traditional fold-up cuff includes some hand sewing. However, a shortcut machine method will save you time. If your machine has a free arm, it's even easier. Be sure you have marked the hem and cuff foldlines.

■ Turn the leg or sleeve inside out and press the hem up.

■ If necessary, finish the raw edge. Then machine-stitch the hem in place. (These hem stitches won't show on the outside of the finished cuff.)

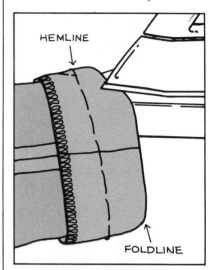

■ Turn the leg or sleeve right side out. Fold the lower edge up along the cuff foldline and press.

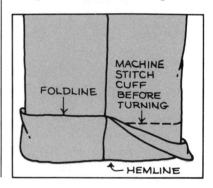

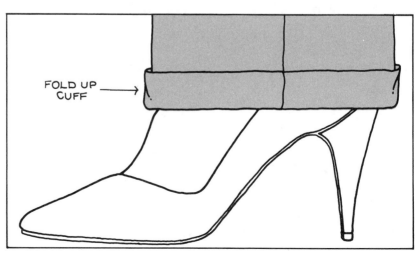

■ To keep the cuff in place, stitch in the ditch at the seams, through all layers.

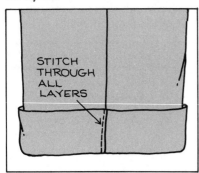

MOCK FOLD-UP CUFF

If your pattern has straight, untapered sleeves or legs, and you want to have cuffs, here's an easy way to fake it.

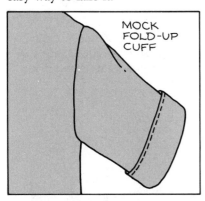

■ Before you cut out your garment, you'll need to alter the pattern. Cut it apart along the hemline, spread it ½″ (1.3cm), and pin or tape it to paper.

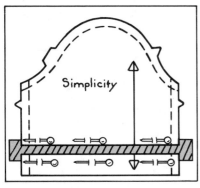

■ When you're ready to hem the garment, fold the edge to the inside along the hemline and press.

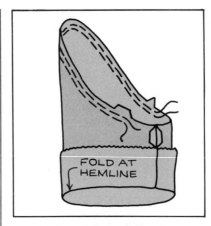

■ Fold the edge up again the same amount and press.

■ Stitch ¼″ (6mm) from the second fold. This will create a tuck and encase the raw edge of the hem.

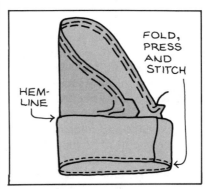

■ Open out the sleeve or pants leg so that you can press the tuck up and the "cuff" down.

S MOCK FOLD-UP OR MOCK BAND CUFF

Like the conventional mock cuff, this technique requires

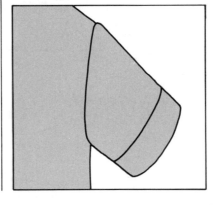

straight, untapered sleeves or legs. It's easier to make this type of cuff before the underarm seam (on sleeves) or the inner leg seam (on pants) is serged.

■ Before you cut out your pattern, make sure that the cuff allowance is twice the width of the finished cuff, plus ¾″ (2cm). If necessary, lengthen the pattern at the lower edge.

■ Measure up from the lower edge of the sleeve or pants a distance equal to the width of the finished cuff, plus ¼″ (6mm). Fold the lower edge of the garment section to the wrong side along this line; press.

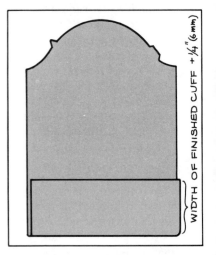

■ Now turn the folded portion of the garment back to the right side; press.

■ Serge along this second fold, being careful not to cut the fabric.

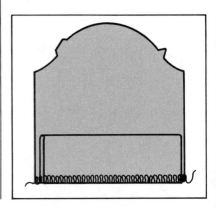

■ Press the cuff down.

■ Beginning at the lower edge of the garment, serge the underarm or inner leg seam.

DARTS

Darts are one of the ways that fabric is molded to conform to the curves of the body.

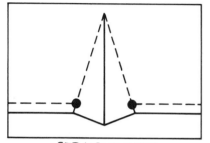

STRAIGHT DART

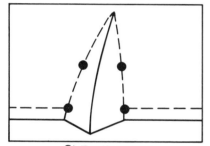

CURVED DART

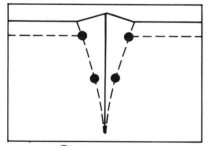

CURVED DART

Darts can be straight, for an easy fit, or curved, for a closer-to-the-body fit. Darts usually start at a seamline, tapering to nothing at their tip. However, a double-pointed dart, found on one-piece dresses and closely-fitted shirts, blouses and jackets, is actually two darts combined into one. The result is a long dart with the widest part occurring at the waist. It

tapers to nothing near the bust (or shoulder blade on the back of a garment) and near the hip.

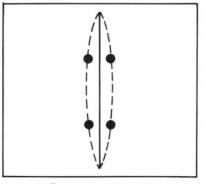

DOUBLE-POINTED DART

MARKING

Examine the shape of your dart. If the stitching line is straight, all you need to do is mark the ●'s. If the stitching line is curved, it's a better idea to mark the entire stitching line. That way, you'll be sure you've stitched the curve exactly right.

STITCHING

■ With right sides together, fold the fabric through the center of the dart, matching the markings and the stitching lines. Place pins at right angles to the stitching lines.

■ Stitch the dart from the wide end to the point. To prevent a bubble at the point, make the last few stitches right at the fold and leave the thread ends long enough to tie a knot. DO NOT backstitch at the point.

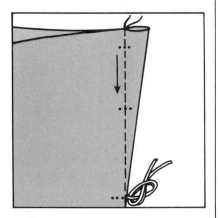

If it is a double-pointed dart, pin and stitch as above, working from the middle to one end.

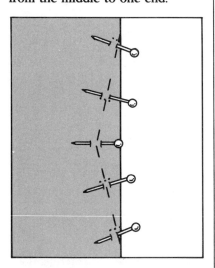

> TIP *When it comes to darts, put your overlock machine aside. It's impossible to get that nice, "tapered-to-nothing" look of a professional dart on an overlock. What you'll end up with is a lumpy, dimpled dart.*

Then, overlapping several stitches, work from the middle to the other end. Carefully clip the dart at its widest point so that it will lie flat.

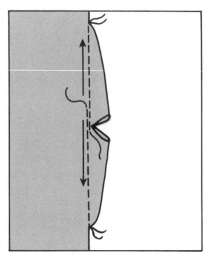

PRESSING

Press the darts flat, then open or to one side, as indicated on your pattern instructions. As a rule, vertical darts are pressed toward the center of the garment and horizontal ones are pressed

downward. Occasionally, your pattern instructions will tell you to slash the dart along the foldline and press it open.

FACINGS

FACING BASICS

A facing is a piece of fabric that finishes a garment edge. Facings are most frequently found at necklines, armholes, front and back openings and, occasionally, at the waistline or the lower edge of a sleeve.

Most facings are created by attaching a separate piece of fabric to the garment edge. However, a garment that opens at the center front or back often has a special facing, called a self-facing, that is cut in one piece with the garment. When this extension is folded back, it serves as the facing for both the opening edges and part of the neckline. To finish off the rest of the neckline, the garment will also have a back neck facing and/or a collar.

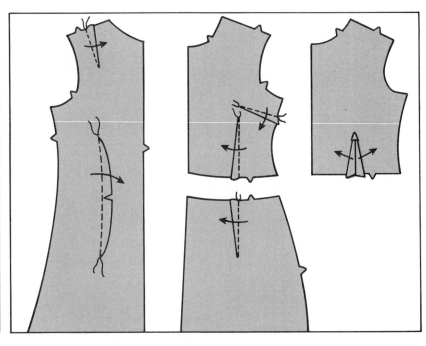

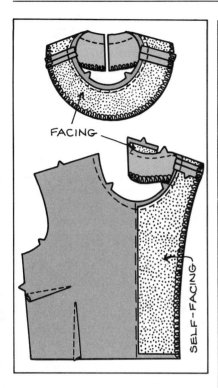

FACING

SELF-FACING

Although the shape and the location can vary, the basics for creating a facing that lies flat and looks professional remain the same.

Staystitch

If the facing is located at the neckline or the waistline, staystitch the neck/waist edges on both the garment and the facing. For armhole facings and front and back edges, staystitching is not necessary.

Interface

Apply interfacing to either the facing section or the garment section, as recommended in your pattern instructions. As a general rule, fusible interfacing is applied to the facing section.

Finish the Edge

Stitch the facing together at the shoulder or side seams, then finish the outer edge. If appropriate, the stitched-and-pinked or the zigzag/overcast finish (see page 99)

will add the least amount of bulk. If your fabric is very bulky and/or ravels a great deal, use the tricot-bound finish, see page 99.

Attach the Facing

Stitch the facing to the garment, as indicated on your pattern instructions. If there are any corners, remember to shorten your stitch length for about 1″ (2.5cm) on either side.

Trim and Grade

To prevent ridges from showing on the outside, remove bulk from the seams by trimming the seam allowances to ¼″ (6mm). On thick fabrics, also trim the facing seam allowance to ⅛″ (3mm) so that the layers are graded. To insure a smooth edge when the facing is turned to the inside, clip or notch curved seam allowances. (See drawing above, at right.)

Press

Press the seam allowances flat to blend the stitches. Next, press

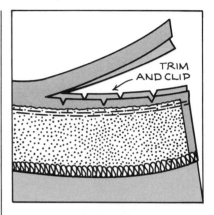

TRIM AND CLIP

them open. Then press them toward the facing.

Understitch

Open the facing out. With the facing on top, stitch through the facing and both seam allowances very close to the seam, as shown below.

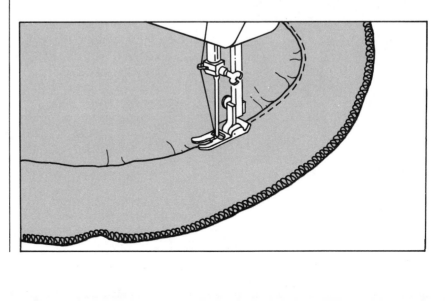

Press Again

Fold the facing to the inside of the garment along the seamline and press.

Tack

To keep the facing from rolling to the outside, secure it at the seam allowances by tacking it by hand, stitching in the ditch, or using a small piece of fusible web.

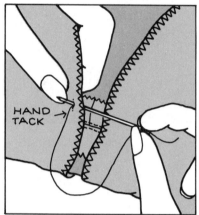

HAND TACK

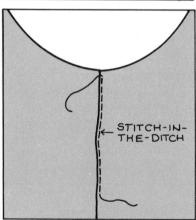

STITCH-IN-THE-DITCH

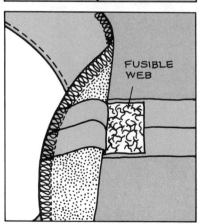

FUSIBLE WEB

TIP *If the garment edge will ultimately be topstitched, there's no need to tack the facing in place.*

S THE OVERLOCK METHOD

When it comes to facings, your overlock machine can save you a lot of time. Use it first to finish the edges of the facing. Then, if the edge to be faced is a straight edge or a gradual curve, you can use your overlock to attach the facing to the garment. Because the overlock automatically gives you very narrow seam allowances, trimming, grading, notching and clipping won't be necessary.

■ Serge the facing pieces together. Press the seams to one side.

■ Finish the facing by serging around the outside edges.

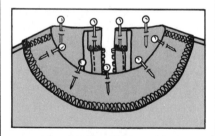

■ Pin the facing to the garment edge. If the faced edge has an opening, fold the garment and facing to the inside along the opening edge and pin as shown.

■ Serge along the 5⁄8″ (1.5cm) seamline, through all layers.

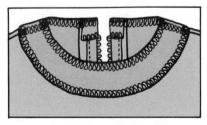

■ Press the seam allowances toward the facing, then understitch on your conventional machine.

TIP *To reduce bulk, make sure the facing seam allowances and the corresponding garment seam allowances are pressed in opposite directions.*

BIAS TAPE FACING

As an alternative to a regular facing, you can substitute single-fold bias tape. It's a quick and easy technique that's particularly popular for children's clothes. Because the tape is made from bias strips of fabric, it will fit smoothly around the curves of neckline and armhole edges.

Purchase either ½″ (1.3cm) or 7⁄8″ (2.2cm) wide single-fold bias tape.

■ Trim the garment seam allowance to ¼″ (6mm).

■ Open out one fold of the tape. If you're facing a curved edge, steam-press the tape and preshape it to match the garment curve.

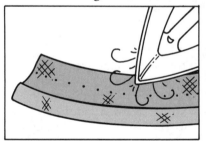

■ With right sides together and raw edges even, pin the tape to the garment. To join the ends of the tape, turn under ½ (1.3cm) on the first end; lap the other

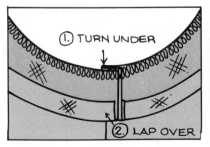

(1.) TURN UNDER

(2.) LAP OVER

end over it. Straight-stitch or serge a ¼″ (6mm) seam.

■ Turn the tape to the inside and press. As you press, roll the tape slightly to the inside of the garment so it will not show on the outside.

■ On the outside, edgestitch close to the garment edge, then topstitch about ⅜″–¾″ (1cm–2cm) away.

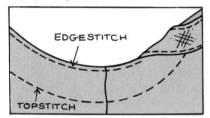

S SERGED NECKLINE

Instead of facing a collarless neckline, serge it! The overlock stitches create a decorative, finished edge. This is a great technique for firmly woven fabrics and knits that don't curl.

Always test first to be sure you like the results before serging your garment's neckline. To test stitching and thread tension, cut the test swatch so that it duplicates the curve of the garment's neckline.

■ Adjust your overlock machine to the appropriate setting; see chart at right.

■ Serge one shoulder seam.

■ Serge around the neckline along the ⅝″ (1.5cm) seamline.

■ Serge the remaining shoulder seam, beginning at the armhole and chaining off 3″–4″ (7.5cm–10cm) at the neckline edge.

■ To secure the stitches at the neckline edge, thread the chain onto a tapestry needle and weave it back through the shoulder seam stitches.

> **TIP** *This technique can be used to replace the facing in other parts of a garment, such as an armhole, hemline or opening edges of a jacket.*

> **TIP** *If your fabric is sheer, you may wish to eliminate the facings and finish the edge with a bias binding cut from your fashion fabric. For more information, see BINDINGS, page 133.*

TYPE OF OVERLOCK STITCH:	3	4	MINE
Stitch Length:	3mm	3mm	
Stitch Width:	Widest	Widest	
Tensions—Needle:	Tight	Tight	
Right Needle:	N/A	Normal	
U. Looper:	Normal	Normal	
L. Looper:	Normal	Normal	

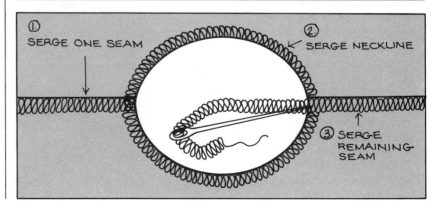

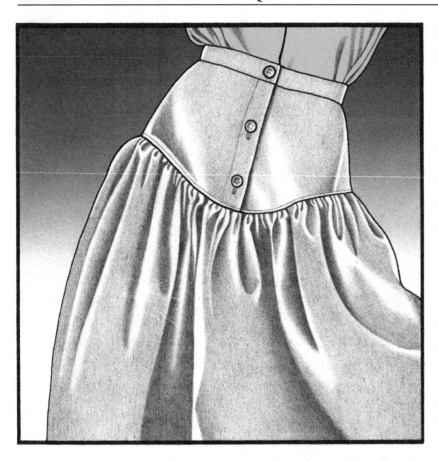

■ Loosen the needle thread tension slightly. This will make it easier to pull up the bobbin thread later.

■ Set the stitch length for a long stitch—the heavier the fabric, the longer the stitch.

■ Working on the right side of the fabric, stitch along the seamline of the area to be gathered. Stitch again, ¼" (6mm) away, within the seam allowance. Be sure to leave long thread tails— and do not backstitch!

■ With right sides together, pin the section to be gathered to the shorter one, matching notches, seams and markings. Pin.

■ Gently pull the bobbin threads at each end, sliding the fabric along until it fits the shorter section. At both ends, wrap the excess bobbin thread around the pins in figure 8's. Distribute the gathers evenly and pin as shown on opposite page, at top.

■ Before machine stitching the

GATHERS

Gathers are used to control fullness in just about any part of the garment. You'll find them at the waistline, at a yoke seam, at the cuff of a full sleeve, or the cap of a puffed sleeve. Gathers are also used to create ruffles.

The fabric you choose will affect the appearance of your gathers. The softer the fabric, the more the gathers will drape and cling to the body. Crisper fabrics create billowy, stand-away-from-the-body gathers.

STRAIGHT STITCH GATHERING

The most common way to create gathers is to use a long, straight machine stitch.

TIP *If the gathers will intersect a previous seam:*

■ *On light and medium weight fabrics, diagonally trim the ends of the seam allowances before stitching the gathers.*

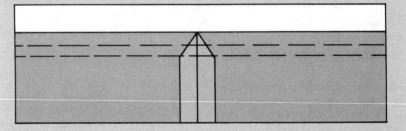

■ *On bulky fabrics, trim ends of seams and stitch up to the seams, keeping the seam allowances free.*

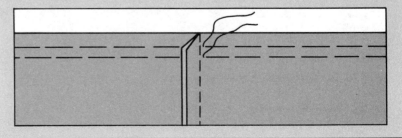

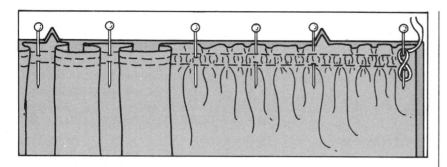

seam, make sure you have re-adjusted the needle thread tension. Working with the gathered side up, stitch just next to the first row of gathers. To keep tucks from forming along the seamline, use the tips of your fingers to hold the fabric on either side of the presser foot.

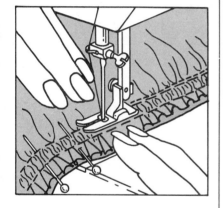

Gathering Long Sections

The longer the area you're working on, the greater the chances of having a thread break while you are forming the gathers. To avoid this:

■ Divide the edges of both the short and long sections into four

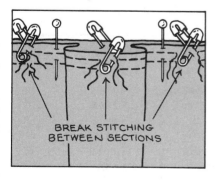

BREAK STITCHING BETWEEN SECTIONS

or eight equal parts and mark with safety pins or straight pins.

■ On the edge to be gathered, make separate rows of gathering stitches for each section.

■ Pin the edges together, distribute the fullness and stitch as for straight stitch gathering.

GATHERING OVER A CORD

This fast method for gathering a long section eliminates any worries about threads breaking.

■ Cut a piece of strong, thin cord, such as pearl cotton, button and carpet thread or lightweight packing string, slightly longer than the edge to be gathered.

■ Set your machine for a zigzag stitch wide enough to stitch over the cord without catching it in the stitches. Position the cord within the seam allowance so that the left swing of the needle falls just short of the seamline. Stitch.

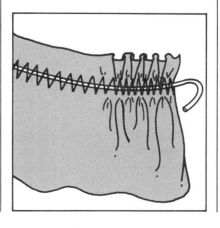

■ Wrap one end of the cord around a pin in a figure 8 to secure it.

■ Pin the two sections together, matching notches, seamlines and markings. To distribute the gathers, hold the cord taut and slide the fabric along it.

■ Working with the gathered side up, stitch along the seamline, being careful not to catch the cord. Depending on the weight of your fabric and the thickness of your cord, you may find it easier to use your machine's zipper foot.

■ When you're finished stitching, just pull out the cord.

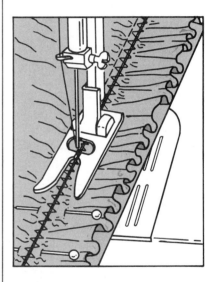

⑤ GATHERING ON THE OVERLOCK

One of the most frustrating things about gathering is that, just when you think you have everything adjusted, you give one last yank, the gathering stitches break, and the whole thing explodes in your lap. You can zigzag over a cord on your conventional machine OR you can put your overlocking machine to work. Here are two overlock techniques. If you use them, remember that the overlock machine will trim your seam allowances to ¼″ (6mm).

TYPE OF OVERLOCK STITCH:	3	4	MINE
Stitch Length:	3mm–5mm	3mm–5mm	
Stitch Width:	Widest	Widest	
Tensions—Needle	Very Tight	Very Tight	
Rt. Needle:	N/A	Tight	
U. Looper:	Normal	Normal	
L. Looper:	Normal	Normal	

S *The Basic Technique*

■ Adjust your overlock machine to the appropriate setting; see chart above.

■ Make a test sample. Soft to medium weight fabrics will gather automatically. For more gathers, tighten the needle thread tension(s). For less gathers, loosen the needle thread tension(s).

■ Place the garment edge wrong side up and serge along the ⅝" (1.5cm) seamline.

■ Remove the fabric from the machine and adjust the density of the gathers by pulling the needle thread(s) along gently.

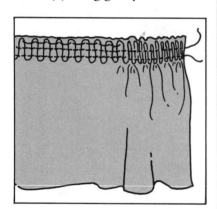

S *Over a Cord*

For heavier fabrics, you may want to gather over a cord for extra reinforcement.

■ Adjust your overlock machine to the appropriate setting; see chart at right.

■ On some overlock machines, the foot has a hole in the front. If yours does, thread a strand of cord, pearl cotton, crochet cotton or topstitching thread through the hole. Work from the front, bringing the thread under the foot toward the back.

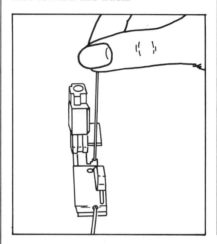

■ If your overlock does not have a hole in the front of the foot, guide the cord over the toe of the foot, over the finger guard and between the stitch fingers. Then bring the cord under the back of the foot.

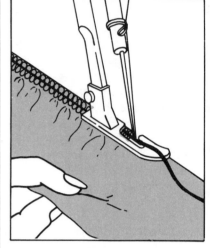

■ Place the fabric wrong side up and serge along the ⅝" (1.5cm) seamline. The stitches will form over the cord.

■ To create the gathers, hold the cord taut and slide the fabric along, as shown below.

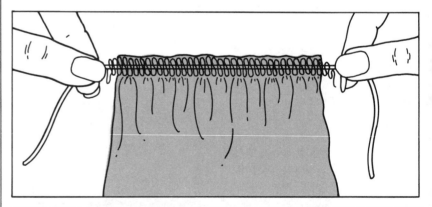

TYPE OF OVERLOCK STITCH:	3	4	MINE
Stitch Length:	2mm–3mm	2mm–3mm	
Stitch Width:	Widest	Widest	
Tensions—Needle	Normal	Normal	
Rt. Needle:	N/A	Normal	
U. Looper:	Normal	Normal	
L. Looper:	Normal	Normal	

HEMS

Hems can be done by hand or by machine. The choice is up to you. If you decide to hem by hand, the stitches should be invisible on the outside of the garment. If you decide to hem by machine, make sure your choice is visually compatible with the other design details on your garment. Occasionally, you might decide to forget about your needle and thread, and simply fuse the hem in place.

HEM BASICS

Regardless of which technique you choose, the basics of preparing the hem are almost the same. However, since some of these procedures may vary slightly depending on the type of hems, read through this section and decide on your technique before you begin. For hemming PLEATS, see page 176.

Marking

When your garment is at that "almost finished" stage, when there's not much left to do but sew on the buttons and put up the hem, it's a good idea to let it hang for 24 hours before you mark it. This gives the fabric grain time to "settle in." This rest period is particularly important for knit garments or for garments with a bias or circular hem. If you skip this step, your finished garment may develop mysterious hemline dips and sags after a couple of wearings.

Once your garment has rested, try it on. Wear suitable undergarments and, if possible, the shoes, belt, etc. that you plan to wear with it. These accessories will affect how the garment hangs, as well as influence the visual proportions. With them on, it will be easier to determine the most flattering hem length.

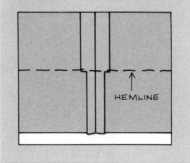

TIP *If your fabric is bulky, trim any seam allowances that intersect with the hem to ¼" (6mm) between the lower edge of the garment and the hemline.*

HEMLINE

The best—and easiest—way to mark a hemline evenly is to enlist the help of a friend. For even results, you stand in one spot, with your feet together; the friend moves around you, using a yardstick or pin-type skirt marker to establish the hem length. Pins

should be placed parallel to the floor about 2"–3" (5cm–7.5cm) apart.

Trimming

Take the garment off, turn it wrong side out and place it over the ironing board or on a table. Turn the hem up along the pin-marked line. Matching the seamlines first, insert pins at right angles to the hemline, through both layers of fabric, then remove the pins that indicate the hemline. Once the hem is pinned up, it's a good idea to try the garment on

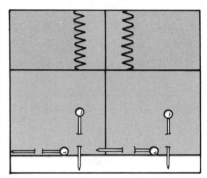

again to check the length and evenness.

Hand-baste the hem about ¼″ (6mm) from the folded edge, removing the pins as you go.
Note: If you're making a machine-rolled hem or a narrow top-stitched hem, you should skip this step.

Measure and mark the desired hem allowance plus ¼″ (6mm) extra for finishing. Trim away the

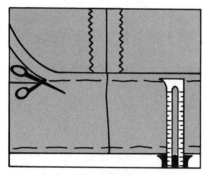

excess. The type of hem you choose, as well as the shape of the hemline, will determine the depth of the hem allowance. On a straight garment, the hem allowance should be no more than 3″ (7.5cm). On a A-line or flared garment, the hem allowance is usually between 1½″–2″ (3.8cm–5cm).

Press the hem. If necessary, put strips of brown paper or adding machine tape between the hem allowance and the garment to prevent ridges. Use a press cloth to protect your fabric.

Easing

If the garment edge is only slightly curved, the hem allowance will have extra fullness. Unless this fullness is eased so that the hem allowance lies flat against the garment, your finished hem will have ripples and ridges.

THE CONVENTIONAL METHOD:

Easing is done after the hem allowance is trimmed but before the raw edge is finished.

■ Ease-stitch ¼″ (6mm) from the edge, remembering to loosen the needle tension slightly.
■ Working on a flat surface, use a pin to draw up the bobbin thread wherever there is extra fullness.

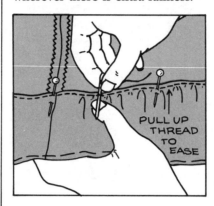

■ Steam-press to shrink out some of the fullness.

S THE OVERLOCK METHOD:

This technique can be used to ease the fullness on the hem allowance on shirttail hems, full, circular and A-line skirts.

■ Adjust your overlock machine to the appropriate setting; see chart below.
■ On the right side of the fabric, serge 3″–4″ (7.5cm–10cm) along the edge of the hem allowance. As you do, hold your forefinger behind the foot so that the fabric piles up. Release the fabric.
■ Repeat, serging all around the raw edge. The hem allowance will automatically roll toward the garment.
■ Steam-press to shrink out some of the fullness.

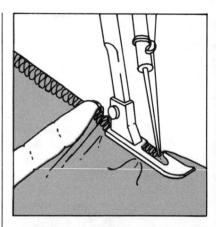

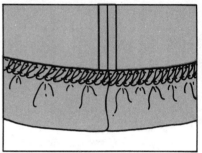

Note: Some fabrics may not ease up enough using this technique. For heavier fabrics, tighten the needle tension even more so that the fabric curls. This will enable you to adjust the gathers.

HAND-SEWN HEMS

Finishing the Edge

If your fabric doesn't ravel, you don't need to finish the edge. However, if a finish is necessary, the stitched-and-pinked, the zig-zag/overcast and the bound seam finishes described under SEAMS, page 99, are all excellent choices . . . or use the overlock technique on page 108.

TYPE OF OVERLOCK STITCH:	3	4	MINE
Stitch Length:	2mm–3mm	2mm–3mm	
Stitch Width:	Normal	Normal	
Tensions—Needle:	Tight	Tight	
Rt. Needle:	N/A	Tight	
U. Looper:	Normal	Normal	
L. Looper:	Normal	Normal	

Other good hem finishes include seam binding or stretch lace. Both these products are applied exactly the same way. However, seam binding is suitable for straight hems only. Stretch lace, because of its flexible properties, is a better choice for knits and for curved hems. To apply, lap the lace or binding ¼" (6mm) over the edge of the hem allowance and edgestitch it in place.

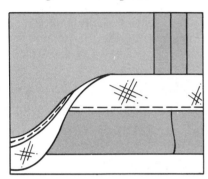

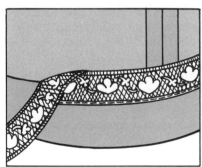

Sewing the Hem

Depending on your fabric, choose the **blindstitch**, the **catchstitch** or the **hemming stitch** (see HAND SEWING, p.119). Use a thread that is the same color or one shade darker than your fabric. (Thread looks lighter when sewn.) To make sure the finished hem is invisible, pick up only one or two garment threads with each stitch.

MACHINE-MADE HEMS

Hems done by machine are a quick and easy alternative to hand sewing. Just be sure the machine

---

> **TIP** *If your fabric is very bulky or if you're letting down a child's garment and you don't have enough fabric for a hem allowance, a faced hem is a good idea. Purchase packaged bias hem facing tape or make your own wide bias strips (see BINDINGS, page 133). Trim the hem allowance to ½" (1.3cm). With right sides together and raw edges even, pin the facing to the hem allowance, lapping the cut edges as shown. Stitch a ¼" (6mm) seam. Press the seam allowances toward the facing. Turn the hem up ¼" (6mm) below the facing seam. Sew the hem in place and slipstitch the ends of the facing closed.*

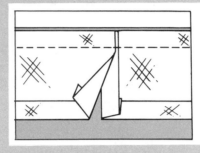
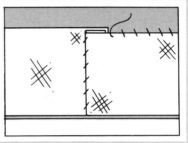

technique you choose is suitable for your fabric.

Machine Blindstitch

Many machines have a built-in stitch that can be used for straight or nearly straight hems on medium weight wovens or stable knits. It is particularly popular for children's playclothes and home decorating. Consult your sewing machine manual for details.

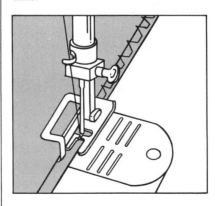

Narrow Topstitched Hem

This finish is suitable for sheer, lightweight or medium weight fabrics.

FOR KNITS: Press under along the hemline, then trim the hem allowance to ⅝" (1.5cm).

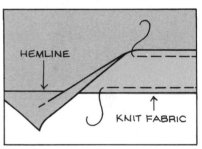

FOR WOVENS: Press under along the hemline, then trim the hem allowance to 1" (2.5cm). Fold the raw edge in to meet the first crease and press again.

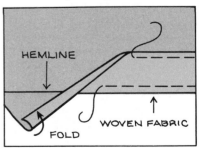

■ Working on the right side, topstitch close to the edge of the hem allowance.

■ If you wish, topstitch again, close to the edge of the garment.

Wide Topstitched Hem

This technique can be used on all fabrics and styles, except for very curved hems. If the hem is slightly curved, be sure to ease-stitch it before topstitching.

For the most attractive proportions, the hem allowance should be 1½"–2" (3.8cm–5cm) wide.

■ Press the hem up along the hemline. Ease in the fullness on any curves.

■ For woven fabrics only, press the raw edge under ½" (1.3cm). For knit fabrics, eliminate this step.

■ Working on the wrong side, stitch close to the edge of the hem allowance.

■ Stitch again, ¼" (6mm) away from the first row of stitching, within the hem allowance.

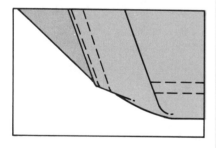

Machine-Rolled Hem

This is a quick and easy way to achieve the narrow rolled hem look that is particularly attractive on sheers, lightweight silk and synthetic fabrics, and for hemming ruffles.

Note: To do this hem, your garment must have at least a ⅝" (1.5cm) hem allowance.

■ Mark the hemline ⅛" (3mm) longer than desired. Fold the garment up along this hemline, then stitch as close as you can to, but not more than ⅛" (3mm) from,

the fold. DO NOT press before you stitch—if the hemline is not on straight grain, pressing first will distort the hem.

■ Using embroidery scissors, carefully trim away the hem allowance above the stitching.

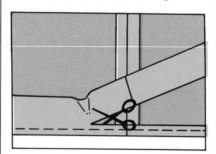

■ Fold the hem allowance up along the stitching line, rolling the stitching line just slightly to the inside of the garment; press.

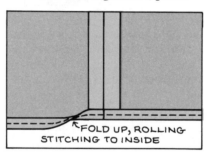

↖FOLD UP, ROLLING STITCHING TO INSIDE

■ Stitch again, close to the inner fold; press.

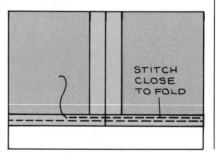

STITCH CLOSE TO FOLD

> **TIP** *When making the machine-rolled hem on sheers, use long basting stitches for the first row of stitching, then remove them when the hem is completed.*

HEMMING ON THE OVERLOCK

Your overlock machine provides you with an array of hemming techniques.

⑤ Overcasting

Serging is an easy way to finish the raw edges of your hem allowance.

■ Plan your hem allowance so there's at least ¹⁄₁₆" (2mm) extra that you can trim off as you serge. This ensures that your fabric "fills" the stitches and that, in time, the stitching won't pull away from the raw edge.

■ Adjust your overlock machine to the appropriate setting; see chart below.

■ Serge along the raw edge of the hem allowance.

■ Secure the thread chains.

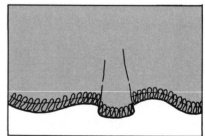

TYPE OF OVERLOCK STITCH:	2	3	4	MINE
Stitch Length:	2mm–3mm	2mm–3mm	2mm–3mm	
Stitch Width:	Normal	Normal	Normal	
Tensions—Needle:	Very Loose	Normal	Normal	
Rt. Needle:	N/A	N/A	Normal	
U. Looper	N/A	Normal	Normal	
L. Looper:	Normal	Normal	Normal	

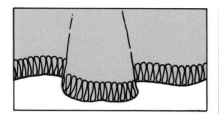

■ Complete your hem, folding up the hem allowance and using the appropriate hand stitches or top-stitching on the conventional machine.

> **TIP** *This same technique can be used to create a finished hem. Using topstitching thread in both the upper and lower loopers, serge along the hemline.*

S *Blind Hem*

Because the stitches will show a little bit on the outside of the garment, this type of hem is more appropriate for children's wear, casual garments and home decorating. The overlock machine finishes and secures the hem in one operation.

■ Adjust your overlock machine to the appropriate setting; see chart above, right.

■ Prepare the hem allowance as for a hand-sewn hem. Then fold the garment back ¼" (6mm) from the raw edge of the hem allowance. Baste or pin in place. Press.

■ Serge along the raw edge so that the needle just catches the fold of the fabric.

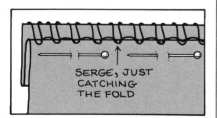

SERGE, JUST CATCHING THE FOLD

■ Remove the pins or the basting stitches. Open out the garment until the stitches lie flat, then

TYPE OF OVERLOCK STITCH:	3	4	MINE
Stitch Length:	Longest	Longest	
Stitch Width:	Widest	Widest	
Tensions—Needle:	Very Loose	Normal	
U. Looper:	N/A	Tight	
L. Looper:	Normal	Loose	

> **TIP** *A special blind hemming foot is available for some overlock machines. It helps you guide the fabric so that the stitches are almost invisible on the outside of the garment.*

press on the wrong side to set the stitches and ease out the fullness.

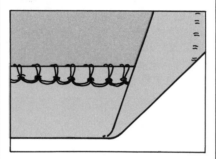

S *Rolled Hem*

The rolled hem, sometimes referred to as a handkerchief hem, is the beautiful and durable finish found on the edges of scarves, napkins, tablecloths and ruffles. Until you bought your overlock machine, there was almost no way you could duplicate the rolled hem at home.

The best fabric choices for a rolled hem are silk or polyester crepe de chine, georgette, lightweight tissue faille, and soft cottons. If you use a washable fabric,

you'll get better results if you preshrink it to remove any sizing.

What gives the hem its finished appearance is the overlock machine's ability to roll the fabric to the underside as the edge is stitched and finished. The thread you see in a rolled hem is the upper looper thread; the lower looper and needle threads are hidden inside the roll. As a first choice, use silk or woolly nylon thread in the upper looper. These threads have the stretch and recovery necessary to help the fabric roll, will lay smooth along the finished edge, and have a beautiful sheen. Use polyester overlock thread in the lower looper and the needle . . . and, if you can't find the right color silk or woolly nylon thread, in the upper looper as well.

■ To make a rolled hem, you should have at least a ½" (1.3cm) hem allowance.

■ Adjust the overlock machine to the appropriate setting; see chart below:

TYPE OF OVERLOCK STITCH	3	MINE
Stitch Length:	1mm	
Stitch Width:	2mm*	
Tensions—Needle:	Normal	
U. Looper:	Tight	
L. Looper:	Very Tight	

* Narrow the stitch width to 2mm or use the presser foot and needle plate especially designed for a rolled hem. Consult your overlock manual for specific information about your machine.

■ Place a test swatch, right side up, under the presser foot and serge. Fine-tune the tension settings until the hem rolls properly.

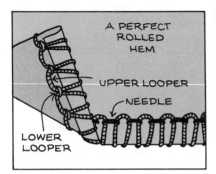

■ If the lower looper thread forms large loops on the underside, loosen the upper looper and tighten the lower looper.

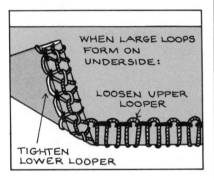

■ If the needle thread is visible on the underside, tighten the needle tension.

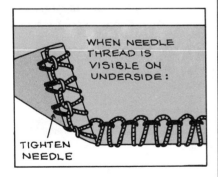

Lettuce Edge

This delicate edge finish works best on very stretchy knits, such

> **TIP** *If you can't get the proper look to the stitch, and your lower looper needs to be set higher than the tightest tension setting, wrap the thread around the tension dial twice. Just remember what you've done and rethread the lower looper before doing any regular serging.*

> **TIP** *When you record your overlock settings for a rolled hem, keep the information with a swatch of the fabric. Rolled hem settings often differ slightly from fabric to fabric.*

as interlocks, tricots and knit ribbing, that are cut and serged across the grain or "with the stretch." You can also achieve good results on lightweight wovens IF they are cut on the bias. The lettuce edge looks great on ruffles, lingerie hems, neck and sleeve ribbings.

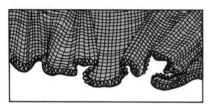

■ Use the same overlock settings as for a rolled hem. Test the settings on a swatch of fabric cut "with the stretch."

■ Place the fabric under the presser foot, right side up, ½" (1.3cm) from the raw edge. Begin serging so that the machine grabs the fabric for a couple of stitches.

■ Continue serging, holding the fabric firmly in front of the foot, so that it's stretched before it's serged. The finished edge will curl just like the edge of a lettuce leaf.

Note: If your knit runs, don't stretch the fabric before you serge. Instead, stretch it after the serging is finished.

Picot (Shell) Hem and Narrow Hem

When you want a softer treatment than a rolled hem, the picot hem and the narrow hem are both ways to edge silks, crepe de chines and soft, scarflike fabrics.

PICOT HEM:

For best results, use polyester overlock thread.

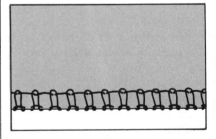

■ Adjust your overlock for the appropriate setting; see chart below.

TYPE OF OVERLOCK STITCH	3	MINE
Stitch Length:	3mm–4mm	
Stitch Width:	Narrowest	
Tensions—Needle:	Normal	
U. Looper:	Tight	
L. Looper:	Very Tight	

TYPE OF OVERLOCK STITCH:	3	MINE
Stitch Length:	1mm–2mm	
Stitch Width:	Narrowest	
Tensions—Needle:	Normal	
Rt. Needle:	N/A	
U. Looper:	Normal	
L. Looper:	Normal	

NARROW HEM:

■ Adjust your overlock for the appropriate setting; see chart above.

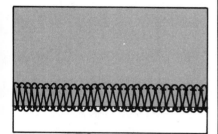

For both hems, set your serger as described above and follow the instructions for the rolled hem. The picot or shell hem is a scalloped, decorative application that's beautiful on lingerie, where a soft hem finish is required. Because the narrow hem is flat, rather than rolled, it's better for heavier fabrics.

FUSED HEMS

This no-sew method of hemming is suitable for all but very sheer or lightweight fabrics. Use packaged strips of fusible web or cut your own from web purchased by the yard.

The strip of web should be narrower than your hem allowance. Sandwich the strip between the hem allowance and the garment, just below the finished edge. Fuse in place following the manufacturer's directions.

To make sure that no ridges appear on the right side of your garment, test the fusible web on scraps first. If ridges show, pink

the edges of the web before applying and try not to rest the iron on the finished edge of the hem allowance.

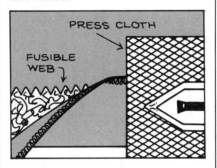

ALTERING A HEMLINE

Fashions change, children grow . . . and hemlines need to be altered.

Shortening a hem is no problem. Just remove the old stitches and proceed as if you were hemming the garment for the first time.

Lengthening can create a few problems.

■ If you don't have a deep enough hem allowance once you let the garment down, add seam binding or stretch lace, or make a faced hem as described earlier in this section.

■ If a good steam pressing doesn't remove the old crease,

make a solution of equal parts of white vinegar and water. Apply it along the crease line using a small brush or an eye dropper, then press. To be sure the vinegar won't affect the color of the garment, test this technique first on an inside seam allowance.

■ If the crease still remains or the color has faded along the former hemline, consider covering the mark with a trim that is compatible with your garment. On children's garments, you might want to forego the vinegar treatment altogether and add some colorful trim.

INTERFACING

Interfacing is an extra layer of fabric that provides shape and support in detail areas of the garment. Interfacing is frequently used in collars, cuffs, lapels, necklines, pockets, waistbands, and opening edges.

TYPES OF INTERFACING

The two basic types of interfacings are sew-in and fusible. Both are available in woven, knitted and nonwoven versions, and in a variety of weights, ranging from heavy to sheer weight. In addition to these specially developed interfacing fabrics, batiste, organza and organdy can be used as interfacings on sheer to light weight fabrics.

The rule of thumb is that the interfacing should always be slightly lighter in weight than the fashion fabric.

TIP *Don't buy exactly the amount of interfacing the pattern calls for. Buy several yards. That way, you can experiment with it on other fabrics. To keep your stash of interfacing neat, store the leftovers in a Ziploc® plastic bag. If it's a fusible, be sure to keep a copy of the fusing directions with the interfacing.*

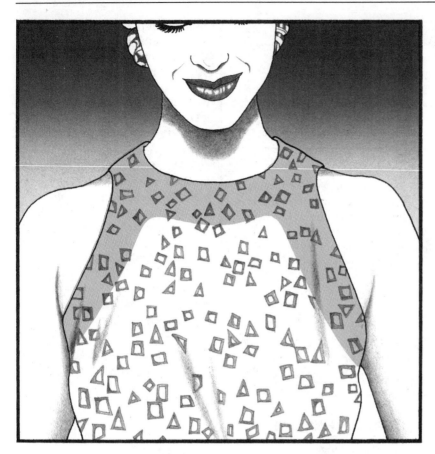

Choosing between a fusible or a sew-in interfacing is really a matter of personal preference. In general, fusibles provide slightly crisper results. Because fusibles "set" the yarns, they're an excellent choice for fabrics that fray. However, some fabrics do not react well to fusibles. These include metallics, beaded, sequinned or re-embroidered fabrics, rayon and acetate velvets, most brocades, fake furs, leather, vinyl and openwork fabrics, such as lace and mesh. ALWAYS test the fusible interfacing on a scrap of the fashion fabric before you begin to be sure it works and that you like the results. Use the chart opposite to match fabric type with suggested interfacings.

Most people think of fusibles as easier to use and they are—as long as you take the time to follow the manufacturer's fusing directions carefully. The key to suc-

cessful results is the prescribed combination of heat, steam and pressure. In addition, even if the directions do not suggest it, take the time to go through the entire fusing process twice, first on the wrong side, then on the right side of the garment section. This extra step will ensure a strong, even bond.

WHERE TO INTERFACE

Your pattern will tell you which pieces require interfacing and the back of your pattern envelope will tell you how much to buy. If you want to add it to certain areas of your garment, even if the pattern doesn't suggest it, go right ahead. For example, you might want to add a little bit of crispness to a patch pocket.

Don't think that you have to use the same weight interfacing throughout the entire garment.

For example, you might decide that the collar should have softer shaping than the cuffs. If you find this confusing, take a look at some of the better ready-to-wear garments. Note how some detail areas in the same garment feel crisper than others. You can certainly reproduce this concept in the garments you sew.

Interfacing is usually applied to the wrong side of what will ultimately be the outermost layer of fabric—for example, to the upper collar rather than the undercollar, to the cuff rather than to the cuff facing. Since there are exceptions, be sure to follow your pattern instructions.

CUTTING AND MARKING

Woven and knitted interfacings have lengthwise, crosswise and bias grains. The interfacing pieces should be cut out so that the pieces are on-grain as indicated in the pattern layouts.

Technically, nonwoven interfacings do not have a grain. However, this doesn't mean that you can cut out your pieces any old way. Some of these interfacings are stable in all directions, others stretch in the crosswise direction, and still others are all-bias. Read the instructions that come with the interfacing and follow their recommendations for how to place the pattern pieces.

Transfer the pattern markings to the interfacing sections, rather than to the fabric. Buttonhole markings are the exception to this rule. That's because you must be able to see them on the outside of your almost-finished garment.

APPLICATION

Sew-in type: To minimize bulk, trim the outside corners of the interfacing diagonally, just inside

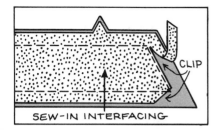

SEW-IN INTERFACING

the point where the seamlines meet. Then pin- or glue-baste the interfacing to the wrong side of the garment section, and machine-baste ½" (1.3cm) from the edges. Trim the interfacing seam allowances close to the stitching and trim off any hem allowances.

Fusible type: Trim the corners diagonally, the same way as for sew-in interfacings and trim off

TIP *Sometimes one edge of the interfacing does not extend all the way to a seamline, for example, on a collarless neckline or on the front of a jacket. With a fusible interfacing, a ridge may be visible on the outside of the garment. To find out, test-fuse a piece of the interfacing to a scrap of the fashion fabric. If a ridge forms, try cutting the edge of the interfacing with pinking shears. If this doesn't help, apply the interfacing to the facing rather than to the body of the garment.*

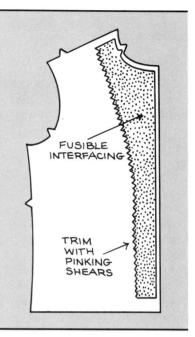

FUSIBLE INTERFACING

TRIM WITH PINKING SHEARS

FABRIC AND USE	INTERFACING	
	For a soft effect	**For a crisp effect**
Very light to lightweight fabrics (voile, gauze, crepe, challis, calico, chambray, interlock knit, jersey, single knit, batiste) Blouses, shirts and dresses	Bastiste; Organza; Sew-in sheer, regular, or stretch very lightweight nonwoven: self fabric	Organdy; Sew-in or fusible lightweight or sheer (nonwoven or woven); Fusible knit
	Do not use fusibles on chiffon or seersucker	
Medium weight fabrics (linen, denim, poplin, flannel, gabardine, satin, duck, chino, velour, stretch terry, double knit, sweater knit)	Sew-in or fusible medium weight woven; Regular or stretch light to medium weight nonwoven; Fusible knit	Sew-in or fusible lightweight hair canvas; Sew-in or fusible medium weight (woven or nonwoven)
Dresses, lightweight suits, active sportswear	Do not use fusibles on rainwear fabrics	
Heavyweight fabrics (corduroy, tweed, worsted, camel hair, melton, sailcloth, canvas, gabardine, coatings) Jackets, suits, coats	Soft, lightweight canvas; Sew-in or fusible medium weight nonwoven	Sew-in or fusible medium weight woven; Crisp medium or heavyweight hair canvas; Fusible heavyweight nonwoven
Leather types (Suede, suede cloth) Do not use fusibles on real leather	Crisp or soft canvas; Fusible or sew-in medium weight nonwoven or woven	
Waistbands	Fusible nonwoven precut strips; Woven stiffener sold by the width; Sew-in or fusible medium to heavyweight (woven or nonwoven)	
Crafts (belts, hats, bags, camping gear, home decorating items)	Sew-in nonwovens in all weights; Fusible medium to heavyweight (woven or nonwoven)	

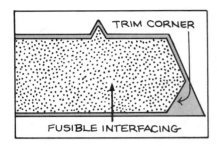

any hem alllowances. Most sewing books will also tell you to trim ½″ (1.3cm) from the seam allowances to reduce bulk. However, on all but the heaviest fabrics, you can eliminate this step. It's just too difficult to get the interfacing positioned correctly on the garment section once it's trimmed. Besides that, the amount of bulk it adds is minimal. Fuse the interfacing in place, following the manufacturer's directions.

SPECIALTY INTERFACINGS

Specialty interfacings have been developed for detail areas, such as waistbands, collars, cuffs and plackets. Many of these are precut into the most common widths. For example, waistband interfacing is available to create 1″ (2.5cm), 1¼″ (3.2cm), 1½″ (3.8cm) and 2″ (5cm) wide waistbands. Some of these interfacings are particularly easy to use because they're perforated to indicate seamlines and foldlines.

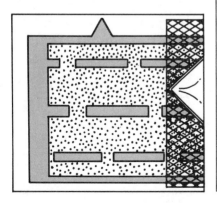

MITERING

Mitering—creating a corner by joining a vertical and a horizontal edge—is one technique that pattern instructions usually assume everyone knows how to do. However, doing it is one thing . . . doing it so that the corners come out crisp and square is quite another.

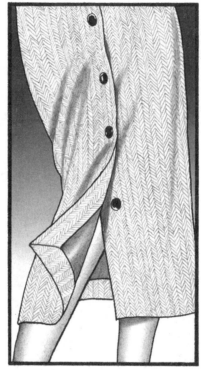

Knowing how to make a professional-looking miter comes in handy when you're turning under a corner in places like a patch pocket (a folded miter), the hem/facing edge of a skirt slit (a stitched miter), or when you're applying trim.

Bindings, because they encase the edge of the fabric, require slightly different techniques for mitering. For more information, see BINDINGS, specifically pages 134–136.

FOLDED MITER

This method works on patch pockets and slit hems.

■ Stitch along the pocket seamlines; then press the seam allowances to the inside along the stitching.

■ Open out the seam allowances at the corners. Fold the corner up diagonally and press, then trim this seam allowance to ¼″ (6mm).

■ Fold all the seam allowances back to the inside. The folded edges will just meet, forming a neat corner.

■ To make sure the corners stay neat as you edgestitch or topstitch the pocket to the garment, slipstitch the edges together, or secure them with glue stick or fusible web. If your folded miter is at the corner of a hem, use slipstitching.

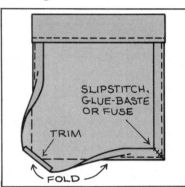

STITCHED MITER

This method is most frequently used at the corner of a turned-up hem.

■ Turn the garment edges to the inside along the seamlines or foldlines; press.

■ Open out the pressed edges. Fold the corner diagonally across

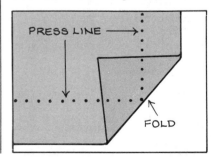

the point so that the pressed lines meet; press.

■ Open out the corner and, with right sides together, fold the garment diagonally through the corner so that creases meet, as shown. Stitch on the diagonal crease line. Trim the corner seam allowance, trimming diagonally at the point.

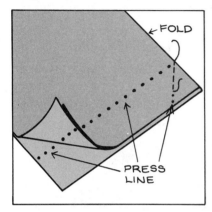

■ Press the corner seam open.

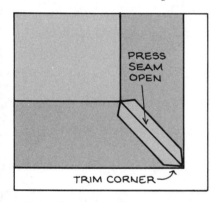

■ Turn the seam allowances or hem and facing to the inside and press.

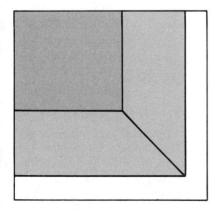

FLAT TRIMS

Flat trims require mitering any time they turn a corner. No matter where the trim is positioned on the garment, the technique is the same. It's the style of the trim—i.e., whether it has two straight edges or one straight edge and one decorative edge—that determines the mitering technique.

If you're applying the trim any place except along the edge of the garment, mark the trim placement line so that it is visible on the outside of the garment. Use a disappearing marking pen, disappearing tracing paper or a line of machine basting—whichever is appropriate for your fabric.

For Trims With Two Straight Edges

Note: With this technique, the right edge of the trim is aligned with the garment edge or the placement line.

■ Pin the trim to the garment edge or along the placement line. Topstitch both edges, ending the stitching when you reach the corner.

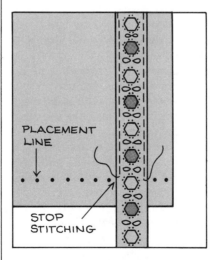

■ Fold the trim back up on itself and press. Then fold the trim diagonally so that it meets the in-

tersecting garment edge or placement line; press again.

■ Refold the trim back up on itself and stitch along the diagonal crease through all the layers.

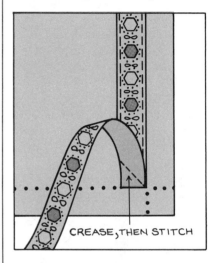

■ Fold the trim back down along the diagonal line of stitching and press. Then continue topstitching along both edges of the trim.

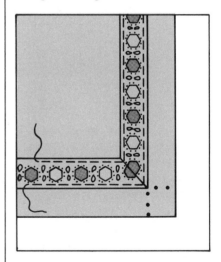

For Trims With One Straight Edge and One Decorative Edge

Note: With this technique, the left (straight) edge of the trim is aligned with the garment edge or placement line.

■ Pin the straight edge of the trim to the garment edge or along the placement line. Topstitch all the way to the corner.

■ Working at your ironing board, fold the trim back up on itself, positioning the fold slightly below the garment edge or placement line. Then fold the trim back down so that it meets the intersecting garment edge or placement line. Secure the trim to your ironing board with a few straight pins; press the corner.

Note: You may have to refold the trim several times until you get it "just right" and are ready to press.

■ Open out the trim and stitch along the diagonal crease through all layers.

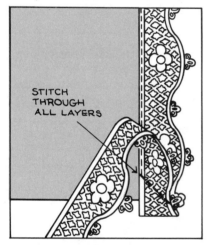

STITCH THROUGH ALL LAYERS

■ Fold the trim back down, press again, and continue stitching the trim to the garment.

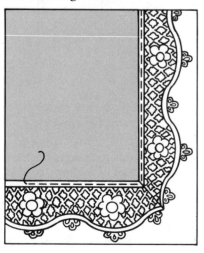

PLEATS

Pleats are folds of fabric that control fullness. They can be soft or crisp, depending on the fabric you choose and whether they're pressed or unpressed.

If you're new to sewing, or your sewing skills are rusty, wait until you've got a little more experience at your machine before you attempt pleats. It's not that pleats are difficult to sew, but they do require accurate cutting, marking and stitching . . . perhaps even more than most other details. Think about it: Pleats usually occur in multiples. Suppose you were making a pleated skirt with eight box pleats. If you were "off" ⅛" (3mm) on each pleat, the skirt would be 1" (2.5cm) too large at the waistline.

Pleats can be formed by working on either the right or the wrong side of a garment. Your pattern instructions will tell you what to do. Mark the pleats on the wrong side of the fabric; then transfer the markings to the right side, if necessary. Mark both the foldlines and the placement lines. If you're using tracing paper or basting, use a different color paper or thread so you can quickly distinguish between the two types of lines.

BASIC PLEAT FORMATIONS

Knife or Straight Pleats

These pleats all face in the same direction. To make them, fold the fabric on the solid line and bring the fold to the broken line, following the arrows printed on the

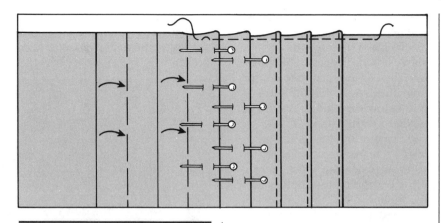

pattern piece. Hand-baste or pin the pleats along the folded edges; then baste across the top of all the pleats. If the pleats are to be pressed, do it before the pleated section is attached to the rest of the garment.

Box Pleats

Each pleat consists of two straight pleats facing in opposite direc-

tions. Following your pattern instructions, fold, baste and press as for straight pleats.

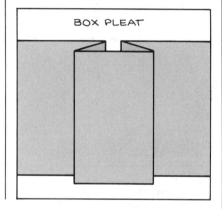

BOX PLEAT

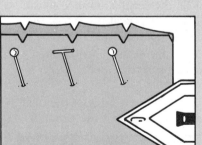

Inverted Pleats

Often used at center front or back, an inverted pleat looks like two straight pleats that face each other, with their folds meeting at the center. Inverted pleats have a pleat underlay. It can be a separate underlay section that is seamed to the garment or it can be formed by basting, then folding and pressing the garment section itself. Your pattern instructions will tell you how to do this.

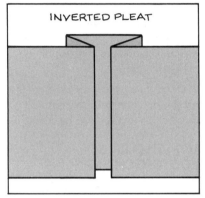

INVERTED PLEAT

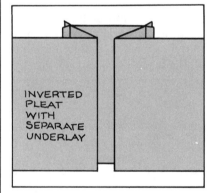

INVERTED PLEAT WITH SEPARATE UNDERLAY

PRESSING

The best-looking pleats are those that have been carefully—and properly—pressed.

Once the pleats are formed, you'll be pressing over several thicknesses of fabric. Since you don't want these layers to create ridges on the outside of your garment, here are a few suggestions:

■ Always use a press cloth. If you haven't got one, use a scrap of your fashion fabric instead.

■ Put strips of brown paper between the garment and the unbasted fold of each pleat.

For Soft (Unpressed) Pleats:
Use a dry press cloth. Hold the iron 2″–3″ (5cm–7.5cm) above the fabric and apply just a little bit of steam. Don't rest the iron directly on the fabric.

For Crisp (Pressed) Pleats:
Use a damp press cloth, lots of steam and the full pressure of your iron. Since the garment still has to be hemmed, press lightly when you get to within 8″ (20.5cm) of the hemline. Once the hem is put in, thoroughly re-press this area.

■ Once you have pressed the pleats, be sure your garment is thoroughly dry before handling it.

TOPSTITCHING/ EDGESTITCHING

Pleats are often topstitched and/or edgestitched to hold them in place. The topstitching, which starts at the waistline and extends into the hip area, is done through all the layers.

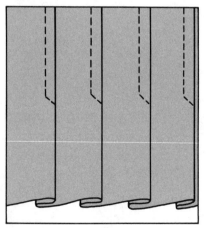

If the fabric does not hold a crease well, it's also a good idea to edgestitch below the hip, catching only the fold of the pleat in your stitching. Do this, too, if you're going to wash your garment, rather than have it dry-cleaned—the pleats will be much easier to re-press if they're edge-stitched.

To make the topstitching above and the edgestitching below the hip look like one continuous line, edgestitch the pleat fold below the hipline first. Edgestitch to within about 8″ (20.5cm) of the hemline. Then, starting at the waistline edge, topstitch between the waist and the hip, overlapping the stitches at the hipline. Once the garment is hemmed, go back and complete the edgestitching.

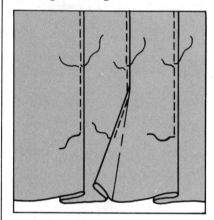

HEMMING

If a seam falls at the inside fold of a pleat, you'll need to perform a little magic with your scissors to make sure everything lies flat.

■ Clip the seam allowance to the line of stitching at the top of the hem allowance.

■ Press the seams open below the clip and trim them to ¼″ (6mm).

■ Finish the raw edge of the hem allowance and hem the garment.

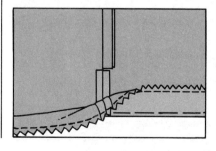

■ Working on the inside of the garment, edgestitch the pleat fold within the hem allowance to keep it flat.

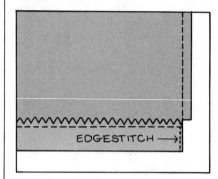

EDGESTITCH →

Once your garment is hemmed, you'll need to go back and repress the lower edges of the pleats.

POCKETS

Pockets should be more than just an attractive design feature. In order to be functional they should be constructed so that they can withstand the wear and tear of frequent use!

PATCH POCKETS

Patch pockets come in an assortment of sizes and shapes, creating design interest on skirts, blouses, pants and jackets. Patch pockets can be lined, unlined or self-lined. Although your pattern will include only one of these techniques, you can easily convert any patch pocket to the treatment you prefer.

Unlined Pockets

Unlined pockets are the easiest to make. They're particularly popular on casual clothes and children's garments in light to medium weight fabrics.

To create the facing:

■ Press under ¼″ (6mm) on the upper edge of the pocket and edge-

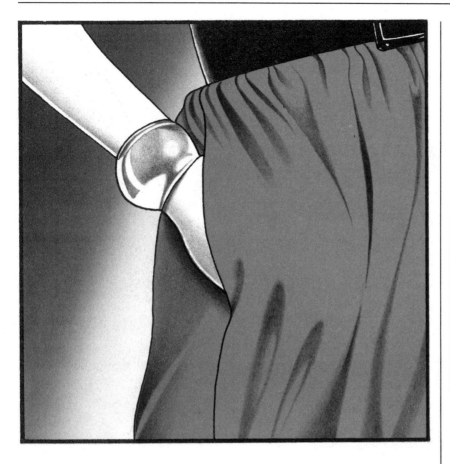

■ Turn the facing to the wrong side pushing the upper corners out with a pin or a point turner.

■ Pull up the gathering threads to shape the curve; then press under along the seamline, rolling the stitching to the wrong side. Press the facing seams and the fold.

■ To eliminate bulk, notch out the fullness in the seam allowance at the curves as far as the machine-basting stitches.

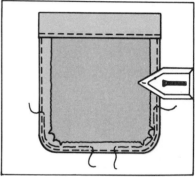

S *For a curved patch pocket on your overlock machine:*

■ Adjust your overlock to the appropriate setting; see chart below.

■ Working on the right side of the pocket, serge around the

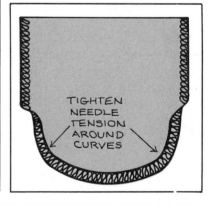

stitch . . . or finish the upper edge on your overlock machine.

■ To create the pocket facing, fold the upper edge to the right side along the foldline; press.

■ Starting at the fold, stitch along the seamline, backstitching at the beginning and the end.

■ Trim the seam allowances in the facing area only to ¼" (6mm). If your fabric is bulky, diagonally trim the corners.

How you complete the patch pocket depends on how it is shaped.

For a curved patch pocket on your conventional machine:

■ Make a row of machine gathering stitches around the curved edges. Put them ¼" (6mm) away from the first stitching, within the seam allowance.

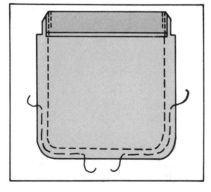

■ If you own a point presser, use it when pressing the seams open in the facing area.

TYPE OF OVERLOCK STITCH:	3	4	MINE
Stitch Length:	3mm	3mm	
Stitch Width:	Widest	Widest	
Tensions—Needle:	Normal to Very Tight	Normal to Tight	
Rt. Needle:	N/A	Very Tight	
U. Looper:	Slightly Tight	Slightly Tight	
L. Looper:	Slightly Loose	Slightly Loose	

pocket on the ⅝″ (1.5cm) seam-line, tightening the needle tension when you reach the curved areas. This will make the seam allowances curl to the inside, easing in the fullness. When you are past the curved area, loosen your needle tension to the normal setting.

■ Press the seam allowances to the wrong side along the stitching line.

For a square or rectangular pocket, miter the lower corners, as described in MITERING, page 174.

To finish the patch pocket:

■ Edgestitch or topstitch the facing in place OR secure it to the pocket with a strip of fusible web.

> **TIP** *Interface the pocket with a lightweight fusible interfacing. Cut the interfacing from the pocket pattern piece, eliminating the seam allowances and the facing. This will provide you with an accurate guide for shaping the curves or mitering the corners. In addition, it will help the finished pocket retain its shape.*

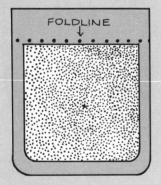

Lined Pockets

There are times when a pocket lining makes a nice finish. You can add this touch even if your pattern doesn't include it.

■ Once the pocket is cut out, fold the pocket pattern piece along the foldline to omit the facing. Use this new shape to cut the lining.

■ Fold under along the upper edge of the lining. The width of this fold should be equal to half the depth of the original pocket facing. Press.

■ With right sides together, pin the lining to the pocket, matching sides and lower edge. Turn the pocket facing down over the lining so that all the raw edges match; pin.

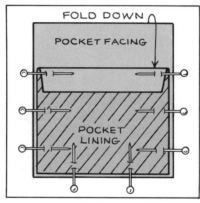

■ Starting at the fold, stitch along the seamline, backstitching at the ends.

■ Trim the seam allowances and corners; notch any curves.

■ Press the lining seam allowance toward the lining.

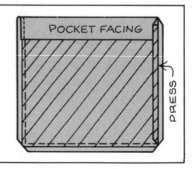

■ Turn the pocket right side out and press, rolling the seam slightly to the lining side.

■ Slipstitch the opening in the lining to the facing.

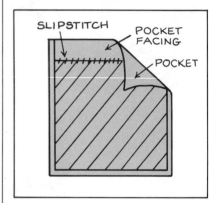

Self-lined Pockets

This super-simple way to line a pocket works best on lightweight fabrics. If your pattern does not utilize this technique, you can easily convert it.

■ When you cut out your pocket, place the pattern piece so that the foldline is on a crosswise fold of the fabric. (The facing part of the pattern will extend beyond the fold and will not be cut.)

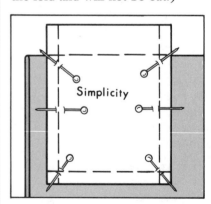

■ To make the pocket, fold it in half with right sides together.

> **TIP** *Trim ⅛″ (3mm) off the sides and lower edge of the pocket lining. Pin the lining to the pocket, matching the raw edges, and proceed as described above. The smaller lining will automatically cause the seams to roll slightly to the inside.*

Stitch, trim, clip and notch as for the lined pocket.

■ Press one seam allowance toward whichever side you wish to designate as the pocket facing.

■ Cut a 1½″ (3.8cm) slash near the lower edge of the pocket facing.

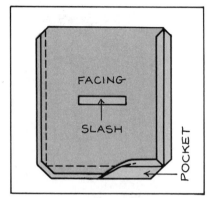

■ Turn the pocket right side out through the slash. Press, rolling the seam toward the pocket facing.

■ Fuse a strip of interfacing or mending tape over the slash.

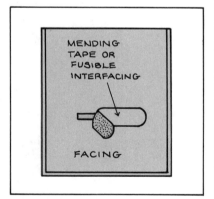

Applying the Pocket

The easiest way to apply the pocket is to topstitch or edgestitch it to the garment.

■ Pin or baste the pocket in place. Glue stick or double-faced basting tape work well.

■ Edgestitch and/or topstitch ¼″–⅜″ (6mm–1cm) from the edge.

TIP *On delicate or hard-to-handle fabrics, such as velvet, it is easier to apply the pocket by hand. To do this, pin or hand-baste the pocket in place. Turn back the pocket edge slightly and slipstitch it to the garment. To secure, take several small stitches at the upper corners of the pocket.*

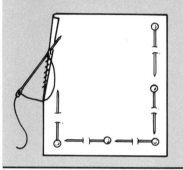

■ To reinforce the upper corners, backstitch or stitch a small triangle.

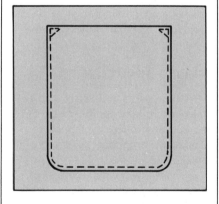

IN-SEAM POCKETS

In-seam pockets can be found at the side seams of dresses, skirts and pants. Often these pockets are created from a separate pattern piece so that the pocket can, if you wish, be cut from a lining fabric.

THE CONVENTIONAL METHOD:

Your pattern instructions will tell you how to make this type of

pocket. There are two important things to remember:

■ Reinforce the corners by shortening your stitch length for about 1″ (2.5cm) on either side of each corner.

■ Clip the garment/pocket back seam allowance ONLY so that you can press the side seams open and the pocket toward the front of the garment.

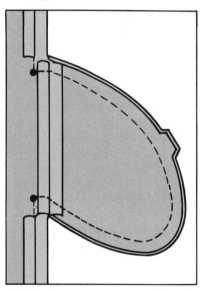

S THE OVERLOCK METHOD:

Use this technique for in-seam pockets on a skirt or pants.

■ If the pockets are separate sections, serge them to the garment front and back along the seamline.

■ With right sides together, pin the pocket/garment sections to-

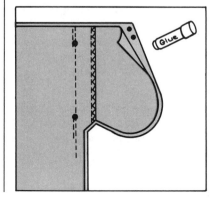

gether at the side seams. On your conventional machine, and beginning at the waistline edge, stitch along the side seam to the first marking; backstitch. Machine-baste to just below the next marking. Switch back to a regulation stitch, backstitch to the marking, then stitch forward for about 3"–4" (7.5cm–10cm).

■ Machine-baste or glue-baste the pocket sections together along the outside edges.

■ Serge the side seams, beginning at the hemline. This is important! If you begin serging from the waistline, it is very difficult to serge around the lower edge of the pocket without cutting into the garment.

■ As you approach the lower edge of the pocket, pull the pocket forward with your right hand to form as straight a line as possible. At the same time, use your left hand to guide the stitches around the curve so they remain on the garment.

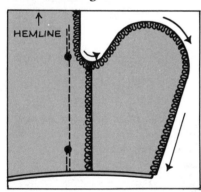

■ Press the pocket toward the center front, then remove the basting stitches from between the markings.

CUT-IN-ONE POCKETS

Some patterns have the pocket shape built into the front and back pattern pieces. This saves time because you don't have to cut out the pockets separately or stitch them to the garment. If your pattern wasn't de-

signed this way, you can use this method as long as your fabric is wide enough.

■ Lap the pocket pattern piece over the garment front pattern piece, matching the seamlines and markings. Pin or tape together. Repeat for the garment back.

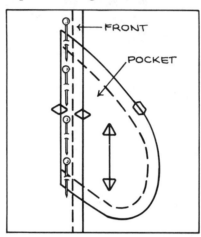

■ Cut out the front and back garment sections.

■ Sew the garment together on either your conventional or your overlock machine, following the guidelines for in-seam pockets.

FRONT HIP POCKETS

Many pants and skirts feature partially hidden hipline pockets, sometimes called slant pockets. The slanted opening may be straight or curved.

Front hip pockets consist of two different-shaped pieces—the pocket, which also becomes part of the main section of the garment at the waistline, and the pocket facing, which finishes the opening edge.

If your pattern features this style of pocket, the pattern in-

structions will tell you how to construct it. However, there are a few extra things you might want to do, depending on your fabric:

■ If your fashion fabric is heavy or bulky, cut the pocket facing from lightweight lining fabric in a matching color.

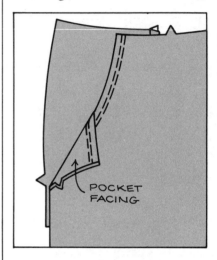

■ If your fabric is very stretchy or very delicate—or if the pocket is going to get lots of use—you

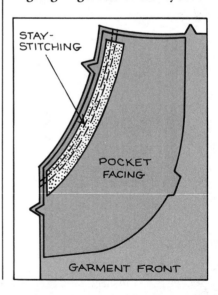

TIP *On a front hip pocket with a straight edge, use a perforated fusible interfacing that is specially designed for facings. Working on the wrong side of the garment, place the interfacing along the opening edge, aligning the perforations with the ⅝" (1.5cm) seamline, and fuse in place.*

might want to reinforce it against the wear and tear it will endure. Cut a strip of interfacing 2″ (5cm) wide and shaped to follow the opening edge of the pocket. Baste or fuse it along the opening edge of the pocket.

S **TIP** *Regardless of your choice of fabric, a front hip pocket will retain its shape better if the opening edge has a pocket stay. If you use your overlock to create the stay, you'll also eliminate the need to interface the edge of the opening:*

■ *With right sides together, pin the pocket facing to the garment front along the pocket opening.*

■ *Serge the seam. As you do this, thread pearl cotton through the hole in the front of your presser foot or guide it over the finger guard of the presser foot so that it's caught in the stitching and acts as a stay in the seam. This technique is the same as the one used for gathering over a cord on page 163.*

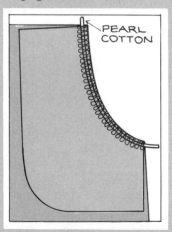

PEARL COTTON

■ *In place of the pearl cotton, you can also feed twill tape under the presser foot as you serge.*

RUFFLES

The two most common types of ruffles are single ruffles and double ruffles.

Single ruffles have one hemmed edge; the other edge is gathered, then incorporated into a seam or attached to an edge.

Double ruffles have two hemmed edges. The gathers can be placed along the center of the ruffle or near one edge. Then the ruffle is topstitched in place on the garment.

HEMMING

Since ruffles are usually made from very long strips of fabric,

you'll want to use a hemming method that's fast and easy. The **narrow topstitched** hem, the **machine-rolled** hem on your conventional machine, or the **rolled** hem or **lettuce edge** hem on your overlock machine are all particularly good choices. See pages 167–170 for information on how to do these hems.

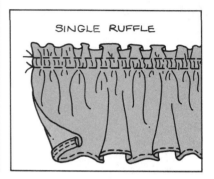

SINGLE RUFFLE

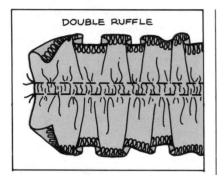

DOUBLE RUFFLE

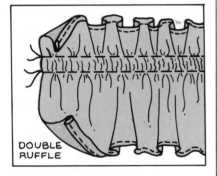

DOUBLE RUFFLE

GATHERING

Hem the ruffle first, then gather it. Gathers in ruffles are handled the same way as gathers in any other part of a garment. (See GATHERS, page 162, for how tos.) For double ruffles, put the gathering stitches along the lines indicated on your pattern pieces.

If you're making a double ruffle, DO NOT use the technique for gathering over a cord. If you do, those zigzag stitches will be visible on the outside of your garment.

ATTACHING THE RUFFLE

A Single Ruffle in a Seam:

■ With right sides together, pin the ruffle to one garment edge, matching notches and markings. Adjust the gathers and machine-baste in place.

■ With right sides together, pin the ruffled section to the remaining garment section. With

the ruffled section on top, stitch along the seamline, just to the left of the basting.

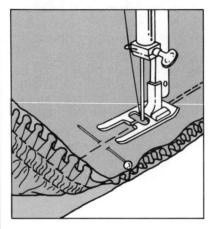

■ Press the seam allowances flat, then press them in the direction indicated on the pattern instructions.

A Single Ruffle at an Edge:

If you're customizing your pattern by adding a ruffle, begin by trimming the garment hem allowance to ⅝″ (1.5cm).

THE CONVENTIONAL METHOD:

■ Press under along the hemline or seamline.

■ Working with right sides up, lap the pressed edge of the garment over the raw edge of the ruffle so that the raw edges meet underneath. Pin, adjusting the gathers to fit and allowing for extra fullness if you're going around any corners.

■ Edgestitch close to the fold through all layers.

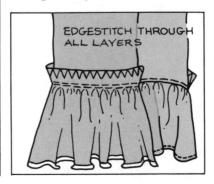

EDGESTITCH THROUGH ALL LAYERS

■ Finish the raw edges of the ruffle by zigzagging, machine overcasting or serging the edges together.

S THE OVERLOCK METHOD:

■ With right sides together, pin the ruffle to the garment edge, adjusting the gathers to fit.

■ Serge the seam, then press the seam allowances toward the garment.

■ Working on the right side, and using your conventional machine, edgestitch close to the seamline, through all the layers.

EDGESTITCH THROUGH ALL LAYERS

Double Ruffle:

■ Pin the wrong side of the ruffle to the right side of the garment,

TIP *If you're making a single ruffle from a lightweight fabric, you can eliminate the need to do any hemming. Cut the strips TWICE the desired depth, plus 1¼″ (3.2cm). Fold the strip in half lengthwise with wrong sides together and gather the raw edges with two rows of stitches.*

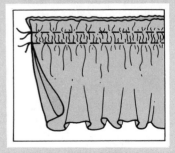

matching all markings. Adjust the gathers to fit.

■ Topstitch over the gathering stitches.

■ Remove the gathering stitches or hide them with a trim, such as ribbon or rickrack.

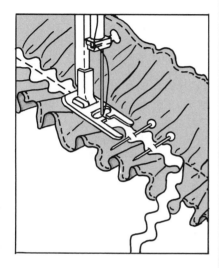

ADDING YOUR OWN RUFFLES

You can add ruffles to your garment even if the pattern does not include them.

Ruffles can be cut on the straight grain or the bias. If the ruffle is very long, you'll probably have to piece it.

As a rule of thumb, the ruffle section should be two to three times the length of the area to which it will be attached. In general, the wider the ruffle or the more sheer the fabric, the fuller the ruffle should be. Cut your ruffle the desired finished width,

> **TIP** *Adding a single ruffle to the bem edge is a good way to lengthen a child's dress, particularly when there isn't enough bem allowance to let down. If the old bemline leaves permanent marks, cover it with ribbon or trim.*

> **TIP** *Use ribbon as a substitute for ruffles. Because the long edges are already finished, there's no need to finish the bem. For best results, the ribbon must be at least 1½" (3.8cm) wide.*

plus 1¼ (3.2cm) for hem allowances and seam allowances.

SHOULDER PADS

Shoulder pads are an integral part of today's fashion silhouette. In addition to enhancing the fashion look, shoulder pads can be a quick and easy way to enhance the fit of a garment.

Narrow or Hollow Shoulders: Shoulder pads can fill the natural hollow that occurs just below the shoulder. They can also add width to narrow shoulders.

Uneven Shoulders: This is a common fitting problem that's easily corrected with different-size shoulder pads. The shoulder that's lower gets the thicker pad. Don't try to get away with just one pad for the lower shoulder. The result will be a bumpy, lop-sided appearance.

NARROW SHOULDERS

BEFORE

AFTER

UNEVEN SHOULDERS

BEFORE

AFTER

LARGE BUST

BEFORE

AFTER

Large Bust: Try adding small shoulder pads to your garments. By adding balance to the upper body, shoulder pads can minimize the appearance of a large bust.

WHICH PAD FOR WHICH SLEEVE?

Shoulder pads are available in the traditional style for set-in sleeves, as well as in an extended shoulder style for kimono or raglan sleeves or dropped shoulders.

The type of garment you're making determines the size pad you'll need:

■ Use ¼″–½″ (6mm–1.3cm) thick pads for blouses and

> **TIP** *If your pattern calls for shoulder pads, be sure to use them. Otherwise, you may be disappointed in the way the fabric drapes and flows over your body curves.*

dresses. This size is occasionally used for jackets when a small pad is required.

■ Use ½″–1″ (1.3cm–2.5cm) thick pads for jackets and coats. This size is occasionally used for dresses when an oversized look is the fashion focus.

TRADITIONAL JACKET PAD

TRADITIONAL DRESS PAD

ATTACHING THE SHOULDER PAD

On Set-in Sleeves

■ Pin the shoulder pad to the inside of the garment so that the largest layer of the pad is against the garment. The shoulder line of the pad should match the shoulder seam of the garment and the straightest edge of the pad should extend ½″ (1.3cm) beyond the armhole seam.

■ Try the garment on to check the pad placement.

■ Remove the garment. Then, on the inside, loosely hand-tack the

EXTENDED JACKET PAD

EXTENDED DRESS PAD

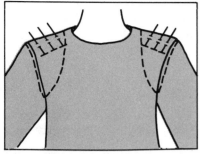

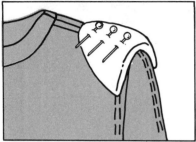

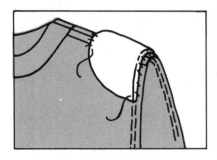

pad in place at the shoulder seam allowance and along the armhole seam allowance.

On Drop Shoulders, Kimono or Raglan Sleeves

■ Try on the garment. Slip the shoulder pad inside and shift the pad over the shoulder until it looks right and feels comfortable. Pin it in place from the outside of the garment.

■ Remove the garment. On the

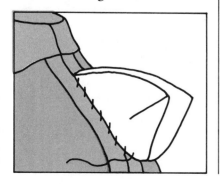

inside, loosely hand-tack the pad to the shoulder seam allowance.

Removable Shoulder Pads

Permanently attaching the shoulder pads may not be the most efficient idea. Suppose they need to be removed when the garment is washed or dry-cleaned . . . or suppose you don't want to invest in multiple sets of pads. The solution? Use self-gripping hook and loop fasteners to make them easy to remove.

■ Using the hook side of the fastener, hand-sew three dots or one strip to the garment along the shoulder line or seam.

■ Try on the garment. Adjust the position of the pad until it looks

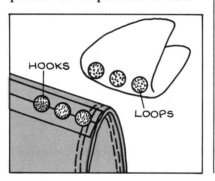

HOOKS

LOOPS

TIP *Keep an extra set of hook and loop fasteners around. Then, when you've removed the shoulder pads for cleaning, you can "cover up" the hook fasteners that are secured to the garment. That way, your hooks won't pick up bits of lint or snag other garments during the cleaning process.*

right and feels comfortable. Pin it in place from the outside of the garment.

■ Remove the garment. On the pad, mark the corresponding position(s) of the loop section(s) of the fastener. Hand-tack them in place.

SHOULDER PAD COVERS

Sometimes, particularly in the case of unlined jackets and coats, you'll want your shoulder pads to be the same color as your garment. Shoulder pad covers are easy to make.

TIP *If you're using lined shoulder pads on a dress or blouse, don't even bother attaching them to your garment. Instead, use ½" (1.3cm) wide strips of hook and loop fastener. Hand-sew the hook side to the top of the pad, along the shoulder line. Position the loopy side on top of the hook side and hand-sew the two sections together at the end nearest the neck edge. To wear the pads, open the fastener, position the pad on your shoulder under your bra strap, and close the fastener.*

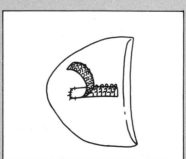

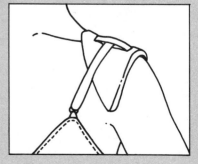

■ Cut a rectangle of lining fabric large enough to cover both sides of the pad, plus ⅝″ (1.5cm) all around.

■ Position the shoulder pad so that the straight edge of the pad is on the bias grainline.

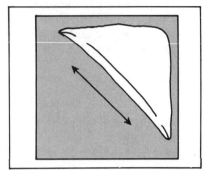

■ Fold the lining over the pad.

S *On your overlock machine:* Serge the edges.

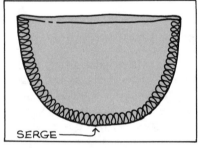

SERGE

On your conventional machine: Straight-stitch along the edge of the pad, trim the seam allowances to ¼″ (6mm) and zig-zag over the raw edge.

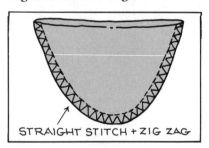

STRAIGHT STITCH + ZIG ZAG

TIP *If your garment is white or a light color, the shoulder pads will be a lot less noticeable if you cover them with a nude color lining fabric.*

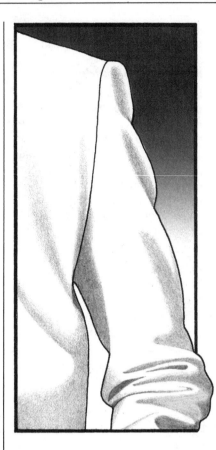

SLEEVES

There are three basic styles of sleeves—set-in, kimono and raglan. Because they're easy to sew and easy to fit, raglan and kimono styles are usually the best choices when you are just learning to sew. However, a garment with a set-in sleeve will soon be at the top of your sewing list. The result you'll want is a smooth fitting sleeve, one that doesn't have any dimples or tucks along the seam of the sleeve cap.

KIMONO SLEEVES

Kimono sleeves are cut as part of the garment front and back. Since there's nothing to deal with but an underarm seam, they're the easiest style to sew.

■ Pin the garment front and back together at the side/underarm seams, matching raw edges, notches and markings.

■ Beginning at the lower edge of the garment, stitch along the ⅝″ (1.5cm) seamline.

■ Reinforce the underarm area by stitching over the first stitching at the curve . . . or center a 4″–5″ (10cm–12.5cm) piece of seam binding or twill tape over the curved area before the seam is stitched and baste it in place. When you stitch the seam, shorten the stitch slightly along the length of the tape.

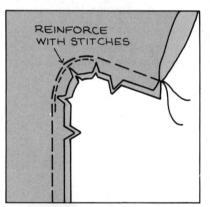

REINFORCE WITH STITCHES

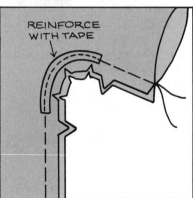

REINFORCE WITH TAPE

■ Clip the curves and press the seam open. DO NOT clip the seam binding.

RAGLAN SLEEVES

Raglan sleeves are joined to the garment front and garment back by diagonal seams that run from the underarm to the neckline. In addition, there may be a shoulder dart or a shoulder seam. To insert the sleeve on your conventional machine, follow your pattern instructions, reinforcing the diagonal seams by stitching again, over the first stitching.

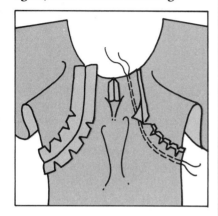

⑤ THE OVERLOCK METHOD:

The flatlock or trellis seam is an easy technique that lends a decorative, ready-to-wear look to any item. Because it's a strong seam that can withstand many washings, it's a good choice for raglan sleeve sweatshirts and children's garments. Consider it, too, if you want to make your raglan sleeve garment reversible.

The two-thread true flatlock seam:

■ Adjust your overlock to the appropriate setting; see chart below.

■ With wrong sides together, serge the seams. Then, working from the right side of the fabric, pull the two layers apart until the seam lies flat.

TYPE OF OVERLOCK STITCH:	2	MINE
Stitch Length:	2mm–3mm	
Stitch Width:	Widest	
Tension—Needle:	Very Loose	
Rt. Needle:	N/A	
U. Looper:	N/A	
L. Looper:	Normal	

TYPE OF OVERLOCK STITCH:	3	MINE
Stitch Length:	2mm–3mm	
Stitch Width:	Widest	
Tension—Needle:	Very Loose	
U. Looper:	Normal to Loose	
L. Looper:	Very Tight	

The three-thread mock flatlock seam:

If your overlock machine does not have two-thread capabilities, here's how to create the same effect with a three-thread stitch. Don't limit its use to raglan sleeves. It's great anyplace else you want a flatlock effect.

■ Adjust your overlock to the appropriate settings; see chart above.

■ Trim the seam allowances to ¼″ (6mm).

■ With the wrong sides together, place the seam allowances under the presser foot so that the raw edge will not be trimmed and the fabric fills up only half of the stitch.

Note: Filling up only half of the stitch ensures that the flatlock seam will lie perfectly flat. Serge a test seam to determine exactly where the raw edge needs to be positioned on your overlock machine.

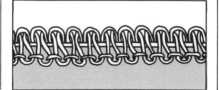

■ Serge the seam. Then, working from the right side of the fabric, pull the two layers apart until the seam lies flat.

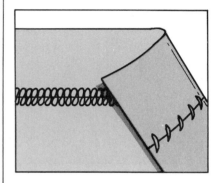

SET-IN SLEEVES

One of the things that distinguishes a set-in sleeve from a kimono or raglan style is the fact that the sleeve itself is slightly larger than the armhole of the garment. The excess fabric occurs in the area between the notches, called the sleeve cap. If the sleeve didn't have this extra fabric, there wouldn't be enough "play" for you to raise your arm. The mark of a professional-looking garment is a set-in sleeve that's properly eased into the armhole, creating a smooth seam and a rounded shape for your shoulder.

Easing the Sleeve Cap—Three Methods

It's much easier to ease the sleeve cap if you do it before the sleeve underarm seam is stitched.

The traditional easing method: Working on the right side of the fabric, ease-stitch the

> **TIP** *For your first set-in sleeve, consider one with a tucked or gathered sleeve cap. Then you won't have to bother about carefully easing in the fullness. Once you've had the experience of setting in a sleeve, go on to a second project that has an eased sleeve cap.*

sleeve cap twice. Ease-stitch first along the seamline between the notches. Then, stitch ¼" (6mm) away, within the seam allowance. Be sure to leave the threads long enough to pull them up to create the sleeve cap.

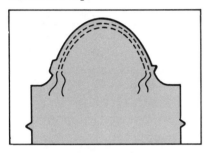

The ease-stitch-plus method: If you are working with a pliable, woven fabric, try this method.

■ Stitch along the seamline, between the notches, with a regular stitch. As you stitch, place one forefinger on each side of the seamline just in front of the needle and pull the fabric horizontally so it's stretched off-grain. While you're doing this, push the fabric back under the presser foot for four or five stitches.

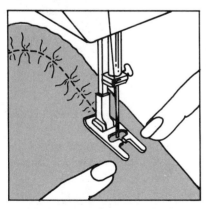

■ Stop stitching, relax the fabric, then repeat, pulling and pushing

the fabric back as you sew. The sleeve will automatically shape itself into a cap.

S *The Overlock Easing Method:*

Easing a sleeve cap on the overlock is simply a matter of tightening the needle tension until the fabric starts to pull up behind the foot. However, once stitched, these gathers can be adjusted only slightly. Test on a scrap of fabric . . . and save this technique until you and your overlock machine are good friends.

Note: Because this technique will cut off the notches, be sure to mark their location with a fabric marking pen or dressmaker's carbon.

■ Adjust your overlock to the appropriate setting; see chart below.

If the fabric is heavy or more easing is required, tighten the needle tension(s) even more. If you need to remove the stitches and start again, see page 115 for the fastest way to rip.

There are two ways to serge your easing stitches:
Technique #1: Working on the wrong side, serge the easing stitches on the ⅝" (1.5cm) seamline. This leaves you with a ¼" (6mm) seam allowancce when

you sew the sleeve to the garment.

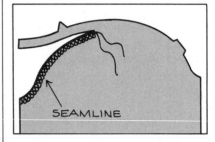

Technique #2: Working on the wrong side, serge the easing stitches, keeping the raw edge of the sleeve cap even with the cutting knife so you don't trim the seam allowance. Later on, when you stitch the sleeve to the garment on your conventional machine, place one forefinger on either side of the presser foot and pull the fabric horizontally so that the sleeve cap is stretched off-grain. It's just like ease-stitching-plus, without pushing the fabric.

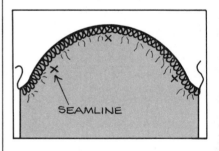

Preparing the Sleeve

Stitch the sleeve seam and press it open. Then finish the lower edge of the sleeve according to the pattern instructions and/or the information provided in

TYPE OF OVERLOCK STITCH:	3	4	MINE
Stitch Length:	Normal	Normal	
Stitch Width:	Normal	Normal	
Tensions—Needle:	Tight	Tight	
Rt. Needle:	N/A	Very Tight	
U. Looper:	Normal	Normal	
L. Looper:	Normal	Normal	

CUFFS, page 152. Now you're ready to pin-baste the sleeve to the garment.

■ Turn the sleeve right side out; turn the garment inside out. Slip the sleeve inside the armhole and pin them together at the sleeve and garment underarm seams, the shoulder markings and notches.

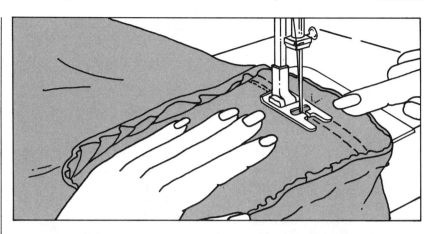

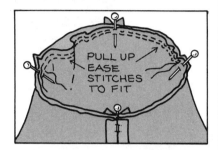

■ Now match the remaining markings and pin these too.

■ Draw up the ease stitching at each end, sliding the fabric along to distribute the fullness evenly in the area between the notches. Your goal is to get the sleeve to smoothly fit the armhole. Pin closely all around the eased area, then pin the underarm area between the notches.

> **TIP** *If you haven't had much experience setting in a sleeve ... or if your machine doesn't stitch over pins ... or if you want to try the garment on to check the fit of the sleeve, hand-baste close to the seamline and remove the pins.*

Stitching the Sleeve

■ With the sleeve side up, begin at the underarm seam and stitch along the seamline, just to the left of the first row of ease stitching. As you stitch, use your forefingers on either side of the presser foot, as shown above, to keep the eased area from puckering under the needle.

■ When you reach the underarm seam, overlap the stitches.

■ Stitch a second row ⅛″ (3mm) away from the first, within the seam allowance.

■ Trim the seam allowance close to the stitching in the underarm area between the notches.

■ To strengthen and reinforce the underarm area, it's wise to finish the seam allowances between the notches by machine zigzagging, overcasting or serging the edges. If your fabric ravels, finish the entire armhole.

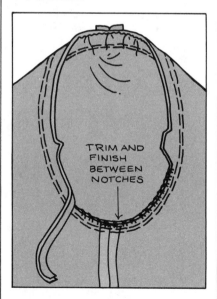

Pressing the Sleeve

■ With the sleeve side up, place the upper portion of the armhole seam (the area between the

> **TIP** *If you're working with a knit that stretches, forget about ease stitching. Working with the garment side up, pin the sleeve to the armhole edge, matching markings. As you stitch, ease in the fullness by stretching the armhole to fit the sleeve cap.*

notches) over the end of a sleeve board, tailor's ham or ironing board.

■ With the point of the iron, press only the seam allowances.

> **TIP** *The shallower the curve of the sleeve cap, the less ease the sleeve has. If your sleeve has very little ease, you may find it easier to attach it to the garment before the underarm seam is stitched. Once the sleeve is attached, the garment side seam and the sleeve seam are sewn in one continuous stitching operation.*

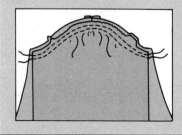

Use steam, if appropriate for your fabric. This blends the stitching and shrinks out some of the fullness. No further pressing is needed—the seam allowances will naturally turn toward the sleeve.

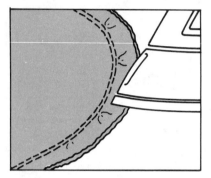

TAILORING—THE SPEED WAY

Tailoring a jacket has never been easier. Today, speed tailoring techniques are synonymous with quality tailoring techniques. The reason: fusible interfacings that replace padstitching and other tedious handwork.

APPLYING THE INTERFACING

The following guidelines are for a woman's lined classic blazer. Although the style of your jacket, as well as the shape and placement of the interfacing sections, may vary, the general principles remain the same.

Take a close look at the accompanying sketches of the collar, undercollar, jacket front, jacket back and facing sections of a classic blazer. You can clearly see the areas where the interfacing should go. For a softer look, you may want to eliminate the interfacing on the facing and the upper collar.

Since most jackets are made

TIP *If it's your first tailoring project, speed tailoring begins with the right fabric. Choose one that is easy to work with. Because it can be easily steamed and molded into shape, your best bet is either a 100 percent wool or a blend with a high percentage of wool. To hide any less-than-perfect stitching, choose a wool with a slight texture, such as a tweed or a double knit, or one with a brushed surface or slubbed yarns.*

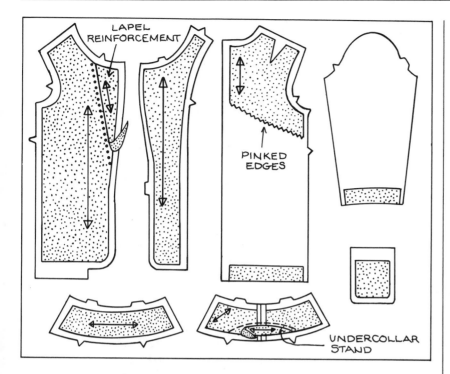

- Using the jacket front pattern piece, trace the shape formed between the roll line and the outer edge of the lapel, eliminating the ⅝″ (1.5cm) seam allowances.
- Draw a new grainline that's parallel to the roll line. Fuse the front interfacing to the jacket front. Then, place the lapel reinforcement over the first layer of interfacing, positioning it a scant ⅛″ (3 mm) from the roll line. Fuse in place.

PRESSING TO ADD SHAPE

Once your interfacings are fused in place, but before sewing any of the garment sections together, use your steam iron to build in some additional shape.

The Undercollar

Fold the undercollar down along the roll line. Using straight pins, fasten it to a tailor's ham the way it would rest on your body. Holding the iron several inches away, apply a generous amount of steam. Be sure the undercollar is thoroughly dry before you remove it from the ham.

The Lapels

Put the jacket front, right side up, on the ironing board. Fold a hand towel lengthwise into several thicknesses and insert it under the curve of the lapel. Holding your iron several inches above the lapel, apply a generous amount of steam. Repeat for the other lapel. Be sure each section

TIP *To prevent the interfacing from creating a ridge across the back of the jacket, pink the lower edge of the back interfacing before fusing it in place.*

from medium to heavy weight fabrics, you'll need to keep the bulk in the seam allowances to a minimum. To do this, trim ½″ (1.3cm) from the seam allowances of all the interfacing sections before fusing them in place.

If the jacket front or back has darts, trim the interfacing away along the dart stitching lines before fusing.

Notice that an extra layer of interfacing has been added to the undercollar and the jacket front. The undercollar stand and the lapel reinforcement shape and stabilize these critical areas, eliminating the need for padstitching.

Undercollar Stand

For this technique, you'll have to create a pattern piece:

- Trace the shape between the roll line and the neck edge on the undercollar pattern piece, eliminating the ⅝″ (1.5cm) neckline seam allowance.
- Change the center back seamline to a "place on fold" line, eliminating the center back seam allowance.
- Draw a grainline that is perpendicular to the foldline.

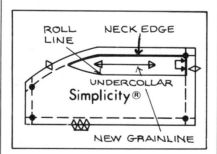

- Cut out the undercollar stand. Position it on the wrong side of the (already interfaced) undercollar, a scant ⅛″ (3mm) below the roll line, and fuse in place.

Lapel Reinforcement

For this technique, you'll have to create a pattern piece:

is thoroughly dry before you remove it from the ironing board.

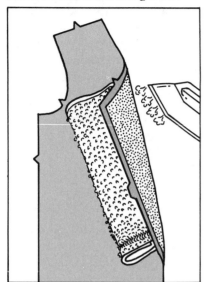

To continue assembling the jacket, consult your pattern instructions.

SPEED LININGS

The traditional way to insert a lining in a jacket is by hand; the modern, speed method is by machine.

To put the lining in by machine, follow these steps:

Step 1: Assemble the body of the jacket, but DO NOT attach the upper collar or the facings or construct the hem.

Step 2: Sew the body of the lining together, including setting in the sleeves.

Step 3: Sew the jacket facings and upper collar together.

Step 4: Sew the facings/upper collar to the lining, beginning and ending the seam approximately 5″ (12.5cm) from the lower edge of the lining.

Step 5: With right sides together, pin the facings/upper collar to the body of the jacket, matching all markings; stitch. Trim, grade and press the seam allowances. Then turn the garment right side out and give it a thorough pressing. (To learn the secret of crisp, neat

SPEED LININGS

STEP 1

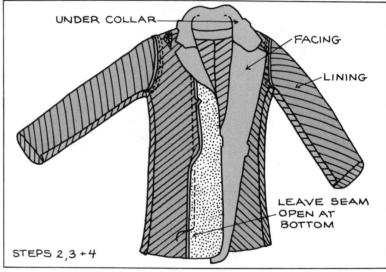

UNDER COLLAR

FACING

LINING

LEAVE SEAM OPEN AT BOTTOM

STEPS 2,3 + 4

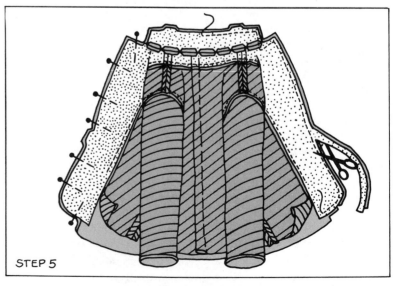

STEP 5

notches, see the accompanying TIP.)

Step 6: Hem the jacket, then hem the lining by slipstitching it in place over the raw edge of the jacket hem allowance and the lower edge of the front facing.

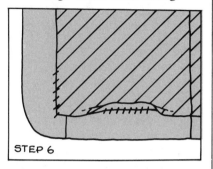

STEP 6

TIP *The first secret to crisp, neat notches is to make sure that the dot that indicates the notch is clearly marked on all sections—the collar, undercollar, jacket front and front facing. The second secret is in the stitching procedure:*

■ *With right sides together, pin the facings/undercollar to the body of the jacket.*

■ *Take one small hand basting stitch through ONLY the jacket and the jacket facing at the notch marking. This will keep the layers from shifting during machine stitching. DON'T catch the seam allowances, the undercollar or the upper collar in the basting stitch. Tie the ends of the thread in a square knot.*

■ *Keeping the seam allowances free, and beginning at the notch marking on the collar/undercollar, machine-stitch from the dot to the center back of the collar.*

■ *Beginning at the notch marking on the jacket front/jacket facing, stitch from the dot to the lower edge of the jacket, keeping the seam allowances free at the notch marking. Tie the thread ends at the notch in a knot.*

■ *Repeat for the other side of the jacket, overlapping the stitches at the center back of the collar.*

■ *If you look carefully, you'll see that you have a small hole at the lapel notch where you started your stitching. Without it, there wouldn't be enough room for all the layers of fabric that converge at the notch when the jacket is turned and pressed. The hole will magically disappear on your finished jacket.*

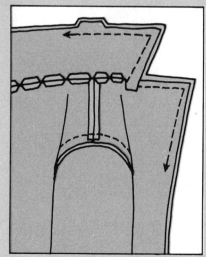

TRIMS

Trims are the finishing touch that give your garment its personality. Go tailored, sportive or feminine—with trims that you purchase by the yard or trims that you create yourself on the overlock machine.

You don't have to be limited by the trim recommendations on your pattern envelope. Feel free, as the fashion mood strikes you, to add trims to any garment. Use them to highlight a seam or detail and bring it into focus.

TRIMMING HINTS

Here are some practical tips to follow when using purchased trim:

■ If you're adding trim to a pattern that does not already call for it, you'll need to determine how much to buy. Measure the area to be trimmed, then add at least ½ yd. (.5m) so you'll have enough extra to join the ends and go around corners and curves.

■ Be sure the trim requires the same care as your garment. Don't put a dry-clean-only trim on a garment you intend to wash.

■ For curves, choose a flexible trim, such as rickrack, bias tape, foldover braid or knitted bands.

■ Use pins, double-faced basting tape, strips of fusible web or fabric glue to hold the trim in place

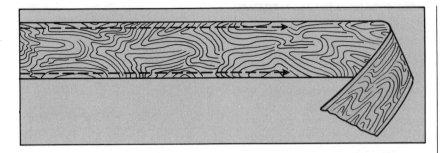

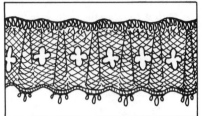

■ Repeat, until you've serged the entire length of the lace.

for stitching. As you do this, keep the trim relaxed, not taut so there won't be any puckering once the trim is permanently stitched in place.

■ Stitch trims in place with a slightly loose thread tension.

■ If the trim needs to be stitched along two edges, for example, when you're applying a ribbon or a band—or if you're stitching parallel rows of trim—always stitch in the same direction. This prevents ripples or puckering.

■ When applying a flat trim at a corner, make sure your corners are neat and sharp. Review the section on MITERING, pages 174–176.

⑤ GATHERING LACE

Occasionally, you may want to use a coordinating straight lace and ruffled lace trim in the same garment. Since it's not always easy to find matching lace, use your overlock machine to transform a piece of straight lace trim into a ruffled trim.

Note: Because lace has a delicate, open weave, this technique dif-

fers slightly from the ones described in GATHERS, pages 162–164.

■ Adjust your overlock machine to the appropriate setting; see chart below.

■ With the right side up, place the straight edge of the lace just to the left of the knife so that you won't cut the lace when you serge.

■ Holding your finger firmly against the back of the foot, begin serging. As you stitch, the lace will pile up behind the foot. Keep serging until you can't hold the lace any longer.

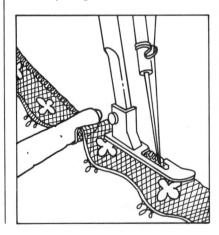

EDGINGS

Trims with at least one decorative edge, such as fringe, piping and pre-gathered ruffles, can be applied in several different ways, depending on where they are located on the garment.

Inserted in a Seam

■ With the wrong side of the trim to the right side of the fabric, place the trim along the seamline so that the decorative edge is toward the garment and the raw edge is inside the seam allowance. For pre-gathered ruffles or piping, place the binding edge just over the seamline; for rickrack, center it over the seamline.

■ Machine-baste the trim in place along the seamline. Use a zipper foot when stitching bulky trims, such as piping or bound ruffles.

■ Pin the garment sections right sides together. Then, using your conventional or your overlock machine, stitch just to the left of the basting.

TYPE OF OVERLOCK STITCH:	3	4	MINE
Stitch Length:	Longest	Longest	
Stitch Width:	Widest	Widest	
Tensions—Needle:	Tight*	Tight*	
Rt. Needle:	N/A	Tight	
U. Looper:	Normal	Normal	
L. Looper:	Normal	Normal	

* For denser gathers, tighten the needle tension.

TIP *Pre-gathered trims require some special handling if they're inserted in a seam:*

■ *To get the trim to lie flat at a corner, some extra fullness is needed. To get it, take a tiny tuck in the trim at the corner before basting it in place.*

■ *If the trimmed edge will be intersected by another garment edge, such as on a collar or a cuff, taper the ends into the seam allowance, clearing the edge that will be stitched to the garment.*

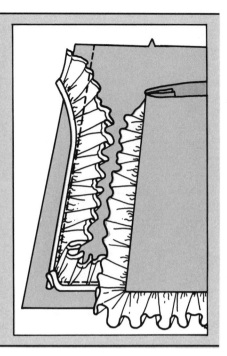

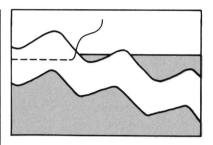

⟦S⟧ *Overlock method:* Use this method to apply lace trim with one straight edge to the raw edge of a garment. This technique can also be used with other straight-edge trims. However, always make a test sample first to make sure the finished effect is not too bulky.

■ If necessary, trim the raw edge of the garment so that there is a ⅝″ (1.5cm) seam or hem allowance.

■ Adjust your overlock machine to the appropriate setting; see chart below.

■ Place the lace and the fabric right sides together, with the straight edge of the lace parallel to and ½″ (1.3cm) from the raw edge of the fabric. Use glue stick or pins to hold the lace in place.

■ Lift the presser foot and place the garment, lace side up, so that

■ Press the seam allowances to one side.

Along an Edge

Topstitched method: Use this technique on a finished garment edge or on a raw edge that has been folded under and pressed.

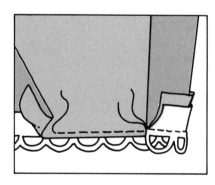

■ Lap the finished edge or the pressed edge of the garment over the straight edge of the trim and topstitch it in place. For rickrack, lap the garment edge so that only one set of points are visible.

■ Trims with two decorative edges, such as scalloped braid or rickrack, can be positioned on the outside of the garment and topstitched in place.

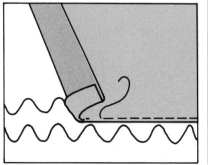

TYPE OF OVERLOCK STITCH:	3	4	MINE
Stitch Length:	2mm–3mm	2mm–3mm	
Stitch Width:	Widest	Widest	
Tensions—Needle:	Normal	Normal	
Rt. Needle:	N/A	Normal	
U. Looper:	Normal	Normal	
L. Looper:	Normal	Normal	

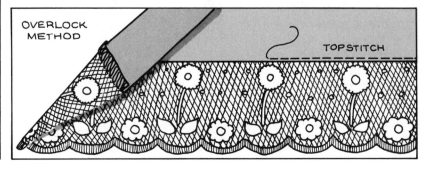

OVERLOCK METHOD

TOPSTITCH

TYPE OF OVERLOCK STITCH:	2	3	MINE
Stitch Length:	2mm–3mm	2mm–3mm	
Stitch Width:	Widest	Widest	
Tensions—Needle:	Very Loose	Very Loose	
Rt. Needle:	N/A	N/A	
U. Looper:	N/A	Loose	
L. Looper:	Normal	Very Tight	

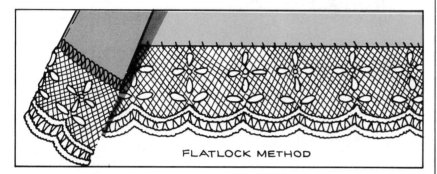

FLATLOCK METHOD

the straight edge of the trim is aligned slightly to the left of the knife; serge, trimming off the excess garment fabric.

■ Press the seam allowance toward the garment.

■ If desired, topstitch on your conventional machine.

Flatlock method: This technique can be used to apply lace with one straight edge to a raw edge or to a finished garment edge.

■ Adjust your overlock machine to the appropriate setting; see chart above, at top.

■ Place the lace and the fabric right sides together, with the straight edge of the lace parallel to and ½″ (1.3cm) from the raw edge of the fabric. Use glue stick or pins to hold the lace in place.

■ Lift the presser foot and place the garment, lace side up, so that the straight edge of the trim is aligned slightly to the left of the knife; serge, trimming off the excess garment fabric.

■ Gently pull on the lace and the fabric until the stitches are flat; press.

Rolled hem method: This technique can be used to apply lace with one straight edge to the raw edge of a garment.

■ Adjust your overlock machine to the appropriate setting; see chart below.

■ Place the lace and the fabric wrong sides together, with the straight edge of the lace parallel to and ½″ (1.3cm) from the raw edge of the fabric. Use glue stick or pins to hold the lace in place.

■ Lift the presser foot and place the garment, lace side up, so that the straight edge of the trim is aligned slightly to the left of the knife; serge, trimming off the excess garment fabric.

■ Gently pull on the lace and the fabric until the stitches are flat; press.

APPLIED TRIMS

Bands or any other trim with two finished edges can be applied almost anywhere on the outside of the garment. Create borders by applying them in parallel rows. Create a checkered or woven effect by crisscrossing them on a bodice, yoke or cuff. Use narrow, flat trims, such as braid or yarn, to create intricate, curved designs.

For a wide trim: Apply it before stitching the garment sections together. That way, the trim ends will be caught in the seams. Topstitch along both trim edges.

TYPE OF OVERLOCK STITCH	3	MINE
Stitch Length:	1mm	
Stitch Width:	Narrowest	
Tension—Needle:	Normal	
U. Looper:	Tight*	
L. Looper:	Very Tight	

* Use woolly nylon or silk thread.

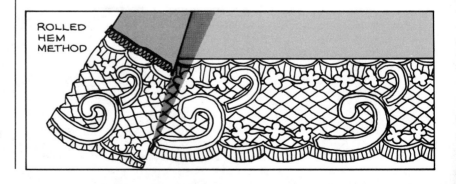

ROLLED HEM METHOD

For a narrow trim: Stitch through the center of the trim or along both edges, depending on the trim's width. For very narrow braid or yarn, use a special braid foot that has a groove to make the application easier.

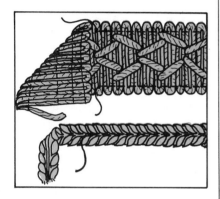

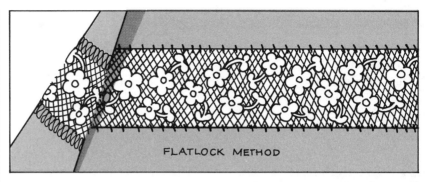

INSERTIONS

See-through trims with two finished edges, such as lace or eyelet, are perfect for insertions on flat garment areas where there are no darts or curved seams.

Apply the insertions to the garment sections before seaming so that the ends of the trim can be included in the seam.

THE CONVENTIONAL METHOD:

■ Pin the trim in place and topstitch close to both edges. For scalloped edges, stitch just inside the points, leaving the decorative edges free.

■ Working on the wrong side of the garment, cut the fabric ONLY between the two rows of topstitching. Press the seam allowances away from the trim.

■ Working on the right side of the garment, edgestitch close to the folds, through all thicknesses.

■ Working on the wrong side of the garment and using your embroidery scissors, trim the seam allowances close to the stitching.

⑤ THE OVERLOCK METHOD:

If your lace has two straight edges, you can insert it using either the Flatlock Method or the Rolled Hem Method described under EDGINGS, page 196.

Before you begin, use a fabric marker, dressmaker carbon or other appropriate method to mark two parallel trim placement lines. The distance between these lines should be ½″ (1.3cm) less than the width of your trim.

To apply the lace:

■ Position one finished edge of the lace between the placement lines so that it overlaps the marking ⅛″ (3mm). For the Flatlock Method, place them right sides together; for the Rolled Hem Method, place them wrong sides together.

■ Adjust your overlock machine and serge, following the directions for either the Flatlock Method or the Rolled Hem Method.

■ Match the other finished edge of the lace with the other placement line and serge.

■ Open out the garment section so the lace lies flat; press.

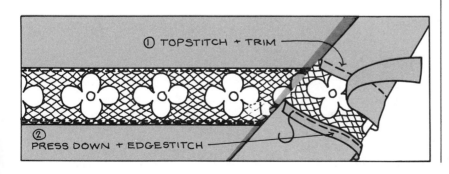

TYPE OF OVERLOCK STITCH:	2	3	MINE
Stitch Length:	2mm–4mm	2mm–4mm	
Stitch Width:	Widest	Widest	
Tensions—Needle:	Very Loose	Tight	
U. Looper:	N/A	"0"	
L. Looper:	"0"	Normal	

⑤ CREATING YOUR OWN TRIM ON THE OVERLOCK

Decorative threads (see Chapter 5, pages 105–106) can be used to create special effects with your overlock machine. Consider threading knitting ribbon (silk or rayon, but not 100 percent polyester) or pearl cotton through the upper looper, then serging around the edges of a wool cape or jacket. Imagine variegated pearl cotton used to serge the neckline, hem and sleeve edges of a dress or tunic. No need for linings, facings or hems!

When working with any decorative thread, use the following procedure:

■ Thread the needle with normal thread.

■ Thread the decorative thread through the thread guides and the upper looper and/or the lower looper.

■ Adjust your overlock machine to the appropriate setting; see chart above.

■ Serge a test swatch on the garment fabric, feeding the fabric so that the seam/hem allowance is trimmed off. Adjust the tensions as necessary so that the decorative thread forms an even stitch. If you get an uneven stitch—or your stitches form an "S" or a zigzag pattern—loosen the tensions even more or bypass the tension assemblies. If the thread still doesn't feed smoothly (a special problem with knitting ribbon), try bypassing the top thread guide of the upper looper.

■ If you're serging in a circle, stop stitching when the stitches meet, then overlap two stitches. Pull on the needle thread just above the needle so that there's about 3″ (7.5cm) of slack. Lift the presser foot and pull the garment out from under the foot. Cut the threads. To secure the thread ends, use a craft or yarn needle with a large eye and tunnel the threads back under the stitching on the wrong side of the garment.

> **TIP** *If you're using decorative three-thread stitching on a garment where both sides of the stitches will show—for example, a cape, poncho or reversible garment—consider using topstitching thread in the needle and the lower looper. The stitches will have a more polished look.*

Shirring

For a smocked, decorative treatment at a waistline or wrist, or on the bodice of a child's dress, use your overlock machine, pearl cotton and narrow elastic cord. This is a quick and easy substitute for conventional smocking or shirring, as well as an attractive substitute for an elasticized casing.

■ Adjust your overlock machine to the appropriate setting; see chart below.

■ With wrong sides together, fold the garment along one smocking line.

■ Thread pearl cotton, knitting ribbon or other decorative thread through the upper looper for three-thread stitching or the lower looper for two-thread stitching.

■ Place the garment section under the presser foot, positioning the fold slightly to the left of the knife so that the fabric fills only half of the stitch. Serge, being careful not to cut the fabric.

■ Repeat, flatlocking as many rows as desired. The shirring will look best if the folds are spaced about ¾″ (2cm) apart.

■ If you own a long, thin loop turner, tunnel it under the stitches on the back of the fabric. Knot one end of a length of ⅛″ (3mm) elastic cord, attach the other end to the loop turner and pull it through the stitches. If you

TYPE OF OVERLOCK STITCH:	2	3	MINE
Stitch Length:	2mm–3mm	2mm–3mm	
Stitch Width:	Widest	Widest	
Tensions—Needle:	Very Loose	Very Loose	
U. Looper:	N/A	"0"	
L. Looper:	"0"	Very Tight	

don't own a loop turner, thread the unknotted end of the elastic onto a blunt tapestry needle and, working on the back of the fabric, gently work the tapestry needle under the stitching.

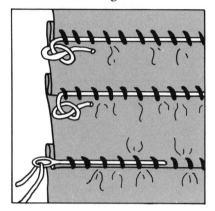

■ Once the elastic is pulled through, adjust the shirring until the garment section is the desired width; then knot the other end of the elastic.

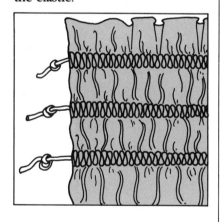

Fagotting

Fagotting is a method of joining two pieces of fabric with visible decorative stitching while leaving a space between the fabric sections. Use it as a delicate, decorative way to join sections of the garment or to add a fine trim to dresses and blouses. If the fagotting is purely decorative, you may find it easier to fagot the fabric first, then cut out the garment, rather than attempting to adjust your pattern to accommodate the fagotting.

TYPE OF OVERLOCK STITCH:	3	MINE
Stitch Length:	4mm	
Stitch Width:	Widest	
Tensions—Needle:	"0"	
U. Looper:	"0"	
L. Looper:	"0"	

■ If your fabric ravels, serge the raw edges of the fabric sections that will be fagotted together. Press the serged edges under ½″ (1.3cm).

■ Adjust your overlock machine to the appropriate setting; see chart above.

■ Place the fabric right sides together so that the folded edges are even. Insert the fabric under the presser foot to the left of the knife so that the needle just catches the fabric; serge.

■ Gently pull the fabric apart. There will be a ⅛″ (3mm) space between the folded edges that is filled with thread. Press.

■ If you want to further embellish your garment, use your conventional machine to topstitch on either side of the fagotting. Use a straight stitch or a decorative stitch. For a rich, custom look, do all your stitching in a thread that matches the fabric.

TUCKS

A tuck is a stitched fold of fabric that controls fullness and/or adds a decorative touch to a garment. Alone or in groups, tucks can be found just about any place—at shoulders, waistline or hipline, or adorning a yoke, a pocket, a cuff or a hemline. A special type of tuck—called a growth tuck—can be incorporated into children's garments so that they can be quickly and easily lengthened.

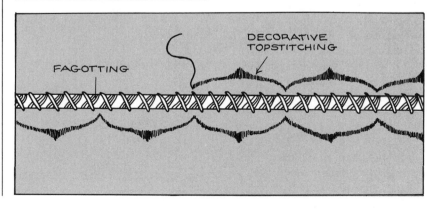

solid lines. Because pin tucks are narrow, the stitching lines are not indicated. Fold the fabric along the solid line and stitch the specified distance from the fold.

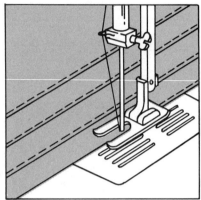

WIDE TUCKS

Wide tucks are indicated on the pattern tissue by a series of solid and broken lines. To create the tuck, fold the fabric on the solid line, matching the broken lines. Then, stitch along the broken lines.

MARKING AND STITCHING

Depending on the design of your pattern, tucks can appear on the outside or be hidden on the inside of your garment. If the tucks will be folded and stitched on the inside of the garment, transfer the markings to the wrong side of the fabric. If the tucks will be folded and stitched on the outside, transfer the markings to the right side of the fabric. Choose a method that won't leave permanent marks on the fabric.

If the tucks are straight and parallel to each other, they'll be easier to stitch if you press in the foldlines first. Then, be sure to stitch all the tucks in the same direction. Press them in the direction indicated on the pattern instructions. Vertical tucks are usually pressed away from the center front or center back; horizontal tucks are usually pressed down.

NARROW OR PIN TUCKS

These are usually indicated on the pattern tissue by a series of

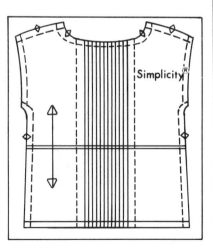

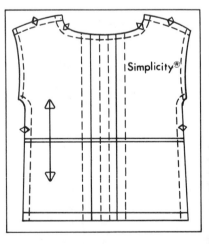

To save time, transfer only the solid lines to the fabric. Fold the fabric on the solid line, then use a stitching guide, such as the markings on the throat plate, a strip of tape placed on the throat plate, or a seam guide, to evenly stitch the specified distance from the fold.

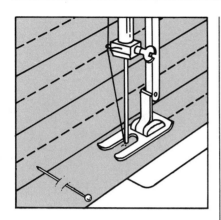

DECORATIVE PIN TUCKS

THE CONVENTIONAL METHOD:

If your sewing machine does decorative stitching with regular thread, you can add pretty shell tucks or tucks with fancy stitches to lingerie, dainty blouses or children's dress-up clothes. On lightweight knits or sheers, create a shell tuck by using a machine

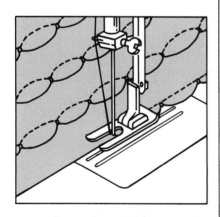

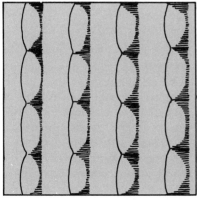

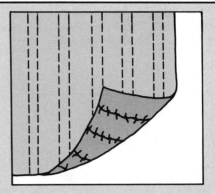

TIP *On light and medium weight fabrics, you can create a tucked effect without actually making tucks. Use a twin needle and two corresponding spools of thread in the top of your machine. The two needle threads combine with the one bobbin thread to create raised rows that look like narrow pin tucks.*

If your sewing machine doesn't have an extra spool holder, put the second spool of thread in a glass placed behind, and to the right of, the machine. It will unwind smoothly without rolling away!

blindstitch over the edge. On crisper fabrics, stitch the tuck with a machine embroidery stitch. Position the stitching so that the design falls within the tuck.

⑤ THE OVERLOCK METHOD:

For colorful, decorative tucks, thread the upper looper with pearl cotton, embroidery floss, variegated crochet yarn, knitting ribbon or metallic thread.

■ Adjust your overlock machine to the appropriate setting: see chart below.

■ Mark and press on the tuck foldline as for conventional tucks.

■ Serge, keeping the fold slightly to the left of the knife so that the

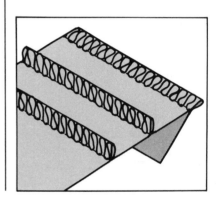

TYPE OF OVERLOCK STITCH	3	MINE
Stitch Length:	3mm–5mm	
Stitch Width:	Widest	
Tensions—Needle:	Normal	
U. Looper:	Loose*	
L. Looper:	Normal	

* Use decorative thread in the upper looper.

TIP *The narrow rolled hem stitch can also be used to make lovely pin tucks. Adjust your machine for its three-thread narrow rolled hem function. Fold the fabric wrong sides together along the tuck line, then serge over the fold. For a satiny appearance, try silk or 100 percent rayon thread in the upper looper.*

fabric isn't cut. Repeat for as many tucks as desired.

■ Press the tucks to one side.

> **TIP** *If you're adding tucks to a pattern that doesn't include them, tuck the fabric first, then cut out the garment. Be sure to purchase extra fabric to accommodate the tucks.*

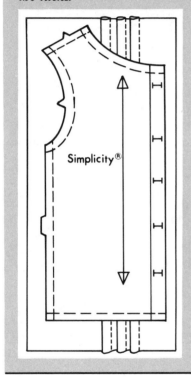

GROWTH TUCKS

Children often grow taller faster than they grow wider. As a result, garments may be too short long before they're too tight. To solve this problem, you can incorporate a growth tuck into the garment. Plan on doing this before the pattern is cut out so you can alter the pattern pieces to allow for the extra length.

Growth tucks can be incorporated into any straight hemline. The most obvious place to allow

for growth is in the skirt hem. However, this technique can also be used on long- or short-sleeve shirts, blouses and pants for both boys and girls.

■ Before you cut out the garment, add 3″ (7.5cm) to the hem allowance.

■ Construct the garment and finish the hem allowance edge.

■ Using a machine basting stitch, form a 1½″ (3.8cm) tuck on the right side of the fabric, within the hem allowance. Press the tuck toward the hemline.

■ When you need to lengthen the garment, remove the basting and press a new hemline. If necessary, stitch ribbon or trim over the old hem crease to disguise it.

On a dress with a waistline seam, you can incorporate the growth tuck in the bodice area.

■ Before you cut out the garment, lengthen the front and back bodice 1″–3″ (2.5cm–7.5cm).

■ Sew the bodice together at the side seams.

■ On the inside of the bodice, baste a tuck half as wide as the amount you lengthened the bodice. Position the tuck so it is

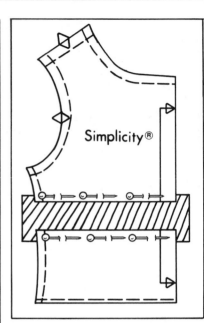

about ¼″ (6mm) above the waistline seam.

■ Press the tuck up, then join bodice to skirt and complete the garment.

■ When the garment needs to be lengthened, simply release the tuck. If there is a zipper, rip out the lower part, release the tuck and re-stitch the zipper and the seam. If necessary, cover fade marks with a contrasting ribbon or sash.

WAISTBANDS

There are several different methods for applying and finishing waistbands. Your pattern instructions will include a method appropriate for your garment. You can follow those directions exactly . . . or use one of our easy variations.

INTERFACING

Regardless of the construction method you choose, the waistband must be interfaced so that it retains its shape. For best results, interface the entire waistband, eliminating the seam allowances as described under INTERFACINGS, page 171. If you're using a sew-in interfacing, add a row of basting on the facing side of the waistband, near the foldline. This will keep the interfacing from shifting.

THE NO-BULK WAISTBAND METHODS

For most sewers, the biggest stumbling block to a smooth waistband is learning how to deal with all the layers of fabric that converge at the waistline seam. Both of the following methods solve this problem by eliminating the seam allowance on the waistband facing. These methods are suitable for all fabrics, but are especially good for heavyweight or bulky fabrics. It's up to you whether you prefer machine stitching or hand stitching as your final step.

Stitch-in-the-Ditch Machine Method

Prepare your waistband ONE of the following ways:

■ Cut out the waistband, placing the long, unnotched edge along a selvage (right), and eliminating ¼″

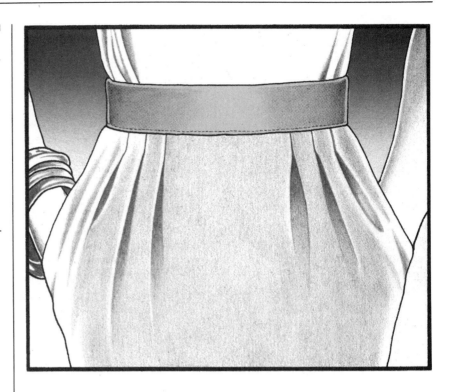

TIP *To save time, fusible interfacing is now available as pre-cut strips in assorted widths. As an extra bonus, some pre-cut strips are perforated to indicate seamlines and foldlines. If you use them, it's a snap to achieve a straight, even waistband.*

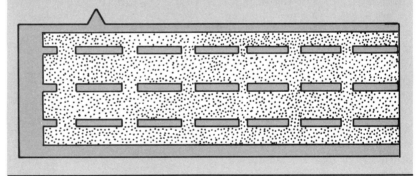

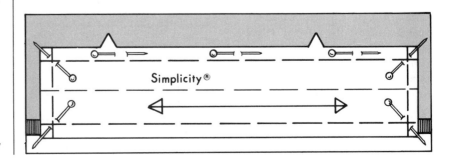

Simplicity ®

(6mm) from the seam allowance. Then fuse the interfacing in place.

OR

■ Cut out the waistband. Apply fusible or sew-in interfacing. To finish the long, unnotched edge, serge, trimming off ¼″ (6mm) as you stitch. If you don't own an overlock machine, trim off ¼″ (6mm), then overcast the edge on your conventional machine.

To attach the waistband:

■ With right sides together, pin or baste the notched waistband edge to the garment, matching notches, centers and markings; stitch. (a)

■ Press the seam allowances toward the waistband; trim the seam to ⅜″ (1cm). (b)

■ With right sides together, fold the waistband along the foldline and stitch the overlap end. (c)

■ On the underlap, turn the waistband seam allowance down. Beginning at the fold, stitch the end to ⅜″ (1cm) from the lower edge; pivot and continue stitching to the small dot marking. Backstitch to secure. Clip the seam allowances to the dot marking and trim the seams. (d)

■ Turn the waistband right side out so that the finished or selvage edge extends ⅜″ (1cm) below the waistband seam on the inside of the garment; press.

■ On the inside, fold the finished or selvage edge under diagonally at the zipper; pin. On the outside, pin the waistband layers together along the waistband seam. (e)

■ On the outside, stitch in the ditch, or groove, of the waistband seam, catching the finished edge of the waistband and the diagonal turn-under. Remove the pins as you stitch.(f)

Hand Method

Prepare the waistband using one of the following methods:

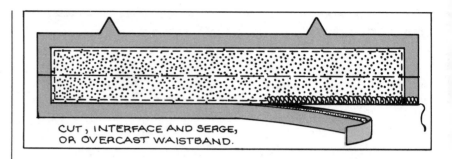

CUT, INTERFACE AND SERGE, OR OVERCAST WAISTBAND.

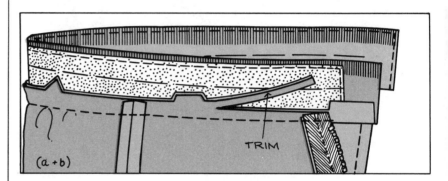

TRIM

(a + b)

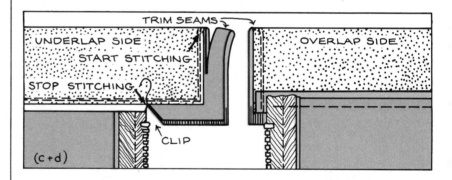

TRIM SEAMS

UNDERLAP SIDE OVERLAP SIDE

START STITCHING

STOP STITCHING

CLIP

(c + d)

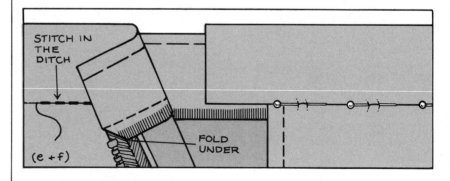

STITCH IN THE DITCH

FOLD UNDER

(e + f)

■ Cut out the waistband, placing the long, unnotched edge along a selvage, eliminating the ⅝″ (1.5cm) seam allowance. Then fuse the interfacing in place.

OR:

■ Cut out the waistband. Apply fusible or sew-in interfacing. To finish the long, unnotched edge, serge, trimming off the ⅝″

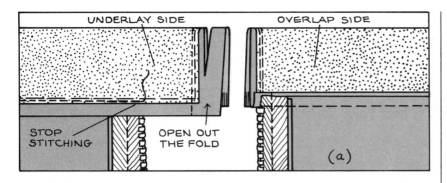

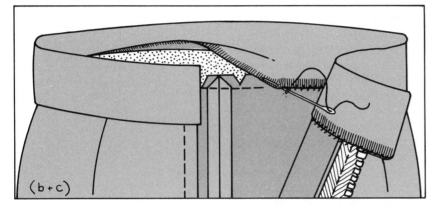

OVERLOCK METHOD

This is a quick way to attach a waistband and finish the raw edges in one step. It's an excellent choice for knits and light to medium weight fabrics.

■ With right sides together, fold the waistband in half lengthwise. Using your conventional machine, stitch across the ends. At the underlap end, pivot and stitch along the waistline seam, ending at the small dot. Backstitch to secure. Clip to the stitching at the dot, then trim the seams. (d), below

■ Turn the waistband right side out and press.

■ Pin both cut edges of the waistband to the outside of the garment, matching notches, centers and markings.

■ With the garment side up, and beginning at the underlap edge, serge along the waistline seam. (e)

■ Press the seam toward the garment and the waistband away from the garment. Hand-tack the

(1.5cm) seam allowance as you stitch. If you don't own an overlock machine, trim off the ⅝″ (1.5cm), then overcast the edge on your conventional machine.

To apply the waistband:

■ With right sides together, pin the notched waistband edge to the garment, matching notches, centers and markings; stitch.

■ Press the seam allowances toward the waistband; trim the seam to ⅜″ (1cm). Then (a):

■ With right sides together, fold the waistband along the foldline. Stitch the seams at both ends of the waistband; trim. *Note:* When stitching the underlap end, open out the fold that was created when you pressed the seam allowances toward the waistband.

■ Turn the waistband right side out so that the finished or selvage edge meets the waistband seam on the inside of the garment and pin; press. (b)

■ On the inside, slipstitch the

serged or selvage edge in place along the entire length of the waistband seam, including the underlap. (c)

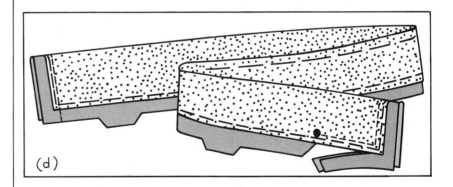

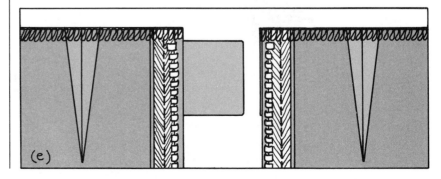

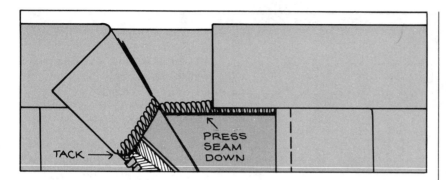

seam allowances in place at the inside edges of the garment opening.

ZIPPERS

Because zippers have a reputation for being difficult to install, many sewers, especially new or returning ones, unnecessarily avoid patterns that feature zippers. Don't

be caught up in that type of thinking! The little tricks that guarantee a perfect zipper are so simple anyone can learn them.

There are four basic zipper applications: centered, lapped, fly-front and separating. Your pattern will give you instructions for the method appropriate to your garment.

In order to easily follow those instructions, as well as the hints given here, check the accompany-

ing diagram so you're familiar with the names of the parts of a zipper.

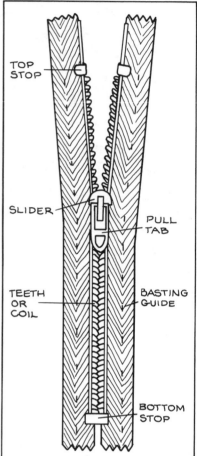

BEFORE YOU BEGIN

■ Check the back of your pattern envelope for the necessary length and type of zipper. If it says "separating zipper," be sure that's what you get. This is a special type of zipper, most frequently used for coats and jackets. It splits open into two separate sections so you don't have to put the garment on over your head.

■ Unless the zipper tape is 100 percent polyester, pre-shrink the tape by plunging the zipper into hot water for a few minutes.

■ Working on the wrong side, press the zipper tape to remove any packaging folds. Don't rest the iron on the teeth or the coils.

INSTALLATION TIPS

Consult your pattern instructions for when and how to put in the zipper. As you follow those directions, keep these tips in mind:

■ ALWAYS use a zipper foot when machine basting and permanently stitching the zipper. It can be positioned either to the right or the left of your needle, making the installation easier and your stitching straighter.

■ To keep ripples out of your finished product, ALWAYS stitch in the same direction: from the bottom of the zipper to the top. This rule holds true for both machine basting and permanent stitching.

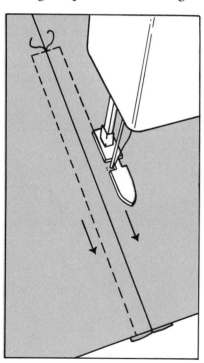

When Basting

■ If the garment seam is basted closed before the zipper is installed, use a long machine basting stitch. Then, before pressing the seam open, clip the basting

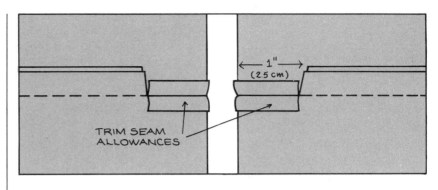

stitches at the bottom of the zipper opening, as well as every 2″ (5cm). This will make them easier to remove once the zipper is installed. Then, if you have trouble grabbing the thread ends, use pointed tweezers.

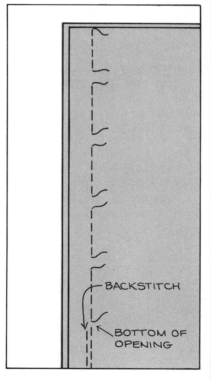

■ If the zipper is going to cross a seam (for example, a center back zipper on a dress with a waistline), you may need to reduce some of the bulk before basting the seam closed. To do this, make a clip in the intersecting seam allowances, 1″ (2.5cm) in from each opening edge. Trim the seam allowances within the

clipped section to ⅜″ (1cm) and press them open.

■ Although machine basting is usually the suggested method for holding a zipper in place for permanent stitching, you may get better results with double-faced basting tape or glue stick. Put basting tape along the outside edge of the zipper tape so you don't stitch through it. You can stitch through glue stick as long as you let it dry for a few minutes first. Otherwise, it will gum up your needle. If you don't have either of these products on hand, use masking tape or transparent tape, positioning the tape along the edge of the zipper tape so that you absolutely DO NOT stitch through it.

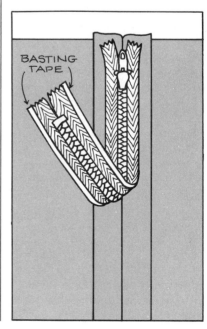

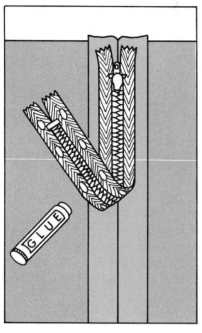

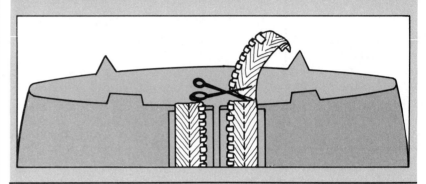

TIP *Another way to avoid stitching around the slider "bump" is to purchase a zipper that's longer than the pattern calls for. When you install the zipper, position it so that the pull tab and slider extend above the edge of the garment. Once the zipper is installed, slide the pull tab down and cut off the excess zipper tape at the raw edge of the garment. The intersecting waistband, seam, facing, etc. will act as the top stop for the zipper.*

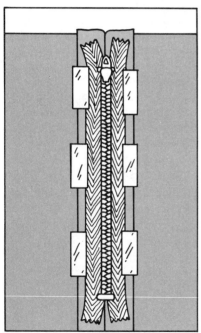

■ As you baste the zipper in place, keep the pull tab flipped up. Later on, this will make it easier to permanently stitch around the pull tab and the slider.

When Topstitching

For a professional-looking zipper installation, the topstitching should be smooth, straight, and a consistently even distance from the edge(s) of the garment all along the length of the zipper. If you can't do it "by eye," try one of the following:

■ Use a ruler and a water-soluble or evaporating fabric marking pen to draw stitching guidelines on the right side of your fabric. Test first to make sure the ink is removable.

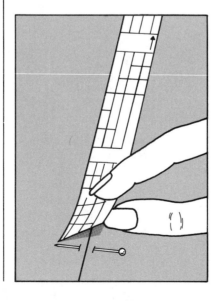

■ Use topstitching or stick-on sewing tape. This tape is perforated so that you can separate it into different widths. Stitch next to the edge of the tape, then pull off the tape.

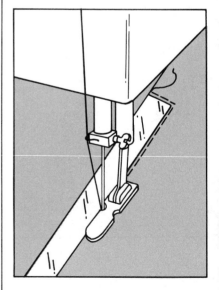

■ If you're inserting a lapped zipper, ½" (1.3cm) wide transparent tape makes a great topstitching guide.

■ To avoid bumpy topstitching around the tab and slider, stop topstitching just before you get to the slider. Leaving the needle in the fabric, raise the presser foot and pull the slider down below the needle. (If you can't work it down gently with your finger, you may have to remove some of the basting that is holding the garment seam closed.) Lower the presser foot and continue topstitching.

THE HAND-SEWN ZIPPER

If your fabric is delicate or requires special handling (for example, chiffon, velvet or lace), consider doing the final row of stitching by hand. In addition, many people prefer the couture look of a hand-sewn zipper for tailored suits and dresses.

The final row of stitching is done with the PICKSTITCH described on Chapter 5, page 120. To keep the stitches straight, use a row of hand basting or any of the topstitching guidelines listed above.

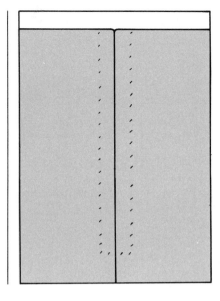

PART THREE

SIMPLY THE BEST PATTERNLESS SEWING PROJECTS

Patternless sewing projects? Yes, patternless! Here's your guide to sewing a smashing new mix-and-match women's wardrobe, suitable for all seasons and where practical, scaled down for children's garments; adorable baby clothes and a super-simple table setting—all sized to Simplicity® standards.

If you don't believe it's possible to sew without patterns, turn to the 8-page color section between pages 224 and 225 to see what exciting results you can achieve by following the easy, self-contained instructions for the projects in this part of the book. You'll be surprised at how easy it is!

A WARDROBE FOR ALL SEASONS

KIMONO (shown in full color)

This versatile kimono can be made in a Misses' hip-length or dress-length version, or for a girl or a boy. As sized for the Misses' Figure, it fits up to a 42″ bust; for Girls, sizes 7–14; and for Boys, sizes 7–12. A baby-sized version appears on page 240. It's wonderful in a variety of light to medium weight fabrics, including silk, linen, terry cloth, broadcloth, chino, poplin, chambray, cotton sateen, shantung, wool flannel, jersey and double knit.

Except for the Cutting Diagrams and the measurement differences indicated in Steps 3 and 4 of the Sewing Directions, the procedures for making the Misses' or the Girl/Boy versions are exactly the same.

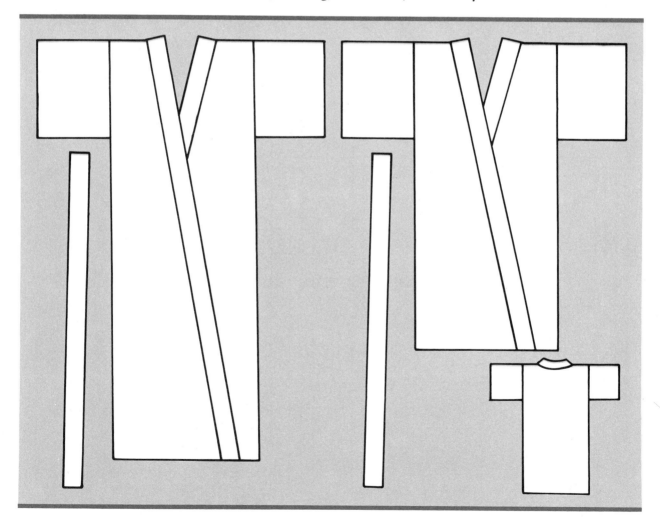

SUPPLIES

For the hip-length Misses' version:

■ 2½ yds. (2.3m) of 44"/45" (115cm) fabric without a nap or one-way design

For the dress-length Misses' version:

■ 3 yds. (2.8m) of 44"/45" (115cm) fabric without a nap or one-way design

For the Girl's or Boy's version:

■ 2 yds. (2m) of 44"/45" (115cm) fabric without a nap or one-way design

For all three versions:

■ thread
■ chalk marking pencil or fabric marking pen
■ yardstick or T-square
■ glue stick (optional)

CUTTING DIRECTIONS

Place your fabric, single thickness and right side up, on a large, flat surface or cutting board. Using the appropriate Cutting Diagram (Diagram A for hip-length,

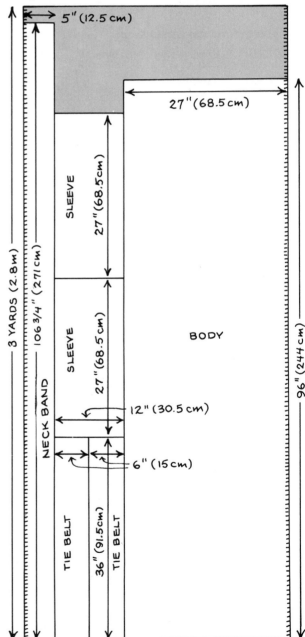

DIAGRAM B - MISSES' DRESS LENGTH

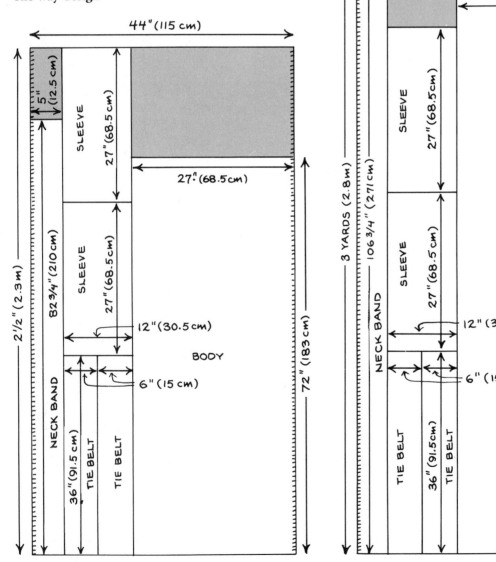

DIAGRAM A - MISSES' HIP LENGTH

Diagram B for dress-length and Diagram C for Girl's or Boy's), plot out and cut the following sections of your kimono:

■ one BODY
■ two BELTS
■ two SLEEVES
■ one NECKBAND

The measurements for each section are indicated on the appropriate Cutting Diagram. Use the yardstick or T-square to get your cutting lines straight, even and parallel.

SEWING DIRECTIONS

Note: All seam allowances are ⅝" (1.5cm). The hem allowance is 1" (2.5cm) at lower edge.

Establishing the Neckline and Center Front Opening

1. With right sides together, fold the BODY in half lengthwise and mark the fold. This is the Center Front/Center Back line.
2. Unfold the BODY and refold it in half crosswise, right sides together; mark the fold. This is the Shoulder Line.

3. The point where the Center Front/Center Back Line and the Shoulder Line intersect is the starting point for establishing the neckline curve.

For the Misses' kimonos only:

■ On the Center Back Line, put a mark ¾" (2cm) from the intersection point.
■ On the Center Front Line, put a mark 10" (25.5cm) from the intersection point.
■ On both sides of the Shoulder Line, put a mark 3" (7.5cm) from the intersection point.

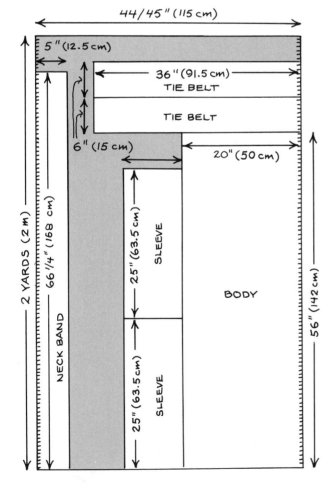

DIAGRAM C – GIRL'S or BOY'S

ESTABLISH CENTER FRONT/BACK AND SHOULDER LINES

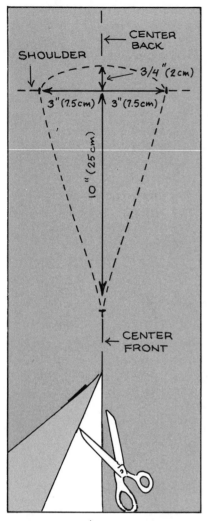

MISSES' NECKBAND

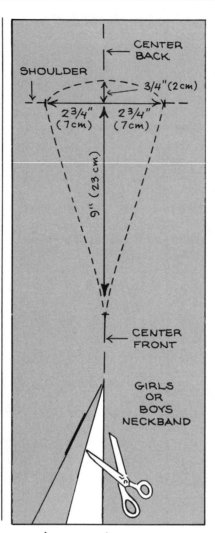

GIRL'S OR BOY'S NECKBAND

Attaching the Neckband

4. To establish the Center Back and Shoulders on the NECK-BAND, fold it in half crosswise and mark at the raw edges. This is the CB marking.

For the Misses' kimonos only:

■ Mark along the raw edges 4⅜" (11.2cm) from the Center Back on each side.

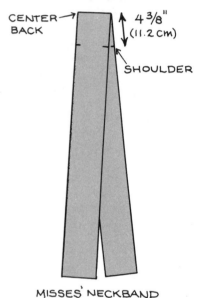

MISSES' NECKBAND

For the Girl's or Boy's kimono only:

■ Mark along the raw edges 4⅛" (10.5cm) from the Center Back on each side.

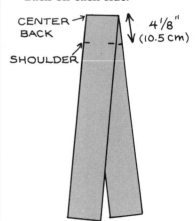

GIRL'S OR BOY'S NECKBAND

These are the Shoulder markings.

For the Girl's or Boy's kimono only:

■ On the Center Back Line, put a mark ¾" (2cm) from the intersection point.

■ On the Center Front Line, put a mark 9" (23cm) from the intersection point.

■ On both sides of the Shoulder Line, put a mark 2¾" (7cm) from the intersection point.

For all versions:

■ To create the neckline, draw a line, as shown, connecting these four marks. Gently curve the line to get rid of the corner at the point where the neckline meets the center front. Be sure that the left side of the neckline matches the right side.

■ Beginning at the lower edge of the Center Front Line, cut the BODY apart until you reach the 10" (25.5cm) mark of the Misses' BODY or 9" (23cm) mark of the Girl's or Boy's BODY, then cut around the neckline.

> **TIP** *You might want to draw one side of the curve, then fold the BODY along the Center Front/Center Back Line and use dressmaker's carbon and a tracing wheel to transfer the curve to the other side.*

5. Staystitch the BODY neckline. Clip the seam allowances just to, but not through, the staystitching all around the neckline, as shown.

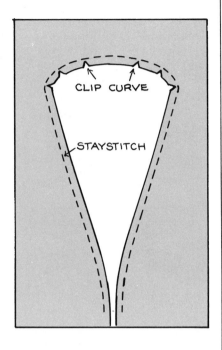

6. With right sides together, pin the NECKBAND to the BODY, matching the CB and Shoulder markings. Be careful not to stretch the band; instead, ease it carefully around the curves. Stitch, trim and clip the seam, or serge it on the overlock.

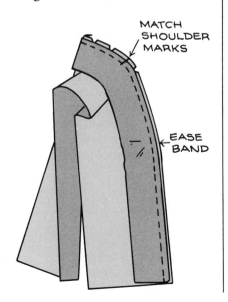

Note: Depending on your fabric and how much easing you have to do, the NECKBAND may extend beyond the lower edges of the BODY. Trim off the excess before hemming the kimono (Step 13).

7. Press the long raw edge of the NECKBAND under ⅝″ (1.5cm). Then fold the band to the inside of the kimono so that the folded edge just covers the seamline. Hand-baste or glue-baste in place, easing it carefully around the curves. Slipstitch in place.

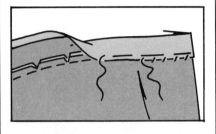

8. Working on the outside of the kimono, edgestitch the NECK-BAND close to the seamline, through all thicknesses.

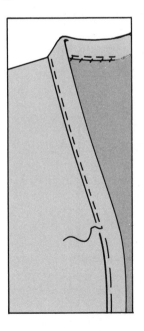

Attaching the Sleeves

9. To find the Shoulder Line, fold each sleeve in half crosswise and mark. Then, along one 27″

(68.5cm) edge of each Misses' SLEEVE or one 25″ (63.5cm) edge of the Girl's or Boy's SLEEVE, mark ⅝″ (1.5cm) in from each outer edge.

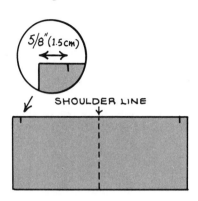

10. With right sides together, pin the SLEEVE to the BODY, matching Shoulder Lines and raw edges. Stitch the seam, beginning and ending the stitching at the ⅝″ (1.5cm) marks. Repeat for the other sleeve, then press both sleeve seams open.

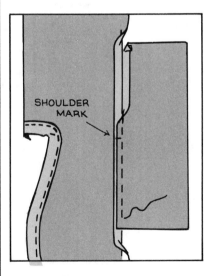

TIP *Both the sleeves and the lower edge of the kimono can be finished on the overlock machine, then turned up and topstitched in place.*

Stitching the Side Seams

11. With right sides together, pin the BODY front and back together at the sides and underarm seamlines.

■ Beginning at the lower edge of the BODY, stitch the side seam. End the stitching when you reach the sleeve seam, keeping the sleeve seam allowances free.

■ Beginning at the lower edge of the SLEEVE, stitch the underarm seam. End the stitching when you reach the ⅝″ (1.5cm) markings, keeping the sleeve seam allowances free. This "break" in the stitching at the underarm area is what makes the underarm seam smooth on the finished kimono.

■ Press the side/underarm seams open.

Hemming the Kimono

12. Narrow hem the lower edge of the sleeves, following the directions for the Narrow Top-stitched Hem, page 167, changing the hem allowance from 1″ (2.5cm) to ⅝″ (1.5cm).

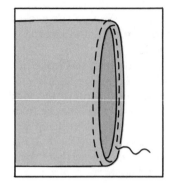

13. Mark the hem at the lower edge of the kimono, then press up along the hemline. Trim the hem allowance to 1″ (2.5cm). Finish, following the directions for the Narrow Topstitched Hem, page 167.

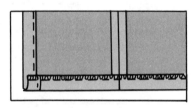

Constructing the Belt

14. With right sides together, serge or stitch the two BELT sections together along one 6″ (15cm) end. Then finish the belt on the conventional or the overlock machine, following the directions for SOFT BELTS, page 129.

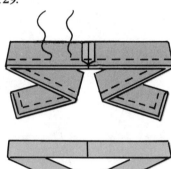

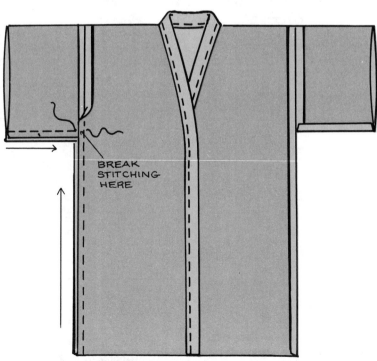

STITCHING THE SIDE SEAMS

BREAK STITCHING HERE

"T" DRESS OR TOP
(shown in full color)

This comfortable, contemporary "T" makes a beautiful dress or top. Choose a soft or crisp, light to medium weight knit or woven. Think silk, linen, cotton, challis, crepe de chine or lightweight wool. The top has been sized for Misses' and Girl's. The dress, sized for Misses' only, features front patch pockets.

Except for the Cutting Diagrams and the measurement differences indicated in Step 3 of the Sewing Directions, the procedures for making the Misses' and Girl's versions are exactly the same.

SUPPLIES

For the Misses' Dress:

■ 2½ yds. (2.3cm) of 44″/45″ (115cm) wide fabric, without a nap or one-way design

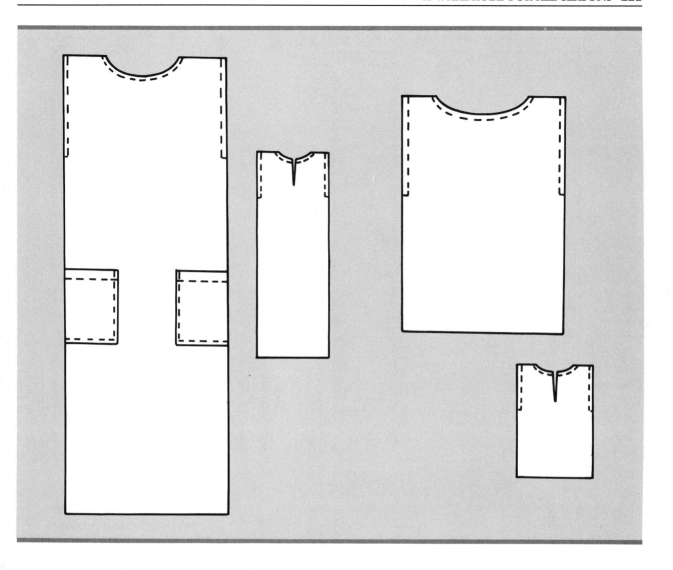

For the Misses' Top:

■ 1½ yds. (1.4m) of 44"/45"
(115cm) wide fabric, without a
nap or one-way design

For the Girl's Top:

■ 44"/45" (115cm) wide fabric,
without a nap or one-way design.
To determine how much fabric to
buy, divide the girl's hip measurement by two, then add 7"
(18cm). Divide this total by 36"
(100cm) to find out what fraction
of a yard (meter) you will need.

For all three versions:

■ thread
■ one ⅜" (1cm) button

■ one package of single-fold bias
tape (for conventional method
only)
■ chalk marking pencil or fabric
marking pen
■ yardstick or T-square

CUTTING DIRECTIONS

Place your fabric, single thickness and right side up, on a large,
flat surface. Using the appropriate
Cutting Diagram (Diagram A for
the dress, Diagram B for the top
and Diagram C for the Girl's top),
plot out and cut the following
sections:

■ one BODY

■ two POCKETS (for the dress
only)

The measurements for each
section are indicated on the appropriate Cutting Diagram. Use
the yardstick or T-square to get
your cutting lines straight, even
and parallel. (See page 222.)

Note: The Misses' dress and top
are cut lengthwise on the fabric
but the Girl's top is cut crosswise.

SEWING DIRECTIONS

Note: The neckline has a ¼"
(6mm) seam allowance. All other
seam and hem allowances are ⅝"
(1.5cm).

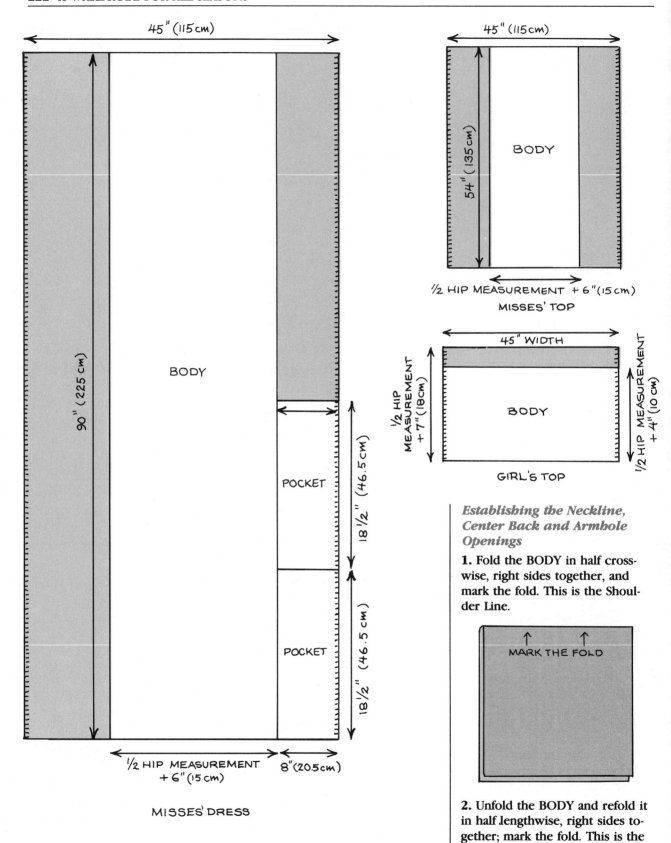

45" (115cm)

90" (225 cm)

BODY

POCKET

18½" (46.5 cm)

POCKET

18½" (46.5 cm)

½ HIP MEASUREMENT + 6" (15 cm)

8" (20.5cm)

MISSES' DRESS

45" (115cm)

54" (135 cm)

BODY

½ HIP MEASUREMENT + 6" (15cm)

MISSES' TOP

45" WIDTH

½ HIP MEASUREMENT + 7" (18cm)

BODY

½ HIP MEASUREMENT + 4" (10 cm)

GIRL'S TOP

Establishing the Neckline, Center Back and Armhole Openings

1. Fold the BODY in half crosswise, right sides together, and mark the fold. This is the Shoulder Line.

MARK THE FOLD

2. Unfold the BODY and refold it in half lengthwise, right sides together; mark the fold. This is the Center Front/Center Back Line.

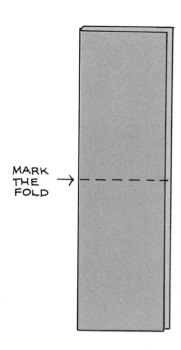

MARK THE FOLD →

3. The point where the Center Front/Center Back Lines and the Shoulder Line intersect is the starting point for establishing the neckline curve and the back opening.

For the Misses' dress or top only:

■ On the Center Back Line, put a mark 1¼″ (3.2cm) from the intersection point.

■ On the Center Front Line, put a mark 3″ (7.5cm) from the intersection point.

■ On both sides of the Shoulder Line, put a mark 4¼″ (11cm) from the intersection point.

For the Girl's top only:

■ On the Center Back Line, put a mark 1¼″ (3.2cm) from the intersection point.

■ On the Center Front Line, put a mark 2½″ (6.3cm) from the intersection point.

■ On both sides of the Shoulder Line, put a mark 3¾″ (9.5cm) from the intersection point.

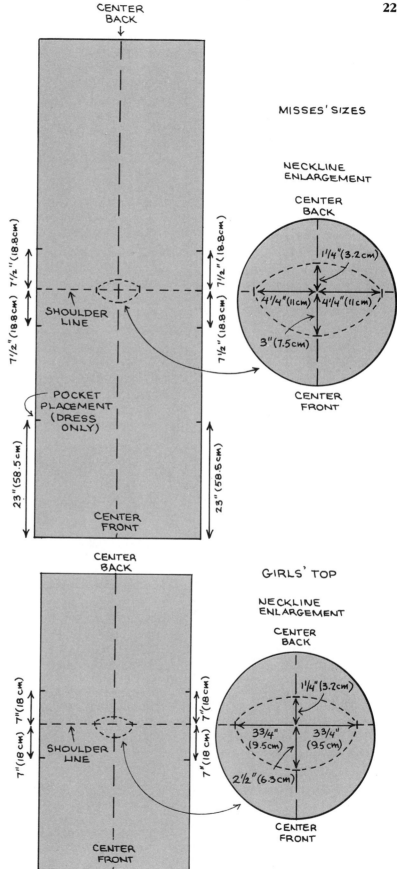

For all versions:

■ To create the neckline, draw a curved line, as shown, connecting these four marks. Be sure that the curve on the left side of the Center Front/Center Back Line matches the curve on the right side.

■ Cut out the neck opening along this line.

For the armholes on the Misses' dress or top:

■ Put four marks at the side seams, each 7½" (19cm) from the Shoulder Line.

For the armholes on the Girl's top:

■ Put four marks at the side seams, each 7" (18cm) from the Shoulder Line.

For the pocket placement (Misses' dress version only):

■ Put two more marks on the front side seams, each 23" (58.5cm) up from the lower edge.

4. To create the back opening, put a mark on the Center Back Line, 5" (12.5cm) down from the back neck edge. Now put two marks at the back neck edge, each ¼" (6mm) from the Center

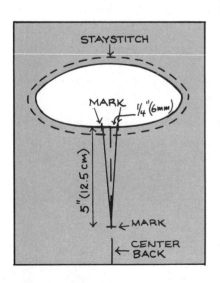

TIP *You might want to draw one side of the curve, then fold the BODY along the Center Front/Center Back Line and use dressmaker's carbon and a tracing wheel to transfer the curve to the other side.*

Back Line. Draw two lines, connecting these three marks into a "V." Do NOT cut along these lines. They are stitching lines.

■ Staystitch the neckline opening ⅛" (3mm) from the raw edge.

Making the Pockets (Misses' Dress version only)

5. Fold the POCKETS in half, right sides together, with the 8" (20.5cm) edges matching. (The fold will be the top of the pocket.) Stitch or serge along the bottom and one side of each POCKET.

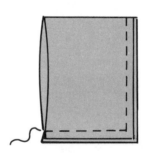

6. Turn the POCKETS right side out and press. Topstitch ¾" (2cm) from the fold. Baste the remaining raw edges together.

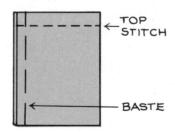

7. Working on the right side, pin one POCKET to each side of the BODY so that the folded edge is

at the pocket placement mark and the raw edges are aligned. Baste the POCKET in place at the sides and bottom. Then topstitch close to the bottom and the finished side edge.

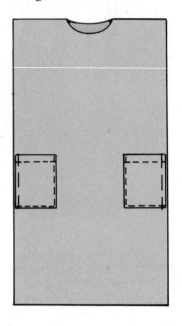

Facing the Back Opening

8. For the FACING section, cut a 3" × 6" (7.5cm × 15cm) rectangle from your leftover fabric.

■ To locate its Center Back Line, fold the FACING in half lengthwise, right sides together; mark along the fold.

■ To finish the sides and lower edge of the facing, serge

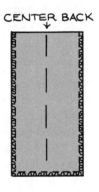

around the edges or trim off to ¼" (6mm) and overcast on your conventional machine.

SIMPLY THE BEST WARDROBE

Whether your goal is to try out some new techniques or polish up rusty sewing skills, these patternless projects are sure to whet your sewing appetite.

■ Simple, elegant and timeless, these styles will look fashionable season after season.

■ Carefully designed for versatility, the shapes mix and match beautifully to create the perfect wardrobe.

■ The easy to follow instructions include conventional and overlock alternatives.

POLISHED PERFECTION!

Long Kimono
+
Top
+
Dirndl Skirt

THE MESSAGE IS PRINTS!

**Top
+
Dirndl Skirt**

Dirndl Skirt   Top

BLACK AND WHITE— ALWAYS RIGHT

Long Kimono
+
Shell Dress

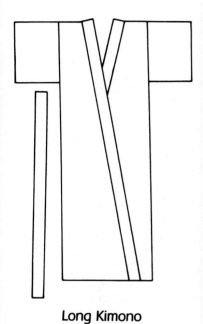

Long Kimono

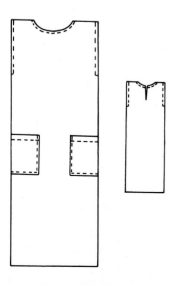

Shell Dress

FOR SIZZLING SUMMER DAYS

Short Kimono
+
Top
+
Pleated Skirt

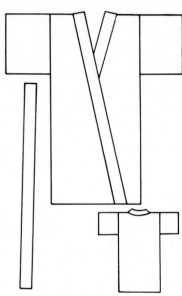

Short Kimono

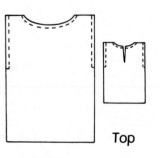

Top

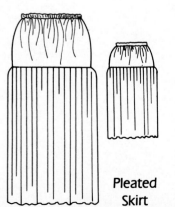

Pleated Skirt

THE CITY SOPHISTICATE

Long Kimono
+
Top
+
Dirndl Skirt

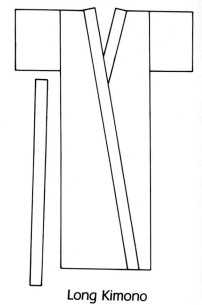

Long Kimono

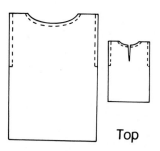

Top

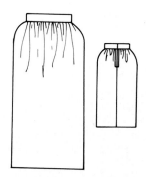

Dirndl Skirt

ACCESSORIES GALORE!

Clutch Purse

Tote Bag

Belt

Clutch Purse

Scarf

Sash

THE KINDER KORNER

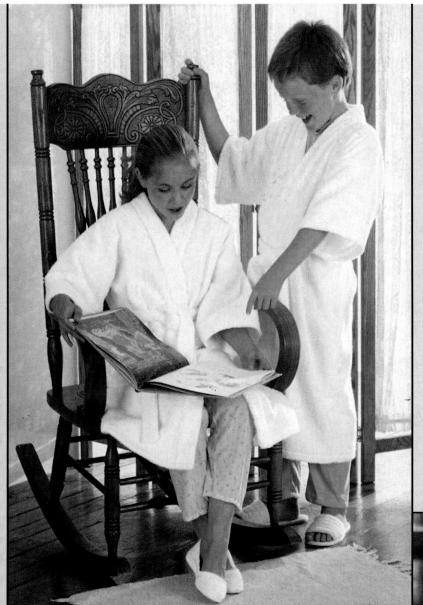

Soft & Cuddly Kimonos

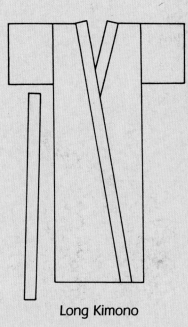

Long Kimono

*purchased pajamas

THE BEST DRESSED BABY

Baby Kimono + Diaper Cover

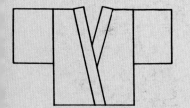

Short Kimono

Diaper Cover

**Tablecloth
+
Napkins
+
Placemats**

9. With right sides together, pin the facing to the back, matching Center Back Lines and the raw edges at the neckline.

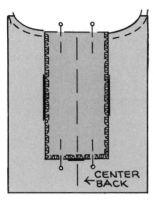

10. With the BODY facing up, stitch along the stitching lines, shortening the stitch for 1″ (2.5cm) on either side of the point. Slash along the Center Back Line, between, and just up to, the stitching.

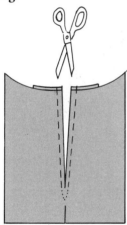

11. Turn the facing to the inside and press. Edgestitch around the opening, as shown.

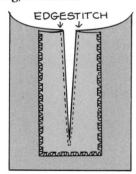

Finishing the Neckline

THE CONVENTIONAL METHOD:

12-A. With right sides together and raw edges even, open out the bias tape and pin it to the neck edge, beginning and ending ⅝″ (1.5cm) from the back opening, keeping the FACING free, as shown. Stitch a ¼″ (6mm) seam.

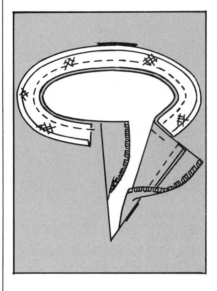

12-B. Press the bias tape up, away from the neckline, then fold it to the inside along the stitching line, clipping where necessary, and press again; baste.

12-C. Fold the upper edge of the FACING and the remaining neckline edge under ¼″ (6mm). Slipstitch the FACING to the neckline edge.

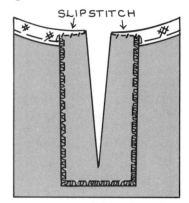

12-D. Topstitch the neckline ¼″ (6mm) from the edge.

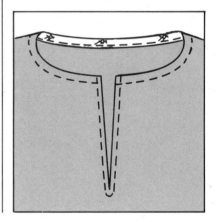

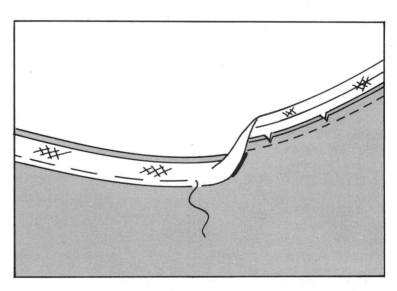

Ⓢ THE OVERLOCK METHOD:

13-A. Baste the FACING to the neckline edge.

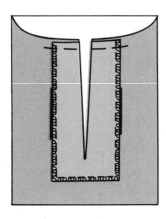

13-B. Serge along the neckline edge, trimming ¼″ (6mm) as you stitch.

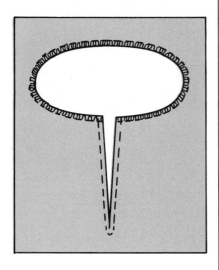

Finishing the Armholes and Stitching the Side Seams

THE CONVENTIONAL METHOD:

14-A. With right sides together, pin the BODY front and back together at the side seams, matching the armhole markings. Starting at the lower edge, stitch the side

seam, between the lower edge and the armhole marking. Backstitch at the armhole marking to reinforce.

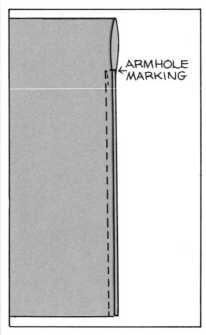

14-B. Finish the armhole edges, following the directions for the Narrow Topstitched Hem, page 167, changing the hem allowance from 1″ (2.5cm) to ⅝″ (1.5cm) and squaring the stitching at the underarm, as shown.

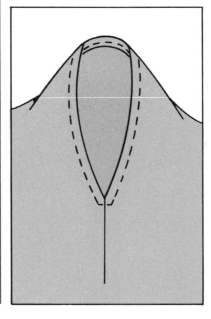

Ⓢ THE OVERLOCK METHOD:

15-A. Serge the armhole edges between the markings, angling the stitches on and off the fabric approximately 1½″ (3.8cm) below the armhole markings, and trimming ⅝″ (1.5cm) as you stitch.

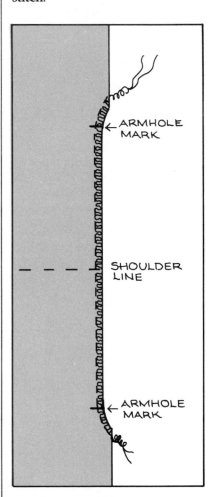

15-B. With right sides together, pin the BODY front and back together at the side seams. Starting at the lower edge, serge a ⅝″ (1.5cm) seam, angling off the fabric at the armhole markings.

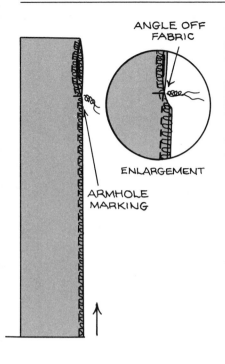

ANGLE OFF FABRIC

ENLARGEMENT

ARMHOLE MARKING

Finishing the Garment

16. Make a thread loop at the left back neck opening. Sew a button to the right back neck opening, opposite the loop.

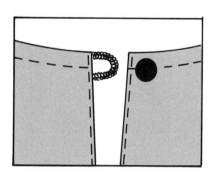

17. Mark the hemline for the lower edge of the garment. To hem the lower edge, review Chapter 6, HEMS, and choose the hand or machine hemming method you prefer. Two good choices, particularly if you are making the Top, would be the narrow topstitched hem (on your conventional machine) or the narrow rolled hem (on your overlock).

PLEATED SKIRT
(shown in full color)

This versatile pleated skirt is suitable for Misses' and Girl's sizes. Make it in a light to medium weight knit or woven fabric. Consider wools, linens and cottons—you'll want to own several versions so you can wear this style all year round.

SUPPLIES

■ 44"/45" (115cm) wide fabric without a nap or one-way design. To determine how much fabric to buy, multiply the hip measurement by 3, then add 4" (10cm). Divide this total by 36" (100cm)—that's how many yards (meters) you'll need.

■ thread

■ one package of ¾" (2cm) wide elastic

■ chalk marking pencil or fabric marking pen

■ yardstick or T-square

CUTTING DIRECTIONS

Place your fabric, single thickness and right side up on a large, flat surface. Using Cutting Diagram A for Misses' sizes and Cutting Diagram B for Girl's sizes, plot out and cut the following sections for the pleated skirt:

■ one SKIRT
■ one YOKE

The measurements for each section are indicated on the appropriate Cutting Diagram. Use the yardstick or T-square to get your cutting lines straight, even and parallel. (See page 228.)

SEWING DIRECTIONS

Note: All seam allowances are ⅝" (1.5cm).

Marking the Pleats

1. Working on the right side (outside) of the SKIRT:

■ Make a mark at the upper right-hand corner that's 1⅝" (4cm) in from the Center Back.

■ Continuing from right to left across the top, make a second mark 2" (5cm) away from the first mark, and a third mark 1" (2.5cm) away from the second. Repeat, alternating 2" (5cm) and 1" (2.5cm) marks across

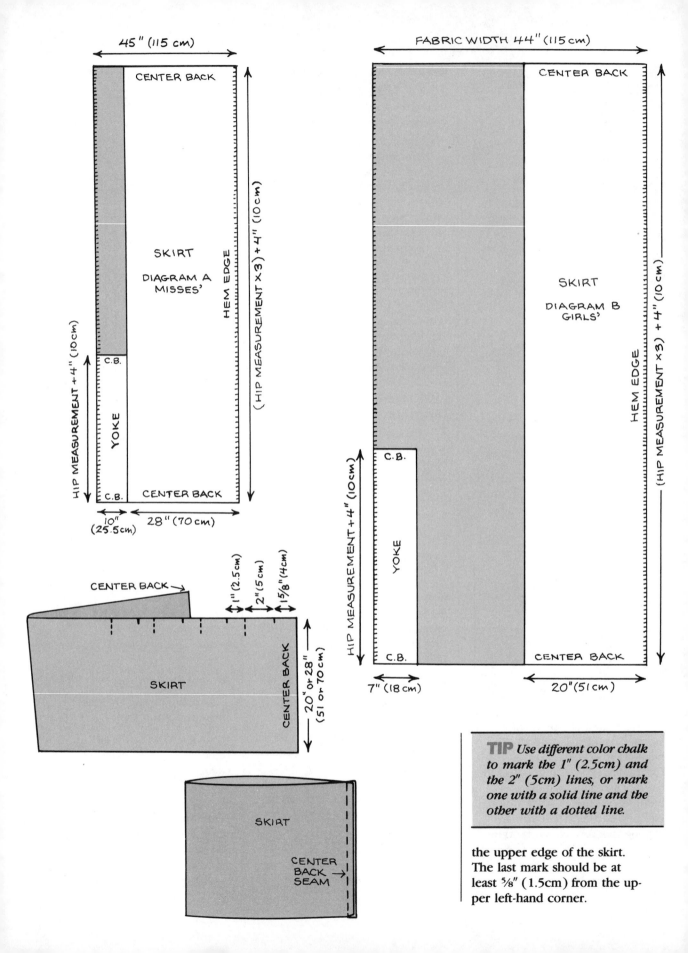

45" (115 cm)

CENTER BACK

SKIRT

DIAGRAM A
MISSES'

HEM EDGE

(HIP MEASUREMENT ×3) + 4" (10 cm)

HIP MEASUREMENT + 4" (10cm)

C.B.

YOKE

C.B.   CENTER BACK

10"
(25.5cm)

28" (70 cm)

FABRIC WIDTH 44" (115 cm)

CENTER BACK

SKIRT

DIAGRAM B
GIRLS'

HEM EDGE

(HIP MEASUREMENT ×3) + 4" (10 cm)

HIP MEASUREMENT + 4" (10cm)

C.B.

YOKE

C.B.   CENTER BACK

7" (18 cm)

20"(51 cm)

CENTER BACK

1" (2.5cm)   2"(5 cm)   1⅝"(4cm)

SKIRT

CENTER BACK

20" or 28"
(51 or 70cm)

SKIRT

CENTER
BACK
SEAM

TIP *Use different color chalk to mark the 1" (2.5cm) and the 2" (5cm) lines, or mark one with a solid line and the other with a dotted line.*

the upper edge of the skirt. The last mark should be at least ⅝" (1.5cm) from the upper left-hand corner.

Constructing the Pleats

2. With right sides together, stitch or serge the SKIRT Center Back Seam.

3. On the outside of the garment, and working from left to right:

■ Bring a 1″ (2.5cm) marking to meet the next 2″ (5cm) marking; pin. Continue across the upper edge of the SKIRT to form all the pleats.

■ Baste the pleats in place across the upper edge of the SKIRT.

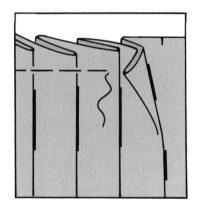

Attaching the Yoke

4. With right sides together, stitch or serge the YOKE Center Back Seam.

5. With right sides together and raw edges even, pin the upper edge of the SKIRT to the lower edge of the YOKE. If necessary, adjust the pleats nearest to the

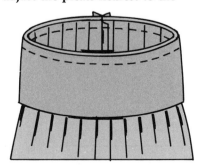

Center Back Seam until the SKIRT fits the YOKE. Stitch or serge the seam.

6. Press the seam toward the YOKE, then topstitch the YOKE, ⅛″–¼″ (3mm–6mm) from the seam.

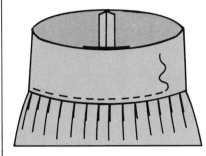

Making the Elasticized Waistline Casing

7. To keep the seam allowances from getting in the way later on when you insert the elastic, use fusible web or machine basting to anchor them to the garment. Do this for about 3″ (7.5cm) from the upper edge of the YOKE.

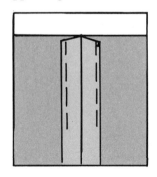

8. To form the casing:

■ Fold under 1¼″ (3.2cm) along the upper edge of the YOKE and press.

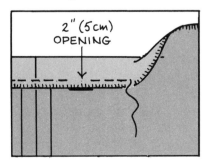

2″ (5cm) OPENING

■ Topstitch 1″ (2.5cm) from the fold, leaving a 2″ (5cm) opening for inserting the elastic.

9. Cut a piece of elastic the person's waist measurement plus 1″ (2.5cm). Insert and secure the elastic, and finish the casing following the directions for Inserting Elastic, page 138.

Hemming the Garment

10. Mark the hem at the lower edge of the skirt, then press up along the hemline. Review Chapter 6, HEMS, to choose the hand or machine hemming technique you prefer. If you can't decide which method to use, experiment on scraps of your fabric.

DIRNDL SKIRT
(shown in full color)

This skirt can be made from almost any fabric, from sensible wools or glamorous satins to soft knits or even casual denims. Its timeless design guarantees that it's a style you'll want to make again and again.

SUPPLIES

■ 44″/45″ (115cm) wide fabric without a nap or one-way design. To determine how much fabric to buy, take your hip measurement, add 12″ (30.5cm), then divide

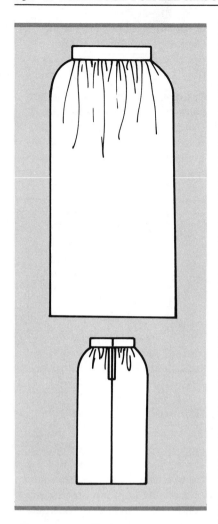

- one SKIRT
- one WAISTBAND

The measurements for each section are indicated on the Cutting Diagram. Use the yardstick or T-square to get your cutting lines straight, even and parallel.

Using your WAISTBAND section as the pattern piece, cut one WAISTBAND INTERFACING.

SEWING DIRECTIONS

Note: All seam allowances are ⅝″ (1.5cm).

Inserting the Zipper

1. On the SKIRT section, the long selvage edge is the lower edge of the skirt; the opposite raw edge is the top edge.

- Put a mark 8″ (20.5cm) down from the top edge, along the Center Back Seam.

- Then, with right sides together, pin and stitch the SKIRT Center Back Seam, from the lower edge to the mark. Backstitch at the mark.
- Machine-baste the remainder of the seam.
- Press the entire seam open.

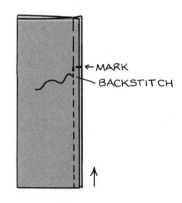

2. Review Chapter 6, ZIPPERS, Installation Tips. Then, place the

this total by 36″ (100cm)—that's how many yards (meters) you'll need.

- 7″ (18cm) skirt zipper
- two hook and eye closures
- fusible interfacing for the waistband
- thread
- chalk marking pencil or fabric marking pen
- yardstick or T-square
- glue stick (optional)

CUTTING DIRECTIONS

Place your fabric, single thickness and right side up, on a large, flat surface. Using the Cutting Diagram as your guide, plot out and cut the following sections for your dirndl skirt:

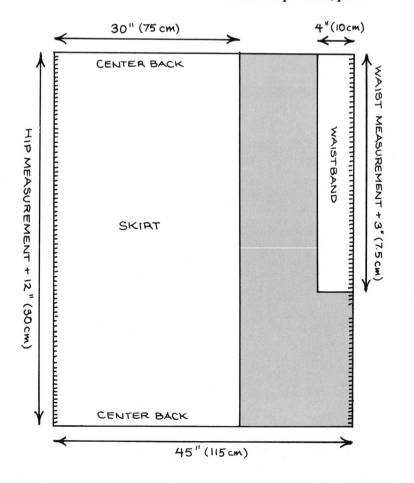

zipper, centered and face down, over the basted part of the seam. The bottom stop should be at the mark and the top stop should be 1″ (2.5cm) from the upper edge. Baste, then topstitch the zipper in place as shown, following the guidelines in Chapter 6, pages 208–211.

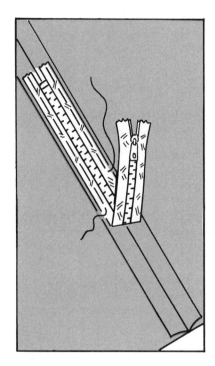

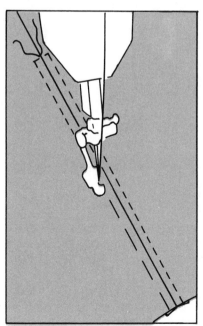

Gathering the Upper Edge of the Skirt

3. Gather the upper edge of the SKIRT, starting and ending the gathering stitches ½″ (1.3cm) from the Center Back. (For a review of gathering techniques, see Chapter 6, GATHERS).

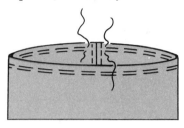

Constructing and Attaching the Waistband

4. Fuse the WAISTBAND INTERFACING to the WAISTBAND, following the manufacturer's fusing directions. Then, place the WAISTBAND flat, with the interfacing side up and selvage edge at the bottom, and mark 3″ (7.5cm) in from the left end of the band. This 3″ (7.5cm) will be the underlap on your finished waistband.

5. Open the zipper. Then, with right sides together:

■ Match the upper edge of the SKIRT to the long raw edge of the WAISTBAND, placing one edge of the zipper opening at the 3″ (7.5cm) mark and the other edge ⅝″ (1.5cm) in from the other end of the waistband, as shown.

■ Pull up the gathering stitches, adjusting the fullness evenly, until the skirt fits the waistband; pin.

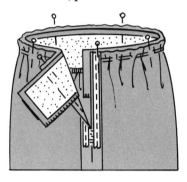

6. Attach and complete the waistband, following the step-by-step directions for the stitch-in-the-

3″ (7.5 cm)

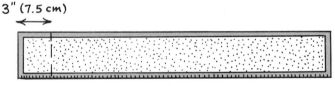

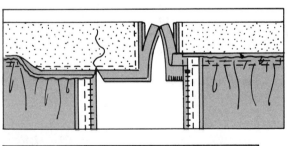

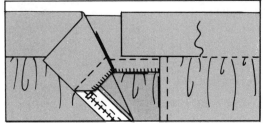

ditch machine method in Chapter 6, WAISTBANDS, page 205.

Finishing the Skirt

7. Lap the ends of the finished waistband, left over right; fasten with the hook and eye closures.

8. Mark the hem at the lower edge of the skirt, then press up along the hemline. Review Chapter 6, HEMS, to choose the hand or machine hemming method you prefer. If you can't decide which method to use, experiment on scraps of your fabric.

SCARF OR SHAWL

Using these same basic directions, you can make a small (36" or 1m) neck scarf, a larger (44" or 1.1m) square that can double as a hip wrap, or an even larger (54" or 1.4m) square that is great as a summer shawl or as an extra layer of warmth over a winter coat or suit jacket. Select a loosely woven fabric, such as a rayon or wool challis, that is easy to fringe.

SUPPLIES

For a 36" (1m) square:

■ 1 yd (1m) of 44"/45" (115cm) wide fabric

For a 44" (1.1m) square:

■ 1¼ yds. (1.1m) of 44"/45" (115cm) wide fabric

For a 54" (1.4m) square:

■ 1½ yds. (1.4m) of 58"/60" (150cm) wide fabric

For all size squares:

■ thread
■ chalk marking pencil or fabric marking pen
■ yardstick or T-square
■ liquid seam sealant (for the overlock method only)

CUTTING DIRECTIONS

Place your fabric, single thickness and right side up, on a large, flat surface.

■ Using the yardstick or T-square, mark and cut a 36" (1m), 44" (1.1m) or 54" (1.4m) square.
■ Draw a line 2" (5cm) in from each edge of the square.

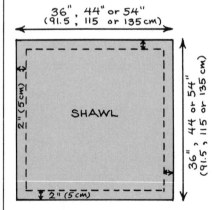

SEWING DIRECTIONS

Finishing the Edges

THE CONVENTIONAL METHOD:

1-a. Machine-stitch along the lines marked on the shawl, using a small, straight stitch.

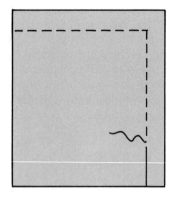

S THE OVERLOCK METHOD:

1-b. Press the shawl under along the marked lines.

■ Adjust your overlock to make a *true or mock flatlock stitch* (see Chapter 6, Raglan Sleeves—The Overlock Method, *page 189*). Serge along each edge from corner to corner, being careful not to cut the fold.

■ When all four sides have been serged, open out the folds and pull on the fabric to flatten the stitches.

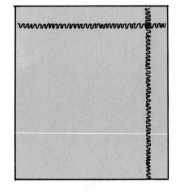

Fringing the Shawl

Note: On some fabrics, the selvage edge will not fringe easily. If this is the case, trim ½" (1.3cm) from all four sides before you begin step 2.

2. Form the fringe by raveling the fabric edges all the way up to the

TIP *For easy fringing, make little cuts all around the shawl every 2"–3" (5cm–7.5cm). Cut just up to the stitching. Then fringe in small sections, using a straight pin or a needle to help pull out the little clumps of thread.*

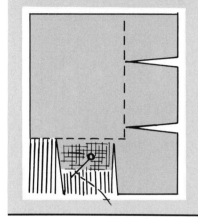

stitching. If you've flatlocked the edges, carefully trim the flatlock stitches from the fringed area and seal the ends of the stitching with a liquid seam sealant.

SASH

Choose any light to medium weight fabric for a soft sash that makes a wonderful waist wrap. Pick a color that matches or contrasts with your outfit. For extra pizzaz, add the optional fringe.

SUPPLIES

■ ½ yd. (45.5cm) of 44"/45" (115cm) wide fabric, without nap or one-way design

■ ½ yd. (45.5 cm) of 6" (15cm) deep fringe trim (optional)

■ thread

■ chalk marking pencil or fabric marking pen

■ yardstick or T-square
■ liquid seam sealant (optional)

CUTTING DIRECTIONS

Place your fabric, single thickness and right side up, on a large, flat surface. Cut a 14" × 41" (35.5cm × 104cm) rectangle.

■ With right sides together, fold the rectangle in half lengthwise and pin. Press the fold.

■ On the long raw edge, mark 3¾" (9.5cm) down from one end. Draw a diagonal line between this mark and the nearest opposite corner. Cut along this line, through both layers of fabric.

■ Remove the pins and cut along the foldline so you now have two sections for your sash.

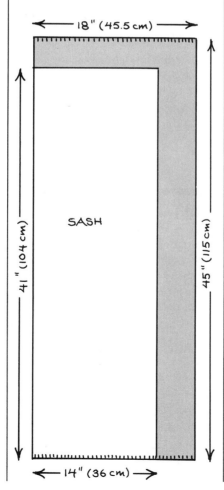

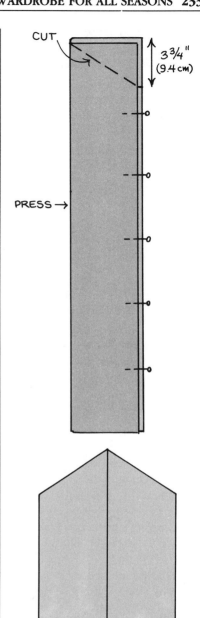

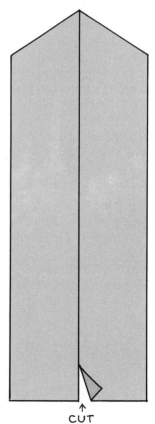

SEWING DIRECTIONS

Sewing the Center Back Seam

1. Sew the two sections of the sash together at the short, straight ends by serging, right sides together, or by stitching a French seam (see Chapter 5, Types of Seams).

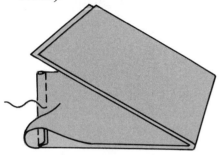

Hemming the Sash

2. To hem the sash, either finish the edges by serging, trimming ⅜″ (1cm) as you go, or do the following on your conventional machine:

- Machine-stitch ⅜″ (1cm) from each raw edge, crossing the stitching at the corners.
- Where the stitches cross, fold the corners diagonally to the wrong side; press. Trim these corner seam allowances to ¼″ (6mm).
- Fold the raw edges to the wrong side so they just meet the stitching line; press.
- Fold up along the stitching line and press again.
- Edgestitch all around the sash, close to the inner fold.

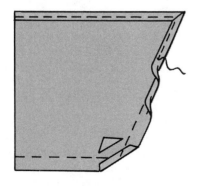

Adding the Fringe (Optional)

3. To finish the sides of the fringe, cut the fringe ½″ (1.3cm) wider than the sash, then fold the

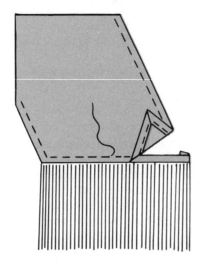

cut ends under ¼″ (6mm), before you topstitch, or cut the fringe to fit and seal the cut ends with a drop of liquid seam sealant.

- With the right sides up, lap the ends of the sash over the straight edge of the fringe.
- Topstitch over the previous stitching.

BELT (shown in full color)

A simple, but versatile, soft belt. Use a medium weight fabric and a beautiful buckle. It's the fashionable answer to pricey ready-to-wear accessories.

SUPPLIES

- ⅜ yd. (34.5cm) of 44″/45″ (115cm) wide fabric
- one 1½″ (3.8cm) buckle
- thread
- chalk marking pencil or fabric marking pen
- yardstick or T-square

CUTTING DIRECTIONS

Place your fabric, single thickness and right side up, on a large, flat surface.

- Cut a 8¾″ × 41″ (22cm × 104cm) rectangle.

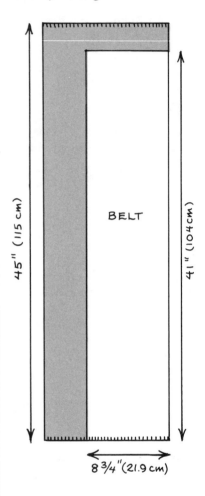

- With right sides together, fold the rectangle in half lengthwise and pin.
- On the long raw edge, mark 3″ (7.5cm) down from one end. Draw a diagonal line between this mark and the nearest opposite

TIP *Leave the belt pinned right sides together, and you're all ready to assemble it.*

corner. Cut along this line, through both thicknesses of fabric.

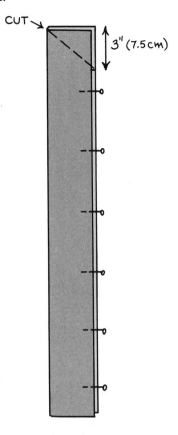

CUT

3" (7.5cm)

SEWING DIRECTIONS

Note: All seam allowances are ⅝" (1.5cm).

Assembling the Belt

1. With the belt pinned right sides together, stitch or serge along the seamline of the long raw edge and the short diagonal end. If necessary, trim and grade the seams.

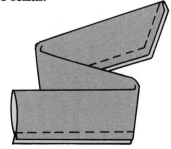

2. Turn the belt right side out and press. Stitch or serge across

the short, straight end, close to the raw edge.

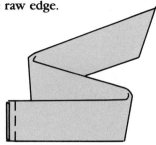

Attaching the Buckle

3. To gather the straight end of the belt, use three rows of long, machine gathering stitches. Place the first row ⅝" (1.5cm) from the end, the second row 1" (2.5cm) from the first, and the third row 1" (2.5cm) from the second.

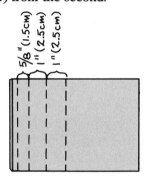

⅝" (1.5cm) 1" (2.5cm) 1" (2.5cm)

4. Pull up the gathers until the end measures 1½" (3.8cm) wide. Tie the threads to fasten.

1½" (3.8cm)

5. Slip the short end of the belt through the buckle and fold, wrong sides together, along the

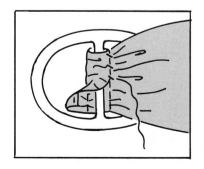

second gathering line. Now, fold the end under along the first gathering line, bring this fold to meet the third gathering line, and slipstitch in place.

CLUTCH PURSE/ EVENING BAG
(shown in full color)

Here's a great place to stash your small "necessaries." Make it to stand alone or in matching fabric as a companion for your tote. Consider glamour fabrics, such as tapestry, satin or brocade, for a smashing evening bag.

SUPPLIES

- ⅜ yd. (34.5cm) of 44"/45" (115cm) wide fabric, without a nap or one-way design
- ⅜ yd. (34.5cm) of 22"–36" (56cm–100cm) wide heavyweight woven or nonwoven, fusible or sew-in interfacing
- Optional: ⅜ yd. (34.5cm) of 44"/45" (115cm) wide lining fabric. (See note under Cutting Directions.)
- one large snap
- thread
- chalk marking pencil or fabric marking pen
- yardstick or T-square

CUTTING DIRECTIONS

Place your fabric, single thickness and right side up, on a large, flat surface. Using the Cutting Diagram, plot out and cut the following sections of your purse:

- one CLUTCH
- one LINING

The measurements for each section are indicated on the Cutting Diagram. Use the yardstick or T-square to get your cutting lines straight, even and parallel.

TIP *Begin by drawing two 12¼″ × 21¾″ (31cm × 55cm) rectangles, then marking one end of each rectangle, as shown, to create the triangular-shaped ends.*

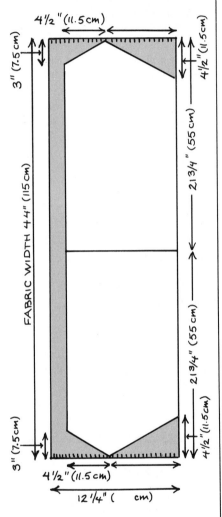

SEWING DIRECTIONS

Note: All seam allowances are ⅝″ (1.5cm).

Using the CLUTCH section as a pattern piece, cut out one INTERFACING.

Note: If your fashion fabric is heavy weight or bulky, cut the CLUTCH from the fashion fabric and the LINING from a lightweight lining fabric.

Preparing the Clutch

1. Baste or fuse the INTERFACING to the wrong side of the CLUTCH.

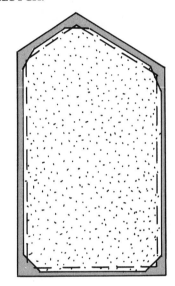

2. Working on the straight, 12¼″ (31cm) edge of the CLUTCH:

■ Fold under 1⅝″ (4cm); press.

■ Measure 6½″ (16.5cm) from the fold and mark a second foldline. Fold the CLUTCH, right sides together, at the markings and press lightly.

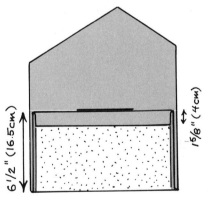

Preparing the Lining

3. Working on the straight, 12¼″ (31cm) edge of the LINING:

■ Fold under 2¼″ (5.7cm); press, then trim to ⅝″ (1.5cm).

■ Measure 6⅜″ (15.9cm) from the fold and mark a second foldline. Fold the LINING, right sides together, at the markings; press lightly.

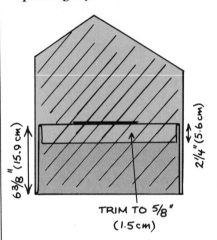

TRIM TO ⅝″ (1.5cm)

Assembling the Purse

4. Place the CLUTCH section, interfacing side down, on a flat surface. Place the LINING on top, as shown, and pin together around the sides and upper edges of the purse. Stitch or serge the sections together as pinned. (DO NOT stitch the folded edges together.) If necessary, trim and grade the seam.

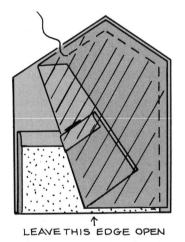

LEAVE THIS EDGE OPEN

Finishing the Purse

5. Insert your hand between the two folded edges, grasp the CLUTCH sections and turn the purse right side out.

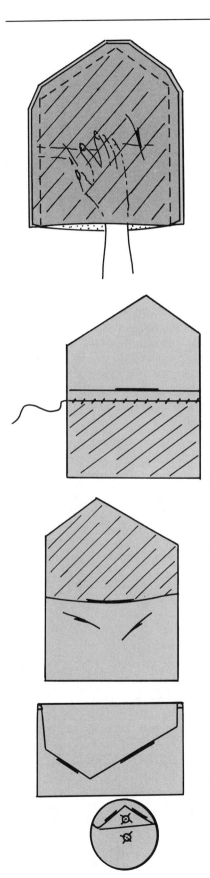

6. Slipstitch the LINING and the CLUTCH together along the inside opening.

7. Turn the lower portion of the CLUTCH right side out over the lower portion of the LINING.

8. Fold the flap down and fasten with a large snap.

TOTE BAG (shown in full color)

This handy tote is the perfect carryall for shopping, office or beach gear. Use a sturdy, medium to heavy weight fabric, such as denim, canvas, sailcloth, synthetic suede or quilted fabric.

SUPPLIES

- 1¼ yds (1.2m) of 44"/45" (115cm) fabric, without a nap or one-way design
- thread
- chalk marking pencil or fabric marking pen
- liquid seam sealant (optional)
- glue stick (optional)

CUTTING DIRECTIONS

Place your fabric, single thickness and right side up, on a large, flat surface. Using the Cutting Diagram as your guide, plot out and cut the following sections of your tote bag:

- one BAG
- one BOTTOM
- two POCKETS
- two HANDLES

The measurements for each section are indicated on the Cutting Diagram. Use the yardstick or T-square to get your cutting lines straight, even and parallel.

SEWING DIRECTIONS

Note: All seam allowances are ⅝" (1.5cm).

Note: Since you will be sewing four or more thicknesses of heavy

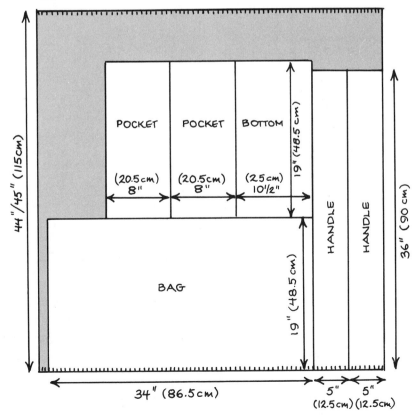

fabrics, the right size sewing machine needle is essential. Use a size 16/100 or 18/100. You may find it easier if you choose a wedge-point needle (the type designed for leather and vinyl) rather than a general purpose needle.

Preparing the Pockets

1. Using chalk or a fabric marking pen, mark both long edges of each POCKET 6¾" (17cm) in from each end, then connect each set of marks, as shown. These are the Handle Placement Lines.

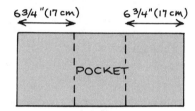

2. To form the pocket facing:

- Fold one long edge of the pocket 1¼" (3.2cm) to the inside and press. Finish the raw edge of the facing. On a conventional machine, finish the edge by turning it under and topstitching; on an overlock machine, serge along the raw edge, trimming off ¼" (6mm) as you stitch.

- Topstitch ¾" (2cm) from the fold.

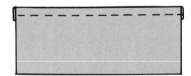

Preparing the Bag and Basting the Pockets in Place

3. Mark both long edges of the BAG 12½" (32cm) in from each

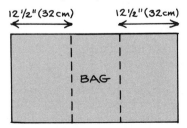

end, then connect each set of marks, as shown. These are the Pocket Placement Lines.

4. Finish the two 19" (48.5cm) edges of the BAG. On a conventional machine, finish the edge by turning it under and topstitching; on an overlock machine, serge along the raw edge, trimming off ¼" (6mm) as you stitch.

- Then, with the wrong side of the POCKET to the right side of the BAG, position the POCKET so that its long raw edge extends ⅝" (1.5cm) beyond the Pocket Placement Line; pin.

- Baste the POCKETS to the BAG along the sides and lower edges of the POCKETS, then along the Handle Placement Lines.

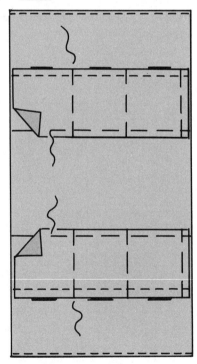

Making the Handles

5. Fold each HANDLE in half lengthwise, wrong sides together; press.

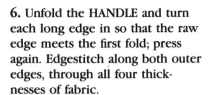

6. Unfold the HANDLE and turn each long edge in so that the raw edge meets the first fold; press again. Edgestitch along both outer edges, through all four thicknesses of fabric.

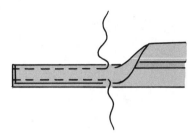

Attaching the Handles

7. Pin or glue-baste the HANDLES to the outside of the BAG over the Handle Placement Lines so that the raw edges of the HANDLES and the POCKETS are even. Topstitch the handle to the

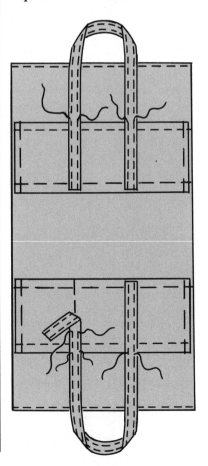

POCKETS and BAG, as shown, over the edgestitching. Stop topstitching at the upper edge of the POCKET and backstitch to reinforce.

Attaching the Bottom Section

8. Press under ⅝″ (1.5cm) on both long edges of the BOTTOM. Then, with the wrong side of the BOTTOM to the right side of the BAG, position the BOTTOM so that the sides are even and the folded edges just cover the Pocket Placement Lines; pin or glue-baste in place.

- Topstitch close to the folded edges of the BOTTOM, catching the POCKETS and HANDLES in the stitching.
- Baste the BOTTOM and BAG together along the remaining edges.

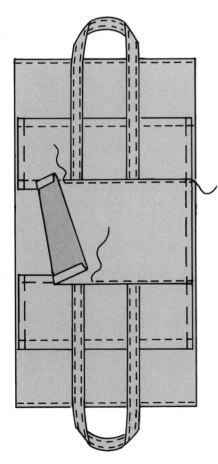

Finishing the Bag

9. Fold the bag in half, right sides together, so that the edges match, and stitch the side seams.

- Stitch along the seamline, then stitch again, ¼″ (6mm) from the first stitching, within the seam allowance. Trim close to the second row of stitching.
- If the raw edges have a tendency to fray, treat them with liquid seam sealant.

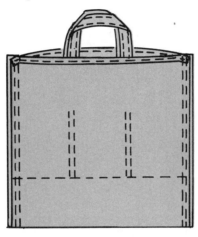

10. To form the BAG facing, fold the finished edge of the BAG 1½″ (3.8cm) to the inside and press. Folding the handles out of the way, topstitch the facing to the BAG 1¼″ (3.2cm) from the fold.

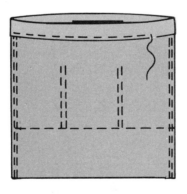

11. On the outside of the BAG, topstitch the HANDLES to the rest of the BAG. To keep the stitching lines smooth and connected, start stitching about 1″ (2.5cm) below the top of the pocket, directly over the previous stitching. To reinforce the handles, backstitch at the upper edge of the bag.

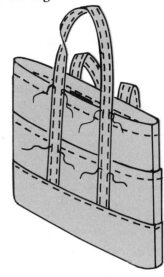

12. If you want your tote to have a flat bottom, fold the bottom corners up 1¼″ (3.2cm), as shown, and slipstitch in place.

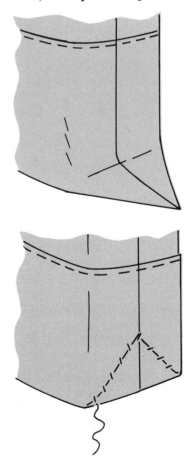

BABY KIMONO
(shown in full color)

Keep baby chic and cozy in this wonderful wrap. Moms will love it, too, because the clever hook and loop closures make it super-simple to dress and undress baby.

This kimono will fit up to size 6 months.

SUPPLIES

■ ½ yd. (45.5cm) of 42"/43" (107–110cm) wide fabric without a nap or one-way design

Note: For children's sleepwear, use fabrics and trims that meet the flammability standards set by the U.S. government.

■ 3 sets of ¾" (2cm) diameter hook and loop fasteners, such as Velcro®

■ 1 yd. (1m) of ⅜" (1cm) wide ribbon

■ thread

■ chalk marking pencil or fabric marking pen

■ yardstick or T-square

CUTTING DIRECTIONS

Place your fabric, single thickness and right side up, on a large, flat surface. Using the Cutting Diagram as your guide, plot out and cut the following sections of the baby kimono:

■ one BODY
■ two SLEEVES
■ one NECKBAND

The measurements for each section are indicated on the Cutting Diagram. Use the yardstick or

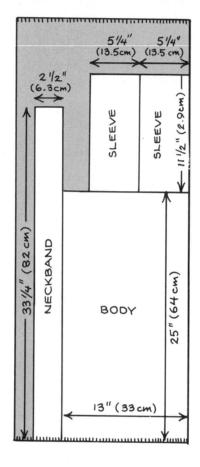

T-square to get your cutting lines straight, even and parallel.

SEWING DIRECTIONS

Note: The seam allowances at the neckline and Center Front opening on the BODY and the seam allowances on the NECKBAND are ¼" (6mm). All other seam allowances are ⅝" (1.5cm).

Establishing the Neckline and Center Front Openings

1. With right sides together, fold the BODY in half lengthwise and

mark the fold. This is the Center Front/Center Back Line.

2. Unfold the BODY and refold it in half crosswise, right sides together; mark the fold. This is the Shoulder Line.

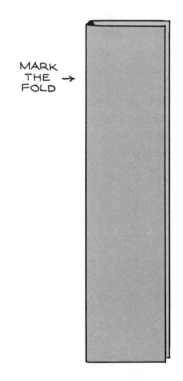

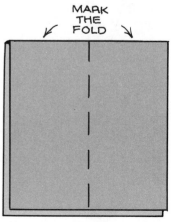

3. The point where the Center Front/Center Back Line and the Shoulder Line intersect is the starting point for establishing the neckline curve.

■ On the Center Back Line, put a mark ⅝″ (1.5cm) from the intersection point.

■ On the Center Front Line, put a mark 3½″ (9cm) from the intersection point.

■ On both sides of the Shoulder Line, put a mark 2¼″ (5.7cm) from the intersection point.

■ To create the neckline, draw a line as shown, connecting

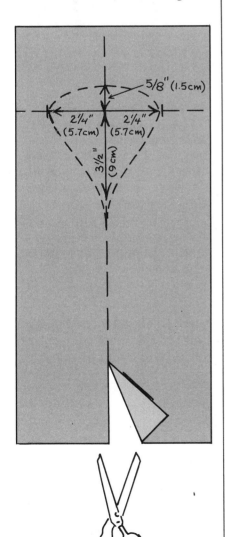

TIP *Draw one side of the curve, then fold the BODY along the Center Front/Center Back Line and use dressmaker's carbon and a tracing wheel to transfer the curve to the other side.*

these four marks. Gently curve the line to get rid of the corner at the point where the neckline meets the Center Front. Be sure that the curve on the left side of the Center Back matches the curve on the right side.

■ Beginning at the lower edge of the Center Front Line, cut the BODY apart until you reach the 3½″ (9cm) mark, then cut around the neckline.

Attaching the Neckband

4. To establish the Center Back and Shoulders on the NECK-BAND, fold it in half crosswise and mark at the raw edges. This is the CB marking. Then mark along the raw edges 3″ (7.5cm) from the Center Back on each side. These are the Shoulder markings.

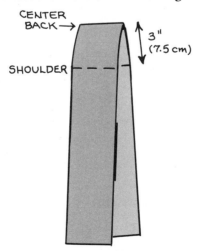

5. Staystitch the BODY neckline a scant ¼″ (6mm) from the raw edge. Clip the seam allowances just to, but not through, the stay-

stitching all around the neckline, as shown.

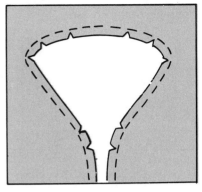

6. With right sides together, pin the NECKBAND to the BODY, matching the CB and Shoulder markings. Be careful not to stretch the band; instead, ease it carefully around the curves. Stitch, trim and clip the seam, or serge it on the overlock.

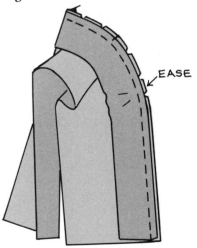

EASE

7. Press the long raw edge of the NECKBAND under ¼″ (6mm). Then fold the band to the inside of the kimono so that the folded edge just covers the seamline. Hand-baste or glue-baste in place, easing it gently around the curves. Slipstitch in place.

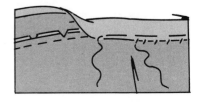

8. Working on the outside of the kimono, edgestitch the NECK-BAND close to the seamline, through all thicknesses.

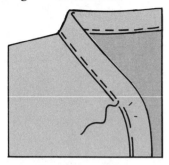

Attaching the Sleeves

9. To find the Shoulder Line, fold each sleeve in half crosswise and mark. Then, along one 11½" (29cm) edge of each SLEEVE, mark ⅝" (1.5cm) in from each outer edge.

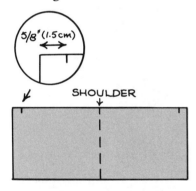

10. With right sides together, pin the SLEEVE to the BODY, matching shoulder lines and raw edges.

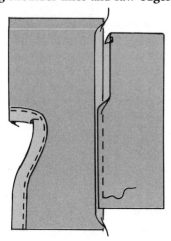

Stitch the seam, beginning and ending the stitching at the ⅝" (1.5cm) marks. Repeat for the other sleeve, then press both sleeve seams open.

Stitching the Side Seams

11. With right sides together, pin the BODY front and back together at the side seams and underarm seamlines.

- Beginning at the lower edge of the BODY, stitch the side seam. End the stitching when you reach the sleeve seam, keeping the sleeve seam allowances free.
- Beginning at the lower edge of the SLEEVE, stitch the underarm seam. End the stitching when you reach the ⅝" (1.5cm) markings, keeping the sleeve seam allowances free. This "break" in the stitching at the underarm area is what makes the underarm seam smooth on the finished kimono.
- Press the side/underarm seams open.

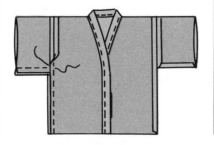

Hemming the Kimono

12. Narrow hem the lower edge of the sleeves and the kimono, following the directions for the Narrow Topstitched Hem, page 167, changing the hem allowance from 1" (2.5cm) to ⅝" (1.5cm).

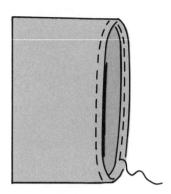

Constructing the Closures

13. On the outside of the right front band, measure up 3½", 5½" and 7½" (9cm, 14cm and 19cm) from the lower edge and mark. Repeat on the inside of the left front band.

- Center the hook parts of the fasteners over the markings on the right front band; hand-or machine-stitch in place.
- Center the loop parts of the fasteners over the markings on the left front band; hand- or machine-stitch in place.

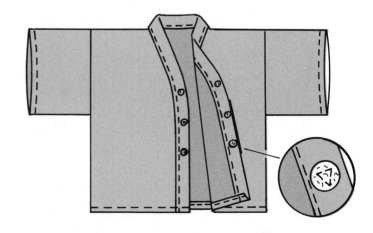

14. Cut the ribbon into three 12″ (30.5cm) lengths and tie each length into a bow. On the outside of the left front band, securely hand-sew the bows in place over the loop sections of the fasteners.

DIAPER COVER
(shown in full color)

For the fashionable little one, make the diaper cover to match the baby kimono. As a beginner's sewing project, this one's a breeze.

SUPPLIES

- ¾ yd. (.7m) of 42″/43″ (107cm–110cm) wide fabric

Note: For children's sleepwear, use fabrics and trims that meet the flammability standards set by the U.S. government.

- thread
- chalk marking pencil or fabric marking pen
- yardstick or T-square

CUTTING DIRECTIONS

Place your fabric, single thickness and right side up, on a large, flat surface. Using the Cutting Diagram as your guide, plot out and cut a 27″ × 31″ (68.5cm × 78.5) rectangle.

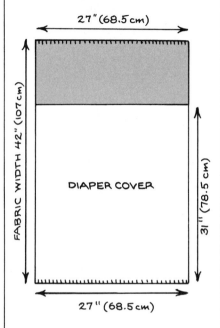

SEWING DIRECTIONS

Hemming on the Overlock Machine:

- Finish the edges with the three-thread overlock stitch or the narrow rolled hem stitch, trimming ⅝″ (1.5cm) as you serge.

Hemming on the Conventional Machine:

- Machine-stitch ⅝″ (1.5cm) from the raw edges, crossing the stitching at the corners.

- Where the stitches cross, fold the corners diagonally to the wrong side; press. Trim these corner seam allowances to ¼″ (6mm).
- Fold the raw edges to the wrong side so they just meet the stitching line; press.
- Fold up along the stitching line and press again.

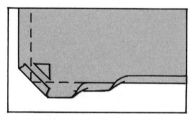

- Edgestitch all around the diaper cover, close to the inner fold.

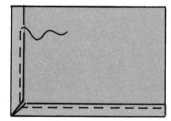

FOR THE HOME

ROUND TABLECLOTH
(shown in full color)

Your choice of fabrics and prints can change this basic round tablecloth to suit any decor, from English country to tailored contemporary.

SUPPLIES

■ Enough fabric for your tablecloth (see below)
■ thread
■ tape measure
■ chalk marking pencil or fabric marking pen

TO DETERMINE HOW MUCH FABRIC YOU NEED:

To get one piece of fabric wide enough to make the tablecloth, you'll need to join several panels together. To do this you must first determine the width of the finished tablecloth, then calculate how many panels you'll need for piecing. This will tell you how many yards of fabric to buy.

1. Measure the width of the table (its diameter) and the distance

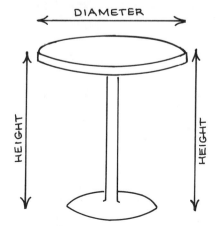

from the edge of the table to the floor (its height). Add:

Height + Diameter + Height + 1″ (2.5cm) for hems = Tablecloth width

2. To determine how many panels you'll need, use the "available width"—i.e., the width of the fabric minus 1″ (2.5cm)* for seam allowances. Now divide the Tablecloth Width by the Available Width. This tells you how many panels you will need. (If you come up with any fractions, count them as a whole panel. For example, if your answer is 2½, you'll need three panels.)

$$\frac{\text{Tablecloth Width}}{\text{Available Width}} = \text{\# of Panels}$$

3. Now use this formula to find out how many yards to buy:

$$\frac{\text{Tablecloth Width} \times \text{\# of panels}}{36″ (100cm)}$$
$$= \text{yds. (m)}$$

SEWING DIRECTIONS

Joining the Panels

1. You want to avoid having a seam run down the center of your tablecloth. Instead, position the seams so that half the additional amount is added to each side of the tablecloth. For exam-

* Check your selvages. You want them to "disappear" into the seam allowances. Some fabrics have color keys or the name of the manufacturer printed along the selvage. If this area is more than ½″ (1.3cm) wide, you'll need to subtract more than 1″ (2.5cm) to get your Available Width.

ple, if your cloth only requires two panels, one will be the center panel. The other should be cut lengthwise in half and then joined to the center panel.

■ Cut the fabric into the required number of panels, each equal in length to the Tablecloth Width.

■ Designate one panel as the center panel. Using the remaining panels, add half the additional amount to each side of the center panel.

■ To join the panels, stitch or serge a ½″ (1.3cm) seam, press the seam allowances toward the outside of the tablecloth, and topstitch ¼″ (6mm) from the seamline.

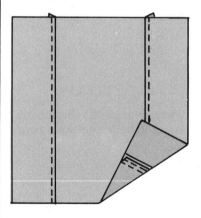

Marking and Cutting the Circle

2. To determine the radius of the tablecloth, divide the Tablecloth Width by 2. Then:

■ Fold the fabric in half, then in quarters, matching seams and edges; pin the layers together.

■ Pin a tape measure to the center point and use it as a

compass to mark the radius with chalk or a marking pen.

■ Cut along the marked line.

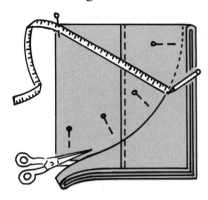

3. *Hemming the Tablecloth*

S THE OVERLOCK METHOD:

■ Either serge along the hemline or finish with a rolled hem, trimming ½″ (1.3cm).

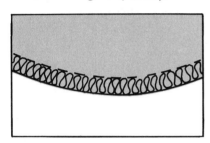

THE CONVENTIONAL METHOD:

■ Ease-stitch (see page 91) around the tablecloth, ¼″ (6mm) from the edge.

■ Press the edge to the wrong side along the stitching line,

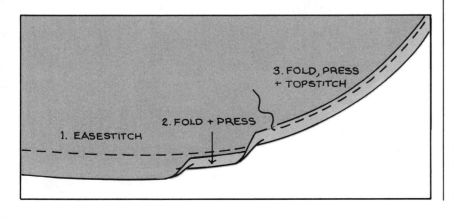

fold the edge over another ¼″ (6mm) and press again.

■ Topstitch close to the inner fold.

PLACEMATS
(shown in full color)

These reversible placemats are a quick way to change the mood of any table setting. Follow these directions to make four 13″ × 19″ (33cm × 48.5cm) placemats.

SUPPLIES

■ ¾ yd. (.7m) of 44″/45″ (115cm) wide reversible fabric

■ 7⅛ yds. (6.5m) of foldover braid or double-fold bias tape (for the conventional method only)

■ decorative thread, such as buttonhole twist or pearl cotton (for the overlock method only)

■ thread

■ chalk marking pencil or fabric marking pen

■ yardstick or T-square

CUTTING DIRECTIONS

Place your fabric, folded wrong sides together and selvage edges matching, on a large, flat surface. Pin together along the selvage and the cut edges. Using the Cutting Diagram as your guide, plot out and cut two 13″ × 19″ (33cm × 48.5cm) rectan-

gles. (Because your fabric is double thickness, this will give you four placemats.)

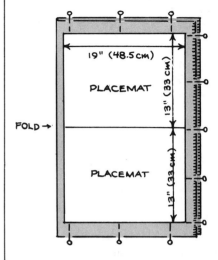

To curve the corners of the placemats, trace the outline of a drinking glass at each corner; trim along the curved line.

SEWING DIRECTIONS

S THE OVERLOCK METHOD:

■ Before you begin, review the section in Chapter 5 on Serging in a Circle, page 114.

■ Finish the edges with the three-thread overlock stitch or the narrow rolled hem stitch, trimming a scant ⅛″ (3mm) as you stitch. Use the decorative thread in the lower looper, and test the stitch first on a scrap of your fabric to determine what tension adjustments are required.

THE CONVENTIONAL METHOD:

- Before you begin, review BINDINGS, pages 132–136.
- Encase the outer edges in foldover braid, using the Edgestitched Application method on page 135, or in double-fold bias tape, using the Two-Step Application Method on page 134.

NAPKINS
(shown in full color)

Beautiful napkins that coordinate with your tablecloth and placemats can be made quickly and easily, especially if you own an overlock. Follow these directions to make four 16″ × 16″ (40.5cm × 40.5cm) napkins.

SUPPLIES

- 1 yd. (1m) of 44″/45″ (115cm) wide fabric
- thread
- chalk marking pencil or fabric marking pen
- yardstick or T-square

CUTTING DIRECTIONS

   Place your fabric, folded wrong sides together and selvage edges matching, on a large, flat surface. Pin together along the selvage and the cut edges. Using the Cutting Diagram as your guide, plot out and cut two 17⅛″ × 17⅛″ (43.5cm × 43.5cm)

squares. (Because your fabric is double thickness, this will give you four napkins.)

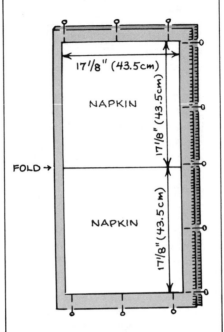

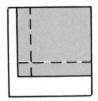

SEWING DIRECTIONS

S *Hemming on the Overlock:*

- Finish the edges with the three-thread overlock stitch or the narrow rolled hem stitch, trimming ⅝″ (1.5cm) as you serge.

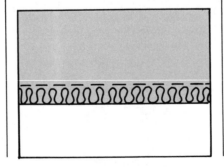

Hemming on the Conventional Machine:

- Machine-stitch ⅝″ (1.5cm) from the raw edges, crossing the stitching at the corners.

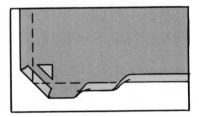

- Where the stitches cross, fold the corners diagonally to the wrong side; press. Trim these corner seam allowances to ¼″ (6mm).

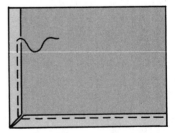

- Fold the raw edges to the wrong side so they just meet the stitching; press.
- Fold up along the stitching line and press again.

- Edgestitch all around the napkin, close to the inner fold.

INDEX

FREE SIMPLICITY® PATTERN OFFER

TO RECEIVE ANY SIMPLICITY® PATTERN OF YOUR CHOICE, FILL OUT THE COUPON BELOW AND SEND $1.00 FOR POSTAGE AND HANDLING ($2.00 IN U.S. FUNDS FOR CANADIAN RESIDENTS). <u>LIMIT</u> ONE FREE PATTERN PER COUPON.

Mail Coupon To: Simplicity Pattern Company
Department C
901 Wayne Street
Niles, Michigan 49121

SIMPLICITY'S SIMPLY THE BEST SEWING BOOK
FREE SIMPLICITY PATTERN OFFER

Simplicity Pattern Number _____ Your Pattern Size _____

Name: _____

Address: _____

City: _____ State: _____ Zip: _____

PLEASE MAKE CHECK OR MONEY ORDER for postage & handling PAYABLE TO SIMPLICITY PATTERN CO.

Please Allow Four To Six Weeks For Delivery.